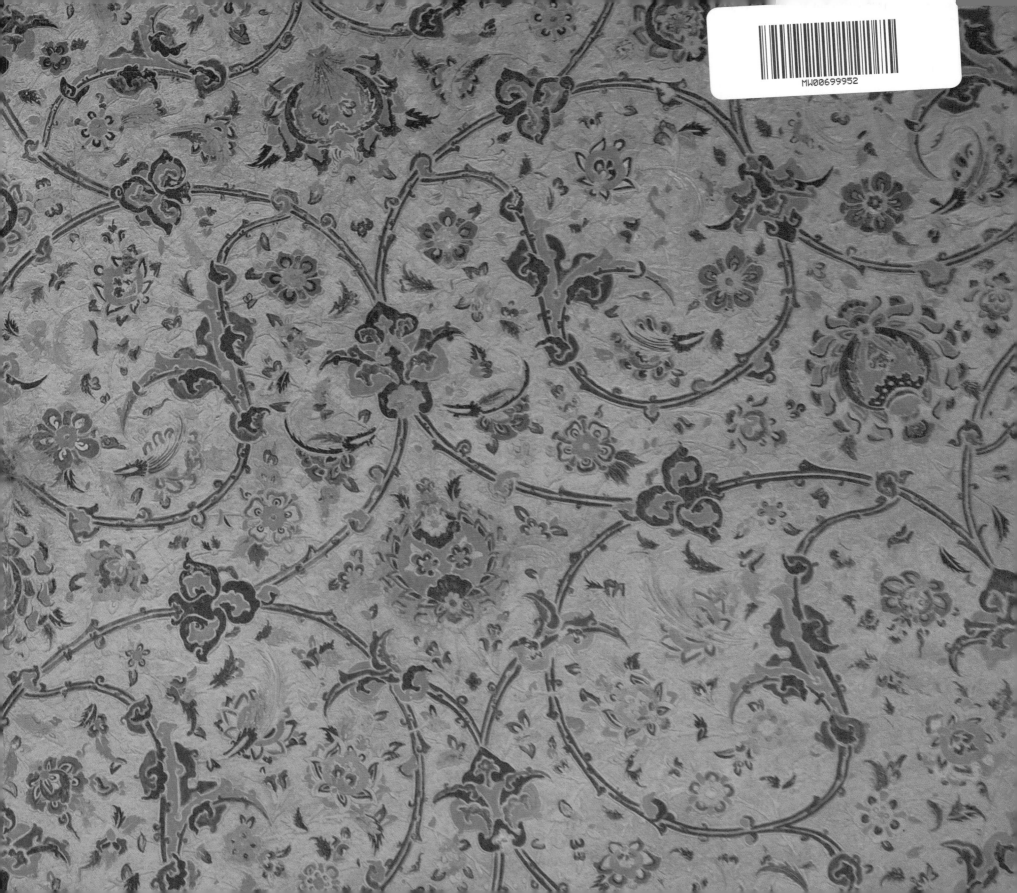

GREG & LUCY
MALOUF

saraban

A chef's journey through Persia

PHOTOGRAPHY BY
Ebrahim Khadem Bayat and Mark Roper

hardie grant books
MELBOURNE · LONDON

Published in 2010 by Hardie Grant Books

Hardie Grant Books (Australia)
85 High Street
Prahran, Victoria 3181
www.hardiegrant.com.au

Hardie Grant Books (UK)
Second Floor, North Suite
Dudley House
Southhampton Street
London WC2E 7HF
www.hardiegrant.co.uk

Designer: Sandy Cull, gogoGingko
Editor: Caroline Pizzey
Photographer (location pics): Ebrahim Khadem Bayat
Photographer (recipe pics): Mark Roper
Stylist: Glen Proebstel
Typesetter: J&M Typesetting
Map (p5): Sandy Cull, gogoGingko

Cataloguing-in-Publication data is available from the
National Library of Australia.

ISBN 978 174066 8 620

Colour reproduction by Splitting Image Colour Studio
Printed and bound in China by C&C Offset Printing

In loving memory of May Malouf, 1932–2010

Contents

Ay saraban, ay caravan

We arrive in the early afternoon, when the sun is at its hottest. After the long, dusty drive we are beginning to understand a little of how it must have felt in the old caravan days, to be part of a camel train moving slowly across the burning desert, with only the low silhouette of distant mountains to hold the eye and the shimmering promise of a far-off oasis to rekindle hope in the heart.

/

We park our car at the edge of the old city and trudge through the sun-baked alleyways to the hotel – our modern-day caravanserai. The ancient wooden door is embedded in a thick mud-brick wall that reveals nothing of what lies within. We push it open and pass through a cool vestibule into a courtyard garden.

/

The hotel is far from luxurious, but on this stifling afternoon it offers a welcome glimpse of Old Persia. The rooms are arranged traditionally around a central courtyard. There are tall trees, colourful flowers and a long pool lined with bright-turquoise tiles. Here is all the promise of paradise: the sound of tinkling water, cool shade that beckons, and rest and refreshment to be enjoyed on low, cushioned daybeds. A young man appears from nowhere bearing a tray of ice-cold watermelon and tall frosted glasses of pomegranate juice. All is languid pleasure, delight upon delight. Within minutes our senses are revived, our good humour restored, and the welcome break in our journey gives us time to pause and reflect.

/

If truth be told, we were singularly unprepared for this Iran. Despite the many months of research and planning, nothing we had read or heard or seen of the country's recent history had suggested that there was anything left here of the old caravanserai romance. In fact it was exceedingly difficult to put together any convincing picture of the place at all. Like the shifting mirage of a desert oasis, Iran itself proved elusive and enigmatic. It often seemed as if the 'real' country – whatever that might be – had dissolved like day into night after the 1979 revolution. Since then, the only perspective that the rest of the world has had is one reflected through a prism of anti-Islamic hostility, particularly in the West, where the very name 'Iran' is weighed down with negative connotations: at best it is seen as mysterious, secretive, baffling; at worst it is a dark, frightening place full of dark, frightening people, geopolitically menacing and religiously intolerant.

/

It is certainly not at the top of many lists as a must-do travel destination, and for months before our departure people had been asking us, 'Why Iran?'. That question, at least, was easy to answer. In our previous books we have explored other cuisines of the Middle East: the Arabian food of Lebanon and Syria, the Ottoman and Anatolian food of Turkey, and the Moorish food of North Africa. And there is no doubt that Persian food is the other great cuisine of the region. There are a number of impressively researched and inspiring cookbooks about traditional Persian food, and we knew from our reading that it is one of the most sophisticated, elaborate and complex food cultures in the world. But unless you live in a city with a flourishing Iranian population (and the diaspora is surprisingly far-flung), there are remarkably few opportunities to eat Persian food. Most Westerners, if they give it any thought at all, would most likely lump it in the general Middle Eastern basket of kebabs and rice and baklava.

/

But we were certain that there was much, much more than this to discover. In the end it seemed that there would be no way around it: if we really wanted to find out about Persian food we would have to go to Iran.

/

Iran or Persia? This proved to be the first of many conundrums, with each name conjuring up different, contradictory images. To many Westerners, Iran is the dour, puritanical place of the present day, while Persia is a romantic world of the distant past: of Scheherazade spinning her tales of one thousand and one nights; of fluffy cats, exquisite miniature paintings and gorgeous carpets; of roses and nightingales; of Omar Khayyam's *Rubaiyat*, and of caravan trails along the ancient Silk Road.

/

There is an element of truth and exaggeration in each version, but they are, of course, one and the same place. For most of its history, Iran has been known outside its borders as Persia, a corruption of the Greek name 'Persis', and it only became Iran in 1935 when Reza Shah Pahlavi declared it to be the country's official name. To Iranians, however, their country has been

known as Iran, the 'land of the Aryans', since the first millennium BC, when Indo-European tribes began to settle on the Iranian plateau.

/

Today 'Iran' and 'Persia' are used seemingly interchangeably – although sometimes with subtle political reasons – and we soon found ourselves quite happily using both, too. For this book we made the decision not to agonise over political or historical correctness, or how and when to use each, so in the pages that follow you'll find both, which seems somehow quite in keeping with the duality of life in this complicated land.

/

This duality, these contrasts, the opaqueness – once we arrived in Iran, we realised that they all contribute to a very real sense of mystery, and of reward. In this ever-contracting and connected world it often seems there are few things left that are strange and new. But as it turned out, this sense of being explorers in an unknown land was one of the most thrilling aspects of our journey around Iran. It felt as if we were being spun back to the days when travel was still an adventure, as if we were seeing places and things about which others from our world knew little.

/

The sad truth is that for a few decades now the beauty of Iran has been largely hidden from Western eyes. But for those who are bold enough to cast prejudice aside, the

rewards are immense. We had been expecting there would be frustrations and for the going to be tough (and it often was), but what we weren't prepared for was the fun, the beauty, the joy.
/

There were, in fact, two journeys, made over a six-month period between October 2009 and March 2010, timed to avoid the blistering heat of the summer months and to take maximum advantage of produce in the markets and bazaars. Because in the end, for all the riches of its archeology, architecture and art and the extraordinary natural beauty, our journey to Iran was always going to be – ostensibly at least – about the food.
/

Perhaps it's truer to say that the food was always to be the starting point. From the travels and research we had done for our previous books, we have found that food – buying it, eating it, sharing it – is an extremely effective way of forging connections with people in other countries, even when you don't speak the same language. Wherever we have gone, food has been a key to unlocking doors into people's lives, and we hoped that it would work a similar magic in Iran.
/

Ultimately, perhaps, there was no great surprise. Middle Easterners are famous for their hospitality, and Iran proved to be even more welcoming than other countries we had visited. We were embraced, without exception, by the rich and poor, orthodox and secular, traditional and modern. Wherever we went we experienced an unprecedented level of hospitality, generosity and friendliness. We were approached time and again by people wanting to talk; by young people in particular, who proved to be educated, informed about the West and internet-savvy and who nearly all spoke a little English. We left Iran having made good friends and feeling more aware of what we all have in common rather than of our differences.
/

And this, surely, is what the future must feel like.
/

We return to our hotel in the early evening. As darkness falls, lamps are lit around the courtyard. Other guests are arriving now, and the spirit of caravanserai romance is in the air. There is a buzz of excitement as people settle into their rooms and then emerge to eat and drink and to swap stories about their day sightseeing in the old city. There might not be camels and horses tied up in the courtyard, and the food may have been served restaurant-style rather than cooked over a campfire, but surely, as new friendships are forged, knowledge is exchanged, and secrets are shared, the soul of the journey is the same as it ever was?

/

We make friends with two fashionably dressed young Tehrani women. They are visiting this place for the first time with their cousin, who is acting as their guide. All three are fascinated by our project and the conversation takes off in lovely mellifluous Farsi. We understand barely a word, but are entranced. Like all Iranians, they speak not just with words, but use their hands and arms and bodies to emphasise a point. The exchange is lively, punctuated with laughter and lines of poetry, but they pause to explain that they are talking about the Silk Road, its past and its travellers.

/

And then one of the young women gets to her feet and, quite unselfconsciously, begins to sing. Her vivid pink headscarf falls back from her forehead and her huge black eyes glitter in the candlelight.

/

Ay saraban, ay caravan
Leilaye man koja mibari …

The melody is hauntingly beautiful and we beg for the translation. The women are laughing now, and hug their cousin affectionately. 'He is our saraban,' they say, and the beauty with the pink headscarf explains further. 'The saraban was the head of the camel train in the olden days. He would lead the travellers safely across the desert to their destination. He was like the modern-day tour guide!'

/

Oh saraban, oh caravan
Where are you taking my Leila?
By taking my Leila away
You take away my heart and my soul.

/

It's a love song, of course, and tells of the doomed passion between folk-hero Majnoon and his Leila. But for many Iranians this song has a deeper resonance: it's a metaphor for the journey of life, but is, above all, a love song for their country.

/

We sit for a while, quiet now in the flickering candlelight, and reflect on the countless other travellers who have passed this way. Most would have been ordinary people like us — merchants, soldiers, pilgrims, tourists even — each with a story, a destiny. Tomorrow our journey will continue. We will have our very own saraban to guide us, and this vast country stretches all around, waiting to be explored, to be revealed — gradually.

/

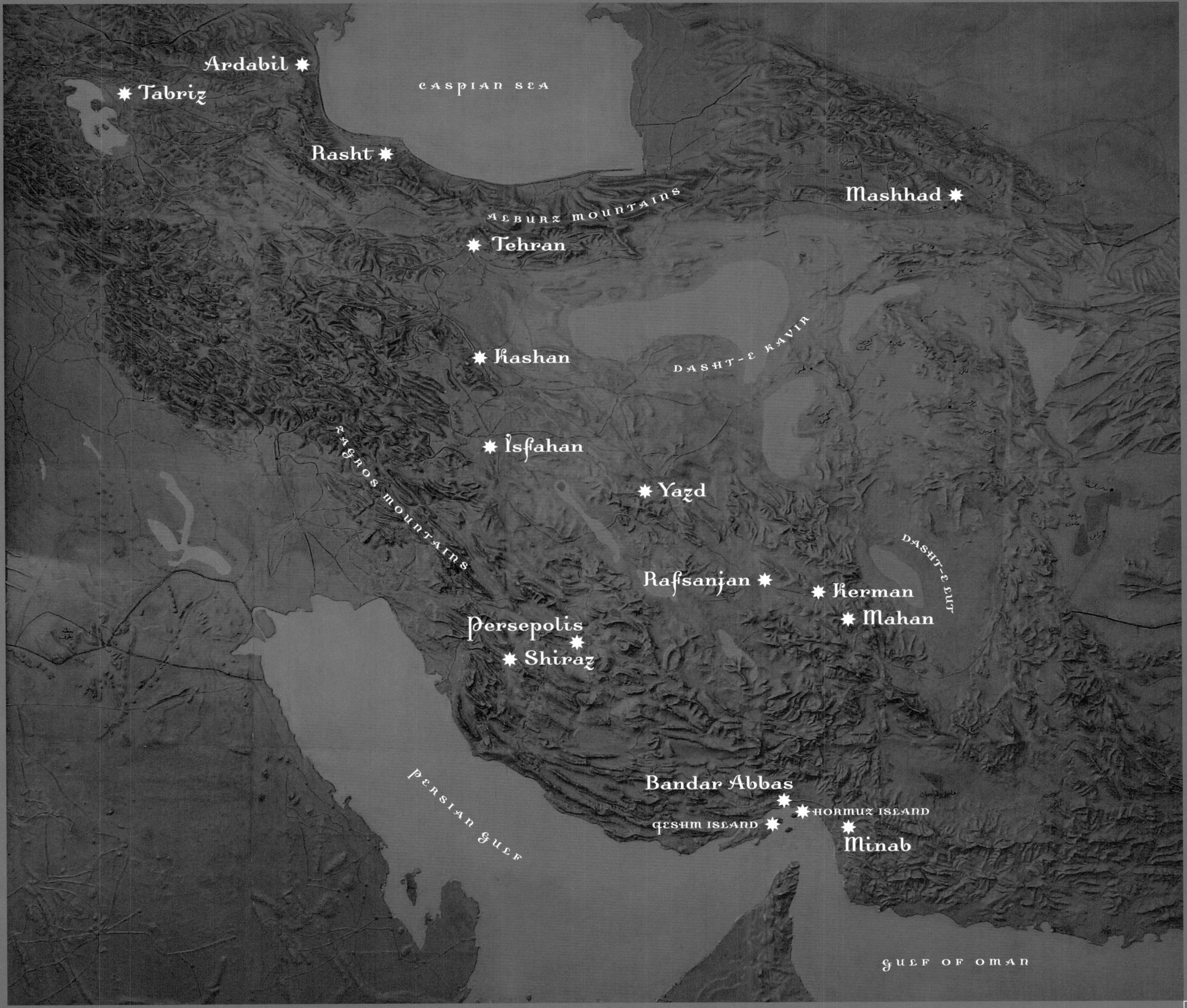

Ardabil ✶

✶ Tabriz

Rasht ✶

CASPIAN SEA

Mashhad ✶

ALBURZ MOUNTAINS

✶ Tehran

✶ Kashan

DASHT-E KAVIR

✶ Isfahan

✶ Yazd

ZAGROS MOUNTAINS

DASHT-E LUT

Rafsanjan ✶

✶ Kerman
✶ Mahan

Persepolis
✶
✶ Shiraz

PERSIAN GULF

Bandar Abbas
✶ ✶ HORMUZ ISLAND
GESHM ISLAND ✶
✶ Minab

GULF OF OMAN

Shia – Sunni: the great divide It began, as do so many great feuds, with a death. In 632 AD the Prophet Mohammed died without naming his successor, leaving open the question of who should assume leadership of the new, and increasingly successful, religion: Islam. Two opposing camps formed: those who believed that succession should pass down through Mohammed's family, and others who could not accept a female line (Mohammed had a daughter, Fatima, and no sons) and so rallied behind Abu Bakr, Mohammed's father-in-law and friend. Abu Bakr became the first Caliph, or Muslim head of state, and to avoid any further confusion after his own death named Umar, from a local Arab aristocratic family, as his own successor. The title was subsequently claimed by other dynasties down through the centuries – the Ummayads, Abbasids, Fatimids and then the Ottomans. Supporters of these Caliphates became known as Sunnis, or followers of the 'sunnah' – an Arabic word that refers to the daily traditions or habits of Mohammed.

/

The other group adopted Fatima's husband, Ali (Mohammed's cousin), as leader, and called themselves Shia'Ali – or followers of Ali. Ali eventually became a Caliph himself, only to be assassinated five years later. When his youngest son, Hossein, was murdered at the Battle of Karbala in 680 AD, the schism between the two factions became irreparable. And permanent.

/

Today Sunnis are the majority, orthodox branch of Islam, with around ninety percent of the world's Muslims adhering to this form of the faith. Shia Islam was linked forever with Persian royalty when Hossein married a Persian princess, and it holds sway only in Iran and southern Iraq, although there are strong communities in other nations, such as Pakistan, Lebanon, Syria and Yemen. To this day, the anniversary of Hossein's martyrdom is one of the most important of Iran's religious calendar, and it is remembered throughout the month of Moharram, which culminates in the day of Ashura – a day of mass public mourning.

/

Shia Muslims believe that the spiritual leadership of Islam is passed down through imams – saints who are descended from the Prophet. While different subgroups of Shi'ism recognise different numbers of imams, the largest group, by far, is the Iranian Twelvers. Twelvers believe in twelve successive imams, the most sacred of whom are Imam Ali, Imam Reza and Imam Hossein, all of whom were martyred. Almost as important is the twelfth imam, the Mahdi or hidden imam, who vanished in 874 AD. Shia Muslims believe that one day the Mahdi will return to earth with Jesus to restore justice – and peace – to the world.

/

Farsi–English Although Farsi and English are both Indo-European languages, the Farsi alphabet is based on Arabic script and English on the Roman alphabet. Transcribing from one to the other is fraught with difficulties (dialects, for instance, can change the sound of a word completely) and formal transliterations from Farsi to English seem to make rather more of a mouthful of the matter than need be!

/

We've adopted a simple phonetic approach, but fully accept that it will be flawed. As an example, the Iranian friends we travelled with pronounced Hafez – Iran's most loved poet and admired national icon – 'Haf-ez'. Several English translations of his works choose to spell the name 'Haf-iz'. What to do? Every ingredient and place name we encountered was similarly tricky to pin down. (Another example of quixotic Iran!) In the end we decided not to agonise over it too much, and have opted for the closest possible match to our experience of the sound of the word. We hope that Farsi speakers will forgive any inconsistencies or errors.

/

Introducing Persian food

AS A LEBANESE CHEF RUNNING A MODERN MIDDLE EASTERN RESTAURANT, I HAVE LONG BEEN intrigued by all things Persian. Since writing our first cookbook in 1999 Lucy and I have been struck, time and again, by just how many culinary trails lead back to Persia. And yet it's a cuisine that has been sadly neglected in the West. Indian restaurants abound, everyone is familiar with Lebanese felafel and Turkish doner kebabs, but Persian restaurants (which many people would probably consider to offer some kind of vague amalgam of these cuisines) are thin on the ground, to say the least.

/

It's true that Persian food shares some common ground with all the aforementioned food cultures, but, to be honest, the entire region is such a tangle of culinary threads – of influences and counter-influences – that it's almost impossible to unravel the genesis of many of them. Food historians have varying, often conflicting, theories as to what began where and who bequeathed which dish to whom, but in the end, perhaps, it doesn't really matter – all the world's cuisines are the richer for the melting pot of Middle Eastern influences. One thing is quite clear: Persian food is not the same as Arab food. Nor is it a variation of Indian food or of Ottoman food. It is its own distinct cuisine, with its own distinct history and traditions, and it deserves to be better known and appreciated in the West.

/

Perhaps the first thing to do when embarking upon a study of Persian food is to open an atlas. Persia – modern-day Iran – is a surprisingly large country, stretching roughly three thousand kilometres from north to south, east to west. It forms a natural corridor between the Far East and the Middle East, and its lands are criss-crossed with a fragile skein of well-worn caravan routes that made up the ancient Silk Road.

/

Climate and terrain are two of the key influences on any country's cuisine, and Persia is no different. At first glance it seems that much of Iran is made up of a high desert plateau, and managing the extreme climate has certainly had a significant impact on the country's social and cultural evolution. But the long stretches of mountain ranges that wrap around the desert heartlands are what have really shaped the country. These jagged peaks are covered in snow over the winter months – and some remain ice-capped even in the summer – providing a source of water and cooling blocks of snow and ice for the people in the valleys and nearby desert communities. Several millennia ago Persian engineers constructed a system of underground pipes – qanats – to transport water from the mountains to villages and, crucially, to irrigate fields, thereby ensuring the survival of settlements. They also built yakchal – squat, thick-walled houses purpose-built for storing ice blocks for chilling food and drink through the summer months.

/

Despite the perception that it is largely desert, much of the Iranian plateau is surprisingly fertile and many fruits, vegetables, herbs and nuts are indigenous to the region. Wheat, barley, lentils, almonds, walnuts, citrus fruits, pomegranates, plums, cherries, dates, beans, peas and many, many herbs have all been grown there for centuries. Some ingredients have even given their names to the English language: saffron, pistachio, spinach, orange, lemon, aubergine, tarragon and caviar all derive from ancient Persian words for these foodstuffs, while Shiraz grapes (which some say originated near the city of Shiraz in the Fars Province of Iran) have a particular resonance in Australia, where a modern-day grape of the same name is used to produce iconic wines.

/

As well as being a bountiful garden of produce in its own right, Persia benefitted from its position on ancient trade routes, and all manner of goods have flowed through the country down through the centuries. As the Persian empire swelled and expanded its borders, trade with the East brought in new and exotic spices; rice, sugar and wild fowl arrived from India, and from China came apricots, peaches and tea. By way of return, Persia sent sesame seeds, basil and coriander, a variety of nuts, broad beans and peas.

/

As they amass wealth and lands, all great empires seem to focus on the pleasures of the senses, and food is one of the most important of these. It is, after all, inextricably woven into a nation's culture and history, and associated with religious feast days as well as important family events such as births, marriages and funerals. After the Achaemanids suffered defeat at the hands of Alexander the Great in 331 BC, new empires emerged in Persia, culminating in a golden era of culture under the Sassanids from the third to the seventh centuries. Their imperial courts were quickly filled with culinary riches, as well as other splendours. Although no books of recipes remain from this time, according to eminent Middle Eastern food historian, Charles Perry, in his foreword to Lilia Zaouali's *Medieval Cuisine of the Islamic World*, Persian aristocrats maintained their own volumes of personal favourites. Other Persian texts from the era tell of food served on plates of silver and wine drunk from golden goblets. Rarefied dishes emerged, the precursors to many that are still prepared today: whole beasts were stuffed with fruit and herbs and roasted or braised with sugar and vinegar, nuts were layered with pastry, and sweet jellies and cordials were made from fruit juice.

/

Although the Arabs conquered Persia in the seventh century, they were in turn conquered by the civilising influence of their new subjects. The diet of pre-Islamic Arabia was limited and monotonous, revolving largely around barley, dates and dairy products. But when they discovered the sophisticated Persian court, with its diverse and rich culinary repertoire, they enthusiastically adopted it as their own. In the kitchens of their new capital at Baghdad, the cuisine was further enriched by ingredients and techniques brought back to the court kitchens as their empire expanded. Here, too, for the first time, books of recipes and culinary protocol were written down, following practices thought to have originated in the Sassanid court. The oldest surviving Arab cookbook, the *Kitab al-tabikh*, was compiled in the tenth century, starting a tradition that was continued in the medieval Islamic world, long before Europeans began documenting recipes.

/

One of the most significant impacts that Islam had upon the medieval kitchen was the prohibition of alcohol. It seems, though, that the newly Islamicised Persia was slow to abandon wine – both as a drink and for use in cooking. Wine and wine vinegar were used extensively in the Baghdad Caliphate (although it was eventually replaced by verjuice – sour grape juice – and other souring agents, such as lime or pomegranate juice and tamarind). Wine as a beverage, and the effects of its consumption, are recurring themes in Persian literature and poetry and many Persian poets, from Omar Khayyam to Hafez, have sung its praises.

/

Shah Abbas I, the great king of the Safavid dynasty at Isfahan, was also fond of a drop of wine, and it certainly features abundantly in the gorgeous frescoes reflecting those times that adorn the walls of the Chehul Sotun Palace, built by his successor, Shah Abbas II, in the seventeenth century. Wine was often served chilled with small blocks of ice, as were syrupy cordials or sherbets.

/

It was at the height of the Safavid era, in the sixteenth century, that Persia's famous rice dishes emerged, becoming more and more elaborate concoctions, layered with herbs, nuts, fruits and spices such as saffron. The refinement of these rice dishes proved so exciting that it even led to rice being exported to India, from where the grain originated. This only served to develop the link that had already been forged between Persian and Indian cuisines. Like the Arabs before them, the barbarian hordes of Mongols who smashed into Persia in the thirteenth century quickly absorbed the Persian language, religion and cuisine. One Mongol dynasty – that of Timur the Lame or Tamerlane – was so successful that it branched off to the north of India, where it became known as the Moghul empire, one of the most refined and extravagant courts ever known in that country. The Moghuls took a number of Persian influences with them: linguistic, architectural and, of course, culinary. Many of the popular and famous northern Indian dishes that we know today – biryani, naan bread, koofteh, kebabs, tikkeh and tandoor dishes – can all be traced back to their Persian antecedents.

/

Climate, geography, history have all shaped the evolution of Persian cuisine. Another key influence has been religion. As touched upon above, the arrival of Islam in the seventh century saw the prohibition of alcohol in the daily diet. Pork and unscaled fish were also forbidden, although neither have had much impact on the Persian diet, where sheep provided most meat and fish is consumed only on the shores of the Caspian Sea and the Persian Gulf.

/

Going back further in time, the teachings of the prophet Zoroaster had a far more profound impact. His philosophy of duality – of the eternal struggle between good and evil in the world – also extended to the human spirit and body, with each individual seeking to achieve good health and happiness over sickness and depression. According to Zoroaster, the four elements – earth, air, fire and water – are reflected within the body in our blood, yellow bile, phlegm and black bile. It's a philosophy that was subsequently developed by Hippocrates in his theory of 'humours', and it became the prevailing view of the human body – of a person's mental and physical makeup – until the nineteenth century. Curiously, a similar philosophy – that diet affects one's entire health and well-being – developed quite independently in China's theory of Yin and Yang and in Indian Ayurveda medicine.

/

To achieve balance within the body, and maintain health and happiness, Zoroaster suggested that we must maintain balance in our diet, and thus food was divided into categories of 'hot' or 'cold' (Hippocrates later added two further groups of 'wet' and 'dry').

/

This ancient theory of dietetics is widely followed to this day in Iran, and most people seem to have an instinctive understanding of whether an item of food is 'hot' or 'cold', probably absorbed at the dinner table from their early childhood. Everyday meals are always planned to be in balance both in their own right, and with the circumstances. For example, if you have a fever, or during summer, you need to eat 'cold' foods. Conversely, in the cold winter months you need 'hot' foods. Similarly, one's constitution or personality may also need to be balanced by diet. A person with a 'cold' constitution – someone who is naturally relaxed, patient, sluggish even – should avoid 'cold' foods, while a 'hot' person – quick-tempered, active, restless – should avoid 'hot' foods. Many Iranians are so devoted to this theory that they will always prefer to deal with ailments by tweaking the diet before visiting a doctor.

/

The classification of foods can be hard to work out – it is to do with the intrinsic 'energy' of an ingredient, and bears no relation to temperature – and it can seem rather bizarre to people who are not familiar with it. (Why are apples hot, for example? Or radishes and coffee cold?) To add confusion, some ingredients are classified differently across regions, but the list given here provides the usual hot or cold classification for the majority of common foodstuffs.

/

'Hot' and 'Cold' foods HOT almonds/apples/bananas/butter/cardamom/cherries (sweet)/chicken (hen)/chickpeas/chives/cinnamon/cucumbers/cumin/currants/dates/dill/duck/eggs/fenugreek/figs/garlic/ginger/grapes/honey/kashk/lamb/mangoes/melons (sweet)/mint/mulberries/mushrooms/oils/olives/onions/oregano/peppers/pistachios/quinces/raisins/rosewater/saffron/salt/sesame seeds/split peas (yellow)/tarragon/turmeric/vanilla/walnuts/wheat/

/

NEUTRAL tea/pears/feta/

/

COLD apricots/barberries/beef/beetroot/cabbage/carrots/cauliflower/celery/cherries (sour)/coffee/coriander/eggplants/fish/green beans/kidney beans/lemons (and sweet lemons)/lentils/limes/milk/nectarines/oranges (sour and sweet)/parsley/peaches/peas/plums/pomegranates/potatoes/prunes/pumpkins/radishes/rhubarb/rice/spinach/sugar/sumac/tamarind/tomatoes/turkey/veal/verjuice/vinegar/watermelon/yoghurt/

/

Nowruz Food inevitable plays a major role in festivals and to mark other special occasions. In Iran, the New Year is the grand-daddy of them all. As a celebration, it is like our Christmas, Easter and the summer holiday, all rolled into one, with presents, painted eggs, elaborate table decorations, feasting and a fortnight's holiday. It is far more important to the Iranian heart than any religious event and any discussion about the country would be incomplete without mention of Nowruz.

/

Iran uses a calendar that dates back to pre-Zoroastrian days, and the year still revolves around the vernal equinox – which occurs on March 20 or 21 – when the first day of spring is celebrated. At the moment of the equinox, the sun is directly above the equator, and from this point onwards light once more begins its defeat of the dark. The rituals that surround today's celebrations date back at least to Achaemenid times, and the famous complex at Persepolis is thought to have been built around 515 BC specifically to celebrate the Nowruz festival. Bas reliefs around the ruins depict images of the eternally fighting lion and bull – symbolising light and dark, spring and winter – and the great staircase up to the central Apadana reception hall is lined with carved dignitaries from all the nations of the empire, bringing gifts to the king.

/

As befits a spring festival, many Nowruz rituals revolve around rebirth, new beginnings, and a desire to ensure health and prosperity for one's family in the year ahead. Today in Iran the run-up to New Year's Day involves a flurry of spring-cleaning, the purchase of new clothes and gifts, and filling the house with spring flowers – hyacinths are the traditional favourite. Ten days before Nowruz, children plant trays of edible seeds, which are carefully tended to ensure they will have sprouted by the big day. And, of course, the kitchen becomes a hive of activity, as cookies, pastries and all sorts of sweetmeats are prepared. These days, many people will stock up on these goodies from local pastry and sweet shops (particularly those selling gaz – nougat – which is eaten and given away in prodigious amounts over the holiday), as well as bringing in supplies of fresh and dried fruit and nuts, to serve to guests or to take as gifts when visiting other households.

/

The real climax of the celebrations is the countdown to the exact, magic moment of equinox, which varies from year to year. To greet the arrival of the New Year, families gather around a specially decorated table, which is called the haft sin – or seven S's. The haft sin table is set with seven items that start with the letter 'S', to symbolise the seven elements of life (fire, earth, water, air, plants, animals and humankind) and the seven guardian angels of creation (birth, life, health, happiness, prosperity, beauty and light). The haft sin themselves have evolved over time, but usually include sabzi (sprouts or herbs that symbolise rebirth), samanu (a wheat-paste pudding representing wealth), sib (an apple, for health), senjed (lotus fruit – love), sir (garlic – medicine), somaq (sumac berries – the sunrise), and serkeh (vinegar – age and patience). Other 'S' items might include sekeh (coins, for wealth) and sonbol (hyacinth flowers). Goldfish are another absolutely essential decorative item on the Nowruz table: they represent life within life, and also the sign of Pisces, which the sun is leaving. Each family also has its own special decorative touches: candles, painted eggs, a mirror, an orange, a bowl of rice or a jug of rosewater are all popular. Many families will include a collection of the revered fourteenth-century poet Hafez, and some – the only nod to Islam – a Koran.

/

The first meal of the New Year includes symbolic dishes: sabzi polow (green herb rice) and kuku-ye sabzi (herb omelette) are served with white fish, to represent growth, bounty, rebirth and freshness.

/

During the Nowruz holidays, families and friends engage in a round of socialising, always in a strict order, with younger family members visiting their elders first. On the thirteenth and final day, it is considered bad luck to stay at home, so the whole country goes out on a picnic! This is not a Thermos-of-tea-and-packet-of-sandwiches kind of picnic, though, but rather an elaborate meal of hot rice, fried fish, omelette, bread, lettuce with sekanjabeen, pickles, yoghurt, fruit, pastries, cakes – all spread out on the picnic sofreh. As the celebrations draw to a close, the specially grown herb tray (now beginning to look a little the worse for wear) is discarded into running water (along with the devil), and each family member makes a wish for the year ahead.

/

And then, on the first workday of the New Year, ash-e reshteh, a soup filled with fine noodles that symbolise the threads of life, is served to celebrate new beginnings, and so the cycle begins – until next Nowruz.

/

Eating the Persian way Persian food is one of the most sophisticated and complex cuisines of any in the Middle East, and the influences that prevailed down through the centuries can still be seen in many dishes today. There are some regional differences – the people of the Caspian Sea littoral are big fish eaters, and they also consume huge amounts of locally grown rice; on the Persian Gulf, many more spices are used than elsewhere in the country – and even the occasional touch of chilli-heat, reflecting the long history of trade with nearby India, Africa and Arab countries. On the whole, though, the approach to eating and the dishes themselves remain consistent around the country.

/

Perhaps the one great unifying theme is that of generosity and sharing. Middle Eastern hospitality is legendary – it is after all one of the important tenets of Islam to welcome a guest as a gift of God – and this is no truer than in Iran. Iranian women always seem to be able to cater (in vast amounts) for the unexpected visitor; indeed it would be unthinkable for a family not to invite anyone who happened to be around – friends, friends-of-friends, neighbours, passers-by – to share in mealtimes. And this approach extends from the wealthiest to the very poorest villager.

/

A Persian meal begins even before one sits down to eat. As a guest, one is welcomed into the formal reception room, and plied with an endless succession of little morsels: bowls of dried fruit and nuts, sweets and pastries, chunks of melon or other fruit are served with tea (chai) or sherbet drinks, all accompanied by polite and charming conversation.

/

When the meal is ready, one is invited to the table – although in many homes, whether rural or urban, the meal is often eaten, by preference, on the floor. A sofreh (a cloth or brightly coloured plastic sheet) will be spread out over the carpet and then the real business of eating begins.

/

Persian meals are less structured than we are used to in the West. There are no fixed courses, as such, but instead dishes accumulate on the sofreh and everyone helps themselves to a bit of what they fancy throughout the meal. That being said, there is a definite order to proceedings.

/

All Iranian meals, however humble or elaborate, begin with a dish of mixed fresh herbs, fresh white cheese and stacks of flatbread. The bread is often used instead of cutlery, to scoop up or wrap food, but otherwise meals are eaten with a spoon, or sometimes a fork. Yoghurt dishes, small salads, pickles and wedges of onion, lemon or lime follow in quick succession. A simple meal, or a light lunch or supper, might then include a thick, tortilla-like omelette known as a kuku, or in the winter there might be a hearty soup (ash), thick with pulses and vegetables. For bigger meals, or when entertaining, there will always be rice – either a plain chelow or a more complex polow, served with khoresht (a stew–sauce) or kebabs. The meal ends with more fruit, and soft drinks or dugh, a lightly sparkling yoghurt drink, are drunk throughout.

/

If you would like to experiment with eating the Persian way, then try to plan a simple meal around one rice dish and a khoresht or kebab dish. Select one or two small dishes to begin (and include a basket of fresh herbs, some cheese and bread, of course), and finish with fresh fruit. For a more elaborate meal, build upon this basic structure and add a dessert (a Western rather than Persian touch), and perhaps offer a few sweet treats to go with coffee (or tea) after dinner.

/

How to use this book

WE WOULD LIKE TO STRESS THAT THIS BOOK IS NOT intended to be a traditional, all-encompassing, definitive work about Persian food. There are several excellent Persian cookbooks available, written by respected and knowledgeable Iranian authors, where you will find a wide range of authentic and traditional recipes – although we wait with bated breath for Roza Montazemi's comprehensive, classic cookbook, *Honar-e Ashpazi* (The Art of Cooking – in print since the mid-1960s), to be translated from Farsi into English. If you develop the kind of passion for Persian food that we have, we strongly urge you to buy as many of these books as you can, and refer you to page 328 for a list of some of our favourites. Having said that, Persian cookbooks are sadly underrepresented on bookshop shelves in the West, and we hope that readers will look on our offering as a welcome addition to the repertoire.

/

This, then, is the crux of the matter: the recipes that follow are intended to complement, rather than replace, traditional versions. They are a little bit free-form, a little bit – dare we say it – modern. As such, we hope you will use them in an equally free-form and modern way. Please don't feel that you have to recreate a Persian banquet faithfully in your dining room! Instead, flip between the sections and put together a meal in your own way, with dishes that appeal. Eating should be pleasurable, rather than an academic exercise, after all.

So please also consider that many of the recipes and ideas in the following pages would be just as wonderful as part of a Western meal. Khoresht dishes, for instance, while uniquely Persian and usually served with rice, are also lovely when served with a big bowl of creamy mashed potato, or soft polenta.

/

The sections that follow are arranged somewhat differently from a traditional European cookbook. There are no starters, main courses and desserts, as such, because that is not the way Iranians eat. Instead, the recipes are organised to reflect, more or less, their role in a Persian meal. So you'll find sections covering the staples (breads and rice – pages 40–69) around which every meal revolves; small dishes (pages 40–69); soups and 'ash' (pages 134–149); stews and sauces (pages 134–149) to accompany rice; grills, roasts and fried dishes (pages 210–235); sweets (which include pastries, cakes, sweetmeats, ice-creams and a selection of Persian-inspired desserts – pages 254–281), and, finally, preserves (pickles, relishes, jams and cordials – pages 304–319). Each section includes an explanatory introduction that outlines what to expect from the recipes.

/

At the end of the book you'll find food notes (pages 321–325) to help with any ingredients that might be new or unusual. But, with a few exceptions, most Persian dishes are made from ingredients that you will probably already have in your pantry or that are readily available from supermarkets or providores. After all, most larger supermarkets stock a good selection of formerly 'exotic' ingredients these days – tamarind, flower waters and spices such as saffron and ground sumac can all be found easily. There are a few particularly Persian items – such as barberries, dried limes and liquid kashk – that you may have to hunt down in Middle Eastern or Iranian food stores. But we do urge you to take the trouble to do this when they are called for, as they are often the key to an authentic Persian flavour.

/

You really don't need any special equipment for Persian cooking. Many Iranian families have an electric rice cooker, which makes good sense given the vast amounts of rice they consume, but to be honest once you've familiarised yourself with the technique, a large, heavy-based, lidded saucepan will do the job just as well. Make sure you've also got a metal sieve for straining, a wide, shallow kitchen spoon for mounding the rice gently in the saucepan, and a supply of tea towels to wrap around your lids when steaming. Sharp knives are essential, as in any cuisine, for chopping fresh herbs, and a mortar and pestle will help with grinding spices.

/

Saraban encompasses some of the wonderful dishes, flavours and techniques that we were able to enjoy on our travels around Iran. Some recipes are indeed authentic, and were kindly shared with us by cooks we met on our journey. Others are highly personal interpretations and are offered up by way of being a new take on old favourites and flavours. They might not be strictly traditional, but we hope that they capture the spirit of the traditions from which they emerge, and that they will inspire you to create a bit of Persian magic in your own kitchen.

/

kohan

It is mid-afternoon in the tea house; a quiet, in-between time. Thin sunlight filters in through a glass dome set high in the vaulted ceiling, piercing the subterranean gloom. Suspended beneath the dome is an arrangement of nomad tassels that rotates languorously in the warm air, casting mysterious shadows about the intricately tiled pillars and arches.

/

There are a few tables and chairs set around the room, but, in the main, the handful of customers here at this time of day prefers to recline against heavy carpet-covered cushions on takhts, low Persian daybeds. Apart from the hiss of the samovar and the faint clink of glasses there is sleepy silence.

/

Ali calls softly to the waiter, who fills a flowery china teapot and brings it to our table with a bowl of roughly hewn rocks of sugar. There is a sudden flash of movement behind him and we see a hand raised high towards the light. For a moment, the sun spills onto the stretched parchment of the musician's drum, then a slow, rhythmic beat and his pure tenor voice break the silence.

/

Your dreams are like a boundless ocean with no shores ...

/

It feels like a dream to me.

/

It's a long way from Tehran to Kerman — just over a thousand kilometres — and it's even further away from our expectations of a dark and dangerous Iran. Here in the tea house the atmosphere has changed. The drowsiness has vanished and as the soulful notes echo around the room everyone is focussed intently on the musicians. At the next table an elderly man is leaning back with his eyes closed and I am startled to see a tear roll slowly down his cheek.

/

This particular tea house, Hamam-e Vakil Chaykaneh, is an old converted bathhouse just off the Kerman bazaar. Ali is our saraban — our guide, translator and expert driver — and he has brought us here after a busy morning exploring. He whispers in my ear that the song was written by Iraj Bastami, a classical musician killed in 2003 in the earthquake that destroyed the ancient city of Bam. 'Everyone loved him,' he says. 'People still weep when they hear his music.'

/

The chai is hot and reviving. I drink it black and strong, although Ali and Ebi, our photographer friend, sip it through lumps of sugar, lodged between their front teeth. Greg is still learning this skill, and for now finds it easier to load the hard rocks of sugar into his glass and stir vigorously until they dissolve.

/

We've been in Iran for a few days now, and this must be the fiftieth glass of chai I've drunk. As Ali explained early on, 'In Iran, without chai, nothing happens!'. His words have proved curiously prophetic as Greg and I have fast developed an addiction to Iranian tea and it's become almost essential to our daily well-being. I'm starting to feel that without chai, we don't happen either.

/

A LITTLE WHILE LATER WE ARE BACK OUTSIDE IN THE bazaar. In hot climates, commerce follows the course of the sun; the shutters come down at lunchtime and are only pulled back up again late in the afternoon. Now the shops are starting to reopen and the passageways are bustling with people. Kerman is an ancient city on the edge of the Dasht-e Lut – the Great Salt Desert – and it used to be an important staging post on the Silk Road that carried trade between Asia and Persia. This is one of the oldest bazaars in Iran and it feels a bit wilder than others we've visited in the Middle East. This could be because of its reputation as a centre for the opium that is smuggled in from nearby Afghanistan and Pakistan, but it is also because of the clientele. These are Baluchi people; their skin is dark, their eyes black and intense. There are few black chadors to be seen. Instead the women are swathed in bright orange, pink and purple. The men wear baggy pants and long loose shirts; some sport elaborately wound turbans and curly slippers.

/

We wander idly past mannequins clad in manteaus, an Iranian trenchcoat of sorts, and stalls crammed with bolts of sheer, shimmering fabrics. There are dusty shops overflowing with cheap plastic toys and shelves of stoppered glass perfume bottles. Another arcade opens onto a broad square and is crowded with brightly painted tin trunks, towers of beaten metal pots and vast copper cauldrons. We stop to admire an attractive display of

dried herbs and try to identify mysterious twigs, petals, seeds and nuts. Elegant brass dishes display fragrant spices of all the colours of the rainbow, and we notice a predominance of cumin, the locally grown spice that gives Kerman its name.

/

Further along we admire ancient wooden doors set into intricately carved stonework and Ali points out lions, dragons and radiant suns in the tile-work. We pause at the high arched portal to the Ganj Ali Khan bathhouse, where the ceiling is painted with lively frescoes in chalky shades of red and blue, then continue down the tiny flight of stairs and enter the magnificently restored hamam itself, complete with alabaster pools of goldfish and rather bizarre wax effigies depicting traditional bathhouse scenes.

/

It is cool in the hamam, but back in the bazaar, despite the lateness of the afternoon, it is hot and dusty. Lunch seems a long time ago and we duck into a traditional ice-cream shop for refreshments. Two young women at the next table are eating saffron ice-cream studded with pistachios, but we opt for the local version of an Iranian specialty, faloodeh, a chilled concoction of thin noodles drenched in lime or sour-cherry syrup. In Kerman, faloodeh is more like tapioca and to our Western palates the texture is unusual. But it is icy-cold and revives our spirits.

/

The two women are keen to talk. They have been eyeing me curiously and lean over to ask why I wear no jewellery apart from my wedding ring. I see that their own thin brown wrists are weighed down with gold bangles of varying shapes and sizes. In this part of Iran, traditional families set great store by jewels, in particular gold, which can be converted to cash in times of need.

/

They tell us that they are students, but that the local university has been closed for the last four months in the wake of the country's elections. They are bored. Foreign tourists like us are a rarity and provide a refreshing interlude in their day. I think of my stepson back in Australia grumbling about the number of lectures and seminars he has to attend. 'How do you spend your days if there are no classes?', I ask. They look downcast. 'There is nothing here,' says one of the young women eventually. 'We come to the bazaar and we eat ice-cream with our friends. What else can we do but wait?'

/

THE COUNTRYSIDE BETWEEN KERMAN AND MAHAN TO THE SOUTH IS STONY
and grey. It is separated from the terrible Dasht-e Lut desert by the Payeh
Mountains, a long crease of craggy hills. Although it is early in the day, and
a mere thirty-minute drive, by the time we arrive at Mahan we are hot and
thirsty. It's easy to imagine the exhaustion of travellers crossing such bleak
terrain from the Indian subcontinent, and the relief they must have felt upon
arriving in this oasis town.

/

In the fifteenth century, some of these travellers would have been pilgrims,
coming to visit Shah Ne'matollah Vali, a revered Sufi Dervish and poet who
died in 1431. One of his most devoted followers was Ahmad Shah Dakani, an
Indian king, and it was he who in 1436 began building a shrine to the master.
As our car pulls up out the front, it's hard to miss the pretty turquoise dome
peeping above high brick walls. Although it is more than five hundred years
old, the dome looks strikingly modern with a geometric spiderweb of black
and white tiles traced over its bright-blue surface.

/

Within the walls of the complex is a green, densely planted garden. Pink
oleanders creep up the brickwork and everything is shaded by tall cypress
and pine trees. We wander through peaceful courtyards, past ponds fringed
with flowerbeds and rows of potted geraniums. Even the faintest breeze
blows wonderfully cooling air across the surface of the water.

/

We follow a white-turbanned Sufi through a series of seven ancient wooden doors, symbolising the journey to divine unity – the seven doorways of heaven. We pass by the tomb itself and enter a vast airy prayer hall. The vaults and archways are decorated with exquisite plasterwork – the entire ceiling a delicate canopy of gold stars. Tucked away in a corner is a tiny meditation room where Ne'matollah is said to have spent forty days and nights praying. Spirals of calligraphy in soft shades of dusty red and green cover the walls and ceiling, and feel particularly Indian.

/

I pause in this little room for a while and am suddenly overcome by a strange feeling of ... what? Not peace, exactly, but a sense of calm. For a fleeting moment I can see the appeal of Sufism, this rather abstruse, mystical branch of Islam, with its abandonment of material things and its focus inward on the soul. And then from outside the room I hear a small child giggling. It's a lovely, musical sound. I turn instinctively to find the source, and the spell is broken.

/

It isn't long before our focus is very much back on the body – our stomachs in particular. On the outskirts of Mahan, in the car park outside the Bagh-e Shahzadeh, we buy two heart-shaped loaves of komaj, a bright-yellow flatbread and a local specialty. The seller stuffs them into a plastic bag and drenches them with icing sugar before passing the bag into our eager hands. Ali is just able to prevent us from tucking into the bread straight away with the promise of chai inside the garden.

/

'Bagh' is the Persian word for a formal garden, and this is a true oasis garden where water from the nearby mountains is channelled via the qanat system – underground pipes – into vast cisterns just outside the walls. It is a delight. The gardens stretch upwards before us and we climb a surprisingly steep gradient to the promised tea house at the summit. Water burbles merrily past us down a broad central channel, broken every now and then by dancing fountains. Willow, cypress and pomegranate trees overhang long reflection pools and at the top, in front of the governor's residence, there is a riot of orange, yellow and red flowers. We gaze back down along the avenue of trees, to the fragile pillars and arches of a summer pavilion, framed by a backdrop of lilac mountains and a bright-blue sky.

/

We collapse gratefully onto carpeted daybeds at the tea house, idyllically situated beneath shady trees. The chai comes quickly and we are finally allowed to tuck into the sweet yellow bread. It's filled with dates, walnuts and sugar and flavoured, surprisingly, with turmeric and cumin. It is quite delicious and between the four of us we make short work of the two loaves.

/

I long to laze around in these verdant gardens for the rest of the day. Instead we drive further into the desert.

/

Ali turns the car east and before long we are climbing steadily over the Payeh Mountains. We exit down into a flat, rocky valley and fly through a hot, grey, stony landscape that soon gives way to hot, grey nothingness. Then the colours begin to change and sand drifts onto the road. This is no longer the classic stony Persian desert, but closer to the sandy deserts I've seen before in North Africa, the Gulf countries and Australia. We coast through a rolling sea of dunes and then, suddenly, we're looking out over a vast, empty plain. In the distance we can clearly make out the Kaluts, a long, broad corridor of massive rock formations marching across the horizon.

/

We drive on – by now we've been driving for several hours – and as we get closer a succession of fantastic rocky crags, sand turrets and towers start to spring out of the barren landscape. Ali is beaming. He comes from the north of Iran, where the terrain is very different, and he loves this desert. He is in the middle of telling us about a recent overnight trip he made here with a group of Swedish tourists, when he suddenly jerks the steering wheel and we veer off the road – although not onto any track that I can see. The car struggles higher and higher over the dunes and we finally draw to a standstill atop a sandy cliff.

/

We pile out of the car and immediately a stifling weight of hot, hot air crushes us into the ground. We clamber around for a while, slipping on the constantly shifting sand. An evil wind springs up and eddies around us, rippling the sand and sending great swathes of it over the car, over the rocks and over us. It is wind like this – often called the black winds for the dust they bear – that blasts across the desert from the north-east to create the strange eroded rock formations of the Kaluts.

/

'Here you can sleep in a million-star hotel!' proclaims Ali proudly. And a part of me longs to do just that: to wait until the sun drops into the sand, build a fire, spread out a rug and gaze up at the vast heavens above. But there are still many hours until sunset and the truth is that none of us can contemplate staying in this desiccated wasteland for one second longer. Defeated by the heat and the wind we climb back into the air-conditioned comfort of Ali's Peugeot and start the long drive back to Kerman.

/

WE ARE FOLLOWING ONE OF THE ancient caravan routes between Kerman and Yazd to the north, now a modern highway. Marco Polo travelled this way in the thirteenth century and in his account of the trip he records passing through groves of fine date palms and feasting on an abundance of partridge, quail and other wild game.

/

We see no signs of any of these delights, but near Rafsanjan we pull off the road to watch a group of labourers in a pistachio orchard. The owner, Haj Mahmud, is supervising the harvest from a series of small walled fields. It looks like hot work, but the men and women move quickly, stripping ripe nuts from the branches onto sheets spread on the ground. When the mound of the purple–pink nuts is large enough, the sheet is gathered up and its load is carried to a truck to be delivered to Haj Mahmud's house in the nearby village for processing.

/

We follow the truck to the village and watch as the pistachios are put through a machine that strips away the pretty outer skin, leaving the familiar white split shell and nut within. 'We say these pistachios are smiling,' Haj Mahmud tells us, grinning himself. 'The bigger the smile, the better the nut.'

/

We are invited to lunch! Our first home-cooked Persian meal. Mahmud's wife – Haj Khanum – spreads a bright plastic cloth over the floor of their airy salon and dishes of food appear from nowhere: saffron rice, thin yoghurt with cucumber, thick yoghurt with dates, braised eggplant, sun-dried tomatoes, minced lamb 'cotlets'.

/

There is much friendly conversation. Photos are taken, email addresses exchanged. Best of all, Haj Khanum shows us how to roast a panful of pistachios with saffron and salt. She fills a big bag with the fragrant nuts and, thus prepared for the onward journey, we are sent on our way.

/

THE FINAL PUSH. WE'RE TO SPEND THE NIGHT AT A CARAVANSERAI — AN ancient hostelry from the Silk Road days – about an hour south of Yazd. Night has already fallen by the time we turn off the main highway and the road vanishes into blackness. I'm relieved that Ali knows the way through the desert. We bump along a track over the sand – mercifully only a short distance – and pull to a stop outside a massive building. It's hard to make out the shape in the darkness, but as we climb wearily out of the car, two vast wooden doors are flung open, light spills out and we are admitted to heaven.

/

This is Zein-o Din, an exquisitely renovated caravanserai. No expense has been spared and inside there are all manner of comforts for the weary traveller. There is hot water, for a start, and we gratefully shower away the dust of the day. Next there is reviving food, and after dinner we retire to our own rooms to sort ourselves out. Each of us has a different chore: Ebi must upload and organise his photos, Greg and I must write up our respective notes, and Ali, our fearless saraban, must telephone ahead to confirm our itinerary for the days ahead.

/

The business side of the day completed, I venture out of my room and see the others sitting together on the platform outside Ali's room. It's carpeted and there are soft, long cushions against the walls. The men are eating dates and laughing. They call out to me across the open central courtyard and the voices of travellers past, present and future seem to echo off the walls and disappear up into the night sky.

/

the staples

The Persian Bakery

THERE IS NOTHING QUITE LIKE Iranian bread – and there is plenty of it! People eat naan for breakfast, lunch and dinner – in fact it's the first thing to appear on any table, and all Iranians would consider a meal incomplete without it. Bread's role is not just as a staple consumable; it also has a practical application as it is used instead of a spoon or fork to scoop and mop up food, and for wrapping all manner of ingredients to be eaten by hand.

/

Three basic types of naan are found all around the country – barberi, lavash (or taftoon) and sangak – as well as numerous regional variations. Bread can be thick or thin, soft or firmer, white or wholemeal, sweet or savoury – even crisp. In some parts, it is sprinkled with seeds, flavoured with spices, drizzled with flavourings, or stuffed. That being said, apart from the odd bread roll, a favourite for lunchtime offal sandwiches, bread is always flat.

/

In small villages and rural areas some people still make their own bread in tanoor – wood-, peat- or dung-fuelled ovens that abut the house. In cities and towns, though, bread is so abundant that it is rarely made in the home any more. One of our favourite sights as we travelled around the country was of people – men, women and children – queuing up at their local bakery to collect hot bread straight from the oven. Neighbourhoods have not one but several bakers who each prepare a single kind of bread, several times a day. And their customers, too, come several times a day to stock up on supplies for the next meal.

/

In Iran, it would be unthinkable not to have the freshest bread on offer at every meal. Which is not to say that the older stuff is wasted. If stale bread is not able to be revived with a sprinkling of water and quick warm-through in the oven, it will be torn into pieces and used to bulk up soups or stews, dunked into tea, or turned into crumbs for a stuffing.

/

Bread has a huge symbolic significance in Iran and many older people – especially in conservative parts of the country – believe it is sinful to allow even the meanest crust to lie on the ground, and they will pick it up and place it respectfully on a nearby sill or ledge.

/

Barberi
BREAKFAST BREAD

These huge oval flaps of golden bread are enjoyed for breakfast around Iran with clotted cream and honey, fruit conserves, eggs or a warming soup, all equally wonderful.

In commercial bakeries, the dough for barberi bread is shaped into large ovals, around 60 centimetres long, but for the home baker we suggest making smaller loaves, about half the size. This quantity of dough makes three loaves, sufficient for six people.

2 teaspoons dried yeast

500 ml warm water

750 g strong white flour

1 tablespoon sea salt

50 ml olive oil

fine polenta, for dusting

20 g unsalted butter, melted

sesame or nigella seeds (optional)

Dissolve the yeast in 50 ml of the warm water and set aside in a warm place for 10 minutes.

Combine the flour and salt in the bowl of an electric mixer fitted with a dough hook and make a well in the centre. Mix the oil with the remaining water and stir in the yeast mixture, then gradually work into the flour with your hands. Knead on a slow speed for 10–15 minutes until smooth, shiny and elastic – add more tepid water if necessary. Transfer to a lightly oiled bowl, then cover with a damp tea towel and leave to prove in a warm place for 2 hours or until doubled in size.

Preheat the oven to 220°C. Knock back the dough, then leave to prove for a further 20 minutes. Halfway through the proving time, put a large, heavy baking tray into the oven for 10 minutes or until very hot.

Transfer the dough to a lightly floured work surface and knock back. Divide into 6 portions and shape into oval balls. Working with one piece of dough, stretch it into a 30 cm long oval with your hands. If it is easier, roll the dough out lightly with a rolling pin. Scatter a little polenta over the base of the hot baking tray and transfer the stretched piece of dough. Use a sharp knife or pizza cutter to mark narrowly spaced parallel lines along the length of the dough. Brush with melted butter and sprinkle with the seeds of your choice.

Bake for 6–7 minutes, until slightly risen and a rich golden brown. Transfer the cooked loaf to a wooden board and cover with a clean tea towel.

While the bread is baking, prepare the next loaf. Continue with the remaining balls of dough.

Barberi bread is best eaten warm. Alternatively, leave it to cool completely, then wrap in plastic and freeze for up to 1 month. Thaw at room temperature and reheat in a warm oven. MAKES 3

Lavash
THIN FLATBREAD

Lavash, paper-thin sheets of flatbread, is eaten by everyone, every day at virtually every meal in Iran – in fact lavash is often used instead of cutlery for scooping up food. It is also used to wrap around kebabs or sandwich fillings – the ubiquitous favourite being fresh herbs and soft white cheese for a quick and easy snack.

Taftoon is a slightly thicker variation of lavash that you can make from the same dough. Both styles of bread keep well if wrapped in a damp cloth and refrigerated. Even better, pieces can be wrapped in plastic, stored in the freezer and thawed in no time when required. Although lavash and taftoon stiffen up fairly quickly, they are easily made pliable again if sprinkled with a little water and heated briefly in a warm oven.

2 teaspoons dried yeast
550 ml warm water
850 g strong white flour
1½ tablespoons sea salt
fine polenta, for dusting

Dissolve the yeast in 50 ml of the warm water and set aside in a warm place for 10 minutes.

Combine the flour and salt in the bowl of an electric mixer fitted with a dough hook and make a well in the centre. Stir the yeast mixture into the remaining water, then gradually work into the flour with your hands. Knead on a slow speed for 10–15 minutes until very smooth and shiny. Transfer to a lightly oiled bowl, then cover with a damp tea towel and leave to prove in a warm place for 2 hours or until doubled in size.

Preheat the oven to its highest temperature. Knock back the dough, then leave to prove for a further 20 minutes. Halfway through the proving time, put a large, heavy baking tray into the oven for 10 minutes or until very hot.

Transfer the dough to a lightly floured work surface and knock back. Divide into 6 portions and shape into oval balls. Working with one piece of dough at a time, roll it out as thinly as you can into a rectangular sheet. Scatter a little polenta over the base of the hot baking tray and quickly transfer the sheet of dough, stretching it a little more, if you can.

Bake for 5 minutes, or until a pale golden brown. Wrap in a clean tea towel and leave to cool. The bread might be crisp as it comes out of the oven, but will soften as it cools.

While the bread is baking, prepare the next piece of dough. Continue with the remaining balls of dough. Eat warm or cold. Once cold, wrap in a damp tea towel and refrigerate, or wrap in plastic and freeze for up to 1 month. Thaw at room temperature and reheat in a warm oven. **MAKES 6**

Sangak
STONE BREAD

Spotting a sangak baker on our travels was always cause for celebration as this bread had quickly become our favourite. Sangak – or stone bread – is so-called because it is baked on a bed of small pebbles spread over the base of the baker's oven. These create a distinctive pattern of indentations on the base of the bread, while the surface puffs into lovely brown blisters. The wholemeal flour gives the bread a nutty flavour and slightly chewy texture.

You can, of course, make sangak on a baking tray and still enjoy the flavour and texture. If you want to go the whole way, you will need to find a selection of small, even-sized pebbles – anywhere from 1–5 centimetres is good. The pebbles must be thoroughly washed and dried, then liberally oiled, before use.

2 teaspoons dried yeast
180 ml warm water
270 g wholemeal flour
500 g strong white flour
1½ tablespoons sea salt
300 ml tepid water

Dissolve the dried yeast in the warm water and set aside in a warm place for 10 minutes until frothy.

Combine the flours and salt in the bowl of an electric mixer fitted with a dough hook and make a well in the centre. Stir the yeast mixture into the tepid water, then gradually work into the flour with your hands. Knead on a slow speed for 10–15 minutes until very smooth and shiny. Transfer to a lightly oiled bowl, then cover with a damp tea towel and leave to prove in a warm place for 2 hours or until doubled in size.

Preheat the oven to its highest temperature. Knock back the dough, then leave to prove for a further 20 minutes. Halfway through the proving time, scatter the oiled pebbles, if using, over the base of a large, heavy baking tray and place in the oven for 10 minutes, or until very hot (otherwise just heat the baking tray in the oven).

Transfer the dough to a lightly floured work surface and knock back. Divide into 6 portions and shape into oval balls. Working with one piece of dough at a time, roll it out to a thin rectangle, about 30 cm x 20 cm. Transfer the dough to the hot baking tray and push it fairly firmly into the pebbles.

Bake for 5 minutes, or until a rich golden brown. When cooked, the bread should lift easily away from the pebbles. While the bread is baking, prepare the next piece of dough. Continue with the remaining balls of dough.

Sangak is best eaten hot from the oven as it doesn't keep quite as well as plain white bread. MAKES 6

Komaj
DATE BREAD WITH TURMERIC AND CUMIN

This is our interpretation of a wonderful savoury–sweet bread we tasted in the oasis town of Mahan in the south-east of Iran. Cumin is grown in abundance in the region and is used to flavour many of the local dishes, often in combination with turmeric. The addition of sweet, sticky dates turns this bread into an afternoon treat when served with a cup of fragrant tea.

We use a heart-shaped cutter here to make the buns, as this was the way we enjoyed them in Mahan. But, obviously, you can use any shape cutter of similar dimensions you like.

2 teaspoons dried yeast

50 ml warm water

680 g strong white flour

60 g sugar

1 teaspoon ground turmeric

1 heaped teaspoon sea salt

310 ml tepid water

30 ml olive oil

1 egg

15 fresh dates, pitted and cut into chunks

50 g unsalted butter, softened

2 egg yolks, lightly beaten

1 tablespoon cumin seeds, lightly crushed

icing sugar, for dusting

Dissolve the dried yeast in the 50 ml warm water and set aside in a warm place for 10 minutes.

Combine the flour, sugar, turmeric and salt in the bowl of an electric mixer fitted with a dough hook and make a well in the centre. Whisk the 310 ml tepid water, oil and whole egg in a bowl, then stir in the yeast mixture. Gradually work the yeast mixture into the flour mixture with your hands. Knead on a slow speed for 10 minutes until smooth and shiny. Transfer to a lightly oiled bowl, then cover with a damp tea towel and leave to prove in a warm place for 1 hour or until doubled in size.

Knock back the dough and leave to prove again in a warm place for 1 hour, until doubled in size.

Preheat the oven to 200ºC. Divide the dough into 8 even portions, then cut each in half. Working with one portion at a time, roll it out to a rectangle, about 17 cm x 11 cm (or roll as appropriate for your chosen cutter), and place it crosswise in front of you. Sit a 9 cm x 8 cm heart-shaped cutter on the left-hand side of the dough and place a few pieces of date inside it. Squish on a small piece of butter, then remove the cutter and fold the dough over, from right to left, to cover the filling. Cut out a heart shape and transfer to a baking tray. Repeat with the remaining portions of dough, then reroll the offcuts. You should get around 20 buns in total. Leave the buns to sit on the baking tray for 15 minutes, then brush lightly with the egg yolk and sprinkle on a good pinch of cumin seeds. Bake for 6–8 minutes until puffed and golden.

Remove from the oven and cool briefly (if you have the willpower) on a wire rack before dusting with icing sugar and eating. MAKES 20

Pirashki

SPICY POTATO PIRASHKIS

Pirashkis are a modern – possibly Russian-influenced – version of Sanbuseh (page 50), and can be savoury or filled with a delicate sweet custard. Pirashkis are made with a light yeast dough, rather than pastry, so they puff up like little airy doughnuts. They may be deep-fried, but baking them in the oven gives almost as delectable a result, and is clearly the way to go if you are calorie-conscious.

80 g clarified butter or ghee, for brushing
thick natural yoghurt, to serve (optional)

PIRASHKI DOUGH

2 teaspoons dried yeast
240 g thick natural yoghurt
3 eggs
50 ml olive oil
1½ tablespoons caster sugar
500 g plain flour
good pinch of sea salt

SPICY POTATO FILLING

5 large potatoes, peeled
30 ml olive oil
1 teaspoon mustard seeds
1 teaspoon ground cumin
1 teaspoon ground turmeric
½ teaspoon cayenne pepper
½ teaspoon sea salt
1 large onion, finely chopped
1 leek, finely chopped
1 clove garlic, finely chopped
juice of 1 lemon
½ cup shredded coriander leaves

To make the dough, stir the yeast into the yoghurt. Lightly whisk the eggs with the oil and sugar, then tip into the yoghurt mixture.

Combine the flour and salt in the bowl of an electric mixer fitted with a dough hook. Tip in the yeast mixture and knead on a slow speed for 4–5 minutes until the mixture comes together as a smooth dough. Be careful not to overwork it. Transfer to a lightly oiled bowl, then cover with a damp tea towel and leave to prove in a warm place for 1 hour.

To make the filling, boil the potatoes until just tender, then cut into 5 mm dice. Heat the oil in a heavy-based frying pan over a low heat. Add the mustard seeds and fry until they start to pop. Add the cumin, turmeric and cayenne and stir together briskly. Stir in the salt, onion, leek and garlic and fry gently for 5 minutes, or until the vegetables start to soften. Add the diced potato and mix well. Remove the pan from the heat and leave the mixture to cool. When it is cold, stir in the lemon juice and coriander.

When ready to make the pirashkis, preheat the oven to 180°C and line a baking tray with baking paper. Knock back the dough and shape it into a fat, flattish rectangle. Fold it over and bash it firmly with your hands into another fat, flattish rectangle – or use a rolling pin to roll it out. Repeat another 8–10 times; the idea is to form layers in the dough, which makes the end result lighter.

Divide the dough into 6 equal portions and cover with a damp tea towel. Working with one portion at a time, roll out the dough until about 2 mm thick, then use a 9 cm pastry cutter to cut out 4 rounds. Place a teaspoon of filling in the middle of each round and fold the top over to create a crescent. Press gently to seal. The dough is fairly wet, so should seal without extra water. Cover the completed pastries with a damp cloth. Repeat with the remaining dough and filling. Brush the pirashkis lightly with a little clarified butter and bake for 6–8 minutes or until golden brown. Serve hot with creamy yoghurt, if you like. MAKES 24

Sanbuseh
LITTLE BEEF AND CINNAMON TURNOVERS

Stuffed pastries – both savoury and sweet – feature widely in all Middle Eastern cuisines. In Persia, they came into their own during the elaborate court cooking of the Safavid era, although the tradition is thought to date back several thousand years. Savoury pastries no longer seem to feature widely in Iranian cooking, but when they do pop up, they are known as sanbuseh – and the link to the Indian samosa and the sambusek of the Middle East is obvious on eating.

These little turnovers are my interpretation of a Safavid-style sanbuseh. I think a light dusting of icing sugar really brings out the underlying cinnamon-sweetness of the filling.

20 sheets filo pastry
100 g clarified butter or ghee
2 tablespoons icing sugar
½ teaspoon ground cinnamon

CINNAMON–BEEF FILLING
30 ml olive oil
30 g unsalted butter
1 large onion, finely diced
1 clove garlic, finely diced
1 teaspoon freshly grated nutmeg
1 teaspoon freshly ground black pepper
1 teaspoon sweet paprika
½ teaspoon ground cinnamon
½ teaspoon sea salt
425 g minced beef
2 tablespoons shredded flat-leaf
  parsley leaves

To make the cinnamon–beef filling, heat the oil and butter in a heavy-based frying pan over a low heat. Add the onion and garlic and fry gently until they begin to soften. Add the spices and salt and fry for 5 minutes, then mix in the minced beef, using a wooden spoon to break up any lumps. Fry gently for 8 minutes, or until the beef is just cooked. Remove the pan from the heat and leave the mixture to cool. When it is cold, stir in the parsley.

To make the turnovers, work with 2 sheets of filo at a time and keep the others covered with a damp tea towel. Spread 1 sheet of filo out on the work surface and brush it lightly with clarified butter. Place the second sheet on top and cut lengthways into 4 long strips. Each strip will make a turnover. Brush each strip along its length with butter. Place a teaspoon of filling at one end and fold the corner over it to make a triangle. Continue to fold along the length of the strip of pastry so you end up with a neat, triangle-shaped parcel. Seal any open edges with a little more butter. Repeat with the remaining filo sheets and filling until you have 40 turnovers. At this stage you can freeze the pastries if you like; otherwise, cook them straightaway.

Preheat the oven to 180°C and line a baking tray with baking paper. Brush the turnovers lightly with a little more clarified butter and cook for 6–8 minutes, until golden brown.

Sift the icing sugar and cinnamon together over the hot turnovers and serve immediately. MAKES 40

Cooking Rice the Persian Way

FOR ANYONE USED TO THE sticky clumpiness of Asian rice, Persian rice will come as a revelation. It is light, dry, fluffy and fragrant, and appears at the table in myriad forms. It is the axis around which nearly every Persian meal revolves, whether as a simple platter of buttery saffron rice to accompany kebabs or as a complex layered polow, incorporating meat, vegetables, nuts, herbs and all manner of exotic spices.

/

Rice was brought to Iran from India several thousand years ago and is grown in the northern provinces near the Caspian Sea. There are seemingly endless varieties on offer in Iran. Short, thick and starchy rice is used for stuffings, meatballs and desserts, but the vast majority of Iranian rice dishes are made from long-grain varieties, some of which are considered to be among the finest in the world. In the north the rice is sometimes smoked, too, which gives it a distinctive flavour.

/

It can be difficult to find Iranian rice outside Iran, although if you are lucky you might be able to find sadri, an excellent quality long-grain rice similar to basmati. For most of us, the best choice for Persian rice dishes is indeed basmati, which is what we specify in the recipes in this book.

/

Most rice these days is pretty clean, but it is usually a good idea to keep an eye out for any random twigs or stones. Whichever long-grain rice you use, it is always thoroughly washed before cooking to remove a lot of the starch. In Iran, the locally grown rice is rather hard, and needs to be soaked. Basmati rice doesn't really need this, but we find it still benefits from a quick soak, to loosen the grains and remove some starch. Even 5 minutes, with a bit of gentle swishing, will help.

/

When it comes to cooking Persian rice dishes, there are essentially two basic methods. Kateh, which is mainly used in the Caspian Sea region, is a simple absorption method whereby the rice is first boiled until the water has been absorbed and then steamed, without rinsing or straining, for 30–40 minutes, to create a solid cake with a crusty base.

/

Far and away the most prevalent cooking technique is the parboil–rinse–steam method, which achieves a gloriously fluffy result and is used for plain chelow rice and also for layered polow dishes. Nearly all the recipes that follow use this basic method, and we can almost guarantee that once mastered, you will never cook rice any other way! Although an electric Persian rice cooker (available in specialist Iranian stores) takes much of the effort out of preparing rice, we've found that a normal saucepan does the job well – and non-stick varieties make it a breeze.

/

For Iranians, one of the most important parts of any rice dish is the crunchy layer that forms under the rice as it cooks – the tah-deeg, which literally means 'base of the pot'. We've found that it is best to use oil or ghee to start the tah-deeg, as straight butter burns too easily. For aficionados, there are several popular tah-deeg variations, which are listed on page 53. For a fancy presentation the rice is inverted onto a platter, so the golden crust can be properly admired. But in many households, for everyday eating the rice is spooned onto a platter and the tah-deeg is served on a separate plate for everyone to fight over.

/

Finally, a note about quantities. Most Westerners would blanch at the vast amounts of rice that the average Iranian can put away at mealtimes, so we've scaled back the amounts accordingly. As a basic guide, we suggest 50 grams per person, which should be sufficient as an accompanying dish for all but the hungriest. As the ratio of rice to water in this method is not critical, you can easily alter the quantities.

/

Chelow
CLASSIC PERSIAN RICE

Once you've grasped the basic parboil–
rinse–steam technique of chelow,
you'll be ready to tackle other Persian
rice dishes as most follow the same
method.

water
300 g basmati rice
2 tablespoons sea salt
70 ml vegetable oil
40 g unsalted butter, melted

Wash the rice thoroughly, then leave it to soak in a generous amount of lukewarm water for 30 minutes. Swish it around with your fingers every now and then to loosen the starch.

Strain the rice, rinsing it again with warm water.

Bring 2 litres water to a boil in a large saucepan. Add the salt and stir in the strained rice. Return the water to a rolling boil and cook, uncovered, for 5 minutes. Test the rice by pinching a grain between your fingers or by biting it. It should be soft on the outside, but still hard in the centre. Strain the rice and rinse again with warm water. Toss it several times to drain away as much of the water as you can.

Return the saucepan to a medium heat and add the oil and 2 tablespoons water. As soon as the oil begins to sizzle, spoon in enough rice to cover the base of the saucepan in a thin layer, then spoon in the rest of the rice gradually, building it up into a pyramid. Don't tip it all in at once, as this will squash the rice and you won't achieve the proper fluffy lightness. Use the handle of a wooden spoon to poke 5 or 6 holes down through the rice to the base of the pan to help it steam. Mix 2 tablespoons warm water with the melted butter and drizzle this over the rice. Wrap the saucepan lid in a clean tea towel and cover the pan as tightly as you can.

Leave the pan on a medium–high heat for a 2–3 minutes until the rice is visibly steaming – you will see puffs of steam escaping from the edges of the pan. Turn the heat down to low and leave the pan alone for 40 minutes. Resist the temptation to peek, as this releases the steam and affects the cooking time. The rice can actually sit quite happily over the lowest possible heat for another 20 minutes or so.

When ready to serve, sit the saucepan in a little cold water in the sink; the sudden change in temperature creates a surge of steam that 'shocks' the rice and makes it shrink from the sides, which loosens the crusty bottom.

To serve, invert the pan onto a warm serving platter so that the rice plops out as one glorious, golden-capped mound. Otherwise, spoon the rice into a warm serving dish and when you reach the crispy base, lift it out and drape it over the rice. It doesn't matter in the slightest if the tah-deeg breaks. Alternatively, present it on a separate plate. **SERVES 6**

SAFFRON TAH-DEEG

The simplest tah-deeg can also be jazzed up a bit by sprinkling saffron liquid (page 54) instead of plain water into the sizzling oil just before you add the parboiled rice to the pan.

YOGHURT TAH-DEEG

Beat 2 tablespoons thick natural yoghurt with 1 egg and 1 tablespoon saffron liquid (page 54). Mix this with a generous scoop of the parboiled rice and spread it over the sizzling oil. Spoon in the rice and steam as described.

POTATO TAH-DEEG

Arrange thin, slightly overlapping slices of waxy potato in the sizzling oil. Spoon in the rice and steam as described.

BREAD TAH-DEEG

Lay a piece of Lavash (page 44) or a pita bread split in half in the sizzling oil. Fill any gaps with torn bits of bread. Spoon in the rice and steam as described.

Saffron chelow rice

Saffron is often used as a garnish to liven up plain white chelow rice. The classic presentation is described below, but an alternative method that we like is to drizzle saffron liquid over the parboiled rice before steaming, which creates a pretty marbled effect through the rice as it cooks.

In Iran, it's rare to see whole saffron threads in rice dishes. Saffron is nearly always used in powder form and steeped in a little water to create a saffron liquid. We prefer to buy the best-quality saffron threads we can find and grind them as called for. (If you need more than 2 tablespoons saffron liquid, simply allow 10 saffron threads per each extra 1 tablespoon boiling water and proceed as below.) If you'd rather, however, you can use ¼ teaspoon saffron powder – just mix it with the boiling water and proceed as described below.

water	70 ml vegetable oil	**SAFFRON LIQUID**
300 g basmati rice	40 g unsalted butter,	20 saffron threads
2 tablespoons sea salt	melted	2 tablespoons boiling water

To make the saffron liquid, lightly toast the saffron threads in a dry frying pan over a medium heat for about 30 seconds. While the threads must be totally dry, be very careful not to burn them. As they crisp up, they will begin to release a wonderfully pungent aroma. Tip the saffron into a mortar and leave for a moment or two before grinding to a powder.

Mix the ground saffron with the boiling water and set aside to infuse for at least 1 hour before using. The colour will continue to develop for about 12 hours.

Prepare the rice as described on page 53. Just before serving, remove 2–3 tablespoons cooked rice and mix with the saffron liquid in a small bowl. Set this saffron rice aside to use as garnish.

Tip the remaining rice onto a serving platter. Sprinkle on the saffron rice and serve the tah-deeg separately. SERVES 6

Sabzi polow
RICE WITH SOFT SPRING HERBS

This vibrant green rice dish is wonderful all year round, but is at its best in spring, when fresh herbs – sabzi – are abundant once again. Sabzi polow is especially popular over the Persian New Year when it is traditionally served with fried fish. Saffron can also be used to give this dish a glorious finishing touch – just follow the steps for using saffron liquid on page 54.

water

300 g basmati rice

2 tablespoons sea salt

70 ml vegetable oil

½ cup finely snipped chives

½ cup finely shredded flat-leaf
   parsley leaves

½ cup finely shredded dill
   sprigs

½ cup finely shredded
   coriander leaves

40 g unsalted butter, melted

1 large clove garlic, lightly
   crushed

Wash, soak and parboil the rice as described on page 53.

Return the saucepan to a medium heat and add the oil and 2 tablespoons water. As soon as the oil begins to sizzle, spoon in enough rice to cover the base of the saucepan in a thin layer. Gently toss the remaining rice with the chopped herbs and spoon it into the pan, building it up into a pyramid. Use the handle of a wooden spoon to poke 5 or 6 holes down through the rice to the base of the pan to help it steam. Mix 2 tablespoons warm water into the melted butter and drizzle this over the rice. Sit the garlic on top of the rice and continue as described on page 53. **SERVES 6**

Addas polow
SAFFRON RICE WITH LENTILS

Lentil and rice dishes are popular all around the Middle East, as the combination is a great way of boosting one's protein intake. In this polow, the nutty flavours of the rice and lentils are offset brilliantly by the sweetness of sultanas and toffee-ish dates. This is another dish that works well for vegetarians, but it also makes a good accompaniment to lamb or chicken dishes.

water

300 g basmati rice

2 tablespoons sea salt

100 g brown lentils

2 tablespoons sultanas

100 ml vegetable oil

1 teaspoon ground allspice

½ teaspoon freshly ground black pepper

6 fresh dates, pitted and cut in half

40 g unsalted butter, melted

2 tablespoons Saffron Liquid (page 54)

1 onion, finely sliced

Wash, soak and parboil the rice as described on page 53.

Cook the lentils in boiling water for 20–30 minutes, or until just tender, then drain well and set aside. Soak the sultanas in a little hot water for 20 minutes, then drain.

Return the rice saucepan to a medium heat and add 70 ml of the oil and 2 tablespoons water. As soon as the oil begins to sizzle, spoon in enough rice to cover the base of the pan in a thin layer. Mix the sultanas with the lentils, then stir in the allspice and pepper. Scatter a layer of this mixture over the rice in the pan. Continue to layer the rice and the lentil mixture, building them up into a pyramid. Use the handle of a wooden spoon to poke 5 or 6 holes down through the rice to the base of the pan to help it steam. Arrange the dates on top. Mix 2 tablespoons warm water with the melted butter and the saffron liquid and drizzle this over the rice. Continue as described on page 53.

Meanwhile, heat the remaining 30 ml oil in a frying pan over a low–medium heat and fry the onion for 8–10 minutes until golden brown, stirring continuously.

Garnish the polow with the fried onion before serving. **SERVES 6**

Baghali polow
BROAD BEAN, BORLOTTI AND DILL RICE

Broad beans and dill go beautifully together and we tried several versions of this classic dish while on our travels. It is particularly good served with lamb, but makes a great vegetarian option, accompanied by a big bowl of creamy yoghurt.

You can make this polow quite happily with frozen broad beans, but don't forget to slip them out of their outer skins. The dried mint and lemon peel are not strictly traditional, but they add an extra dimension of flavour.

water
300 g basmati rice
2 tablespoons sea salt
1 kg broad beans in the pod or
   300 g frozen broad beans
600 g borlotti beans in the pod
70 ml vegetable oil
⅓ cup chopped dill sprigs
1 heaped teaspoon dried mint
40 g unsalted butter, melted
1 large clove garlic, lightly crushed
1 long strip lemon peel, all pith removed

Wash, soak and parboil the rice as described on page 53.

Bring a saucepan of water to a boil. Pod the broad beans and borlotti beans, then blanch them briefly, separately, in the boiling water and peel the broad beans. If using frozen broad beans, slip them out of their skins.

Return the rice saucepan to a medium heat and add the oil and 2 tablespoons water. As soon as the oil begins to sizzle, spoon in enough rice to cover the base of the saucepan in a thin layer. Gently toss the remaining rice with the beans, dill and mint and spoon it into the pan, building it up into a pyramid. Use the handle of a wooden spoon to poke 5 or 6 holes down through the rice to the base of the pan to help it steam. Mix 2 tablespoons warm water with the melted butter and drizzle this over the rice. Sit the garlic clove and lemon peel on top of the rice and continue as described on page 53. **SERVES 6**

Reshteh polow
NOODLE RICE WITH MANDARIN ZEST AND CURRANTS

Noodle rice appeals very much to my Lebanese heart, as it's a popular combination in Middle Eastern cooking. This is a really pretty polow, with bright threads of orange mandarin and golden noodles. The word 'reshteh' actually means 'threads' in Farsi, and noodles are used in several Persian rice and soup dishes to symbolise the tangled threads of life. This dish is often served on occasions when a decision is required, or at times of a new start in life, such as New Year. The threads – or reins – of life can literally be taken in hand, and a new way forward determined.

75 g currants

water

zest of 2 mandarins or oranges, cut into julienne strips

125 ml olive oil

100 g vermicelli noodles, broken into 2 cm lengths

300 g basmati rice

2 tablespoons sea salt

70 ml vegetable oil

½ teaspoon ground cardamom

¼ teaspoon ground cumin

40 g unsalted butter, melted

2 tablespoons Saffron Liquid (page 54)

6 fresh dates, pitted and cut in half

2 cinnamon sticks, broken in half

Soak the currants in hot water for 20 minutes, then drain.

Meanwhile, bring a small saucepan of water to a boil. Blanch the mandarin zest in the boiling water for 20 seconds. Drain and repeat twice more to remove any bitterness.

Heat the olive oil over a medium heat in a heavy-based saucepan. Add the noodles and shallow-fry for 2 minutes, or until golden brown.

Wash, soak and parboil the rice as described on page 53.

Return the rice saucepan to a medium heat and add the vegetable oil and 2 tablespoons water. As soon as the oil begins to sizzle, spoon in enough rice to cover the base of the pan in a thin layer. Gently toss the remaining rice with the mandarin zest, fried noodles, currants and spices and spoon it into the pan, building it up into a pyramid. Use the handle of a wooden spoon to poke 5 or 6 holes down through the rice to the base of the pan to help it steam. Mix 2 tablespoons warm water with the melted butter and saffron liquid and drizzle this over the rice. Scatter the dates over the rice, then sit the cinnamon sticks on top and continue as described on page 53.

Remove the cinnamon sticks before serving the rice garnished with the dates. SERVES 6

Zereshk polow
BARBERRY RICE WITH ROSE PETALS

Fresh barberries are mouth-puckeringly tart, but when dried, which is how they are sold in specialist Iranian or Middle Eastern stores, they add little bursts of sweet-sourness to a dish – and they look like little rubies! This polow is especially good with roast or grilled chicken. The rose petals are not strictly traditional, but they look beautiful and their sweet perfume works well with the tart barberries.

75 g dried barberries, stems removed
water
50 g unsalted butter
1 tablespoon caster sugar
2 tablespoons Saffron Liquid (page 54)
300 g basmati rice
2 tablespoons sea salt
70 ml vegetable oil
1 tablespoon rosewater, or to taste
dried rose petals to garnish (optional)

Soak the barberries in cold water for 2 minutes, then drain and dry well. Melt the butter in a small saucepan over a low heat. Add the barberries and fry for 4–5 minutes, stirring constantly. Add the sugar and saffron liquid and cook for another 3–4 minutes, or until the sugar has dissolved. Remove from the heat.

Wash, soak and parboil the rice as described on page 53.

Return the rice saucepan to a medium heat and add the oil and 2 tablespoons water. As soon as the oil begins to sizzle, spoon in enough rice to cover the base of the pan in a thin layer. Scatter some of the barberries over the rice with a little of the buttery saffron liquid. Continue to layer the rice and the barberries, building them up into a pyramid. Use the handle of a wooden spoon to poke 5 or 6 holes down through the rice to the base of the pan to help it steam. Drizzle on 2 tablespoons warm water and any remaining melted butter and continue as described on page 53.

Serve with a sprinkling of rosewater and the rose petals, if using. **SERVES 6**

Morasa polow
JEWELLED RICE

There are many recipes for this king of Persian dishes, some of which are variations of sweet Shirin Polow (page 64). This version is less sweet, which to our mind really allows the flavours and textures of the separate 'jewels' to shine through.

Much of the beauty of this dish is in the presentation — and indeed morasa polow is often served as a centrepiece at lavish wedding celebrations and other feasts. Instead of turning it out with its crunchy tah-deeg crown, we like to spoon the rice into a pyramid shape to really show off the jewels .

water
300 g basmati rice
2 tablespoons sea salt
70 ml vegetable oil
40 g unsalted butter, melted

JEWELS
water
zest of 2 mandarins or oranges, cut
    into julienne strips
50 g caster sugar
2 tablespoons dried barberries, stems
    removed
30 g unsalted butter
2 tablespoons Saffron Liquid (page 54)
2 tablespoons currants
50 g slivered pistachios
50 g flaked almonds, lightly toasted
50 g roasted hazelnuts, skins rubbed off

Wash, soak and parboil the rice as described on page 53.

Return the saucepan to a medium heat and add the oil and 2 tablespoons water. As soon as the oil begins to sizzle, spoon in enough rice to cover the base of the pan in a thin layer. Spoon in the rest of the rice gradually, building it up into a pyramid. Use the handle of a wooden spoon to poke 5 or 6 holes down through the rice to the base of the pan to help it steam. Mix 2 tablespoons warm water with the melted butter and drizzle this over the rice. Continue as described on page 53.

While the rice is cooking, prepare the 'jewels'. Bring a small saucepan of water to a boil and blanch the mandarin zest for 20 seconds. Drain and repeat twice more to remove any bitterness. Add the sugar and 100 ml water to the pan. Bring to a boil, then reduce the heat and simmer gently for 10 minutes. Allow to cool, then strain off the syrup and reserve the zest and syrup separately.

Soak the barberries in cold water for 2 minutes, then drain and dry well. Melt the butter in a small saucepan over a gentle heat. Add the barberries and fry for 4–5 minutes, stirring constantly. Remove from the heat and reserve.

Just before serving, remove 2–3 tablespoons of the cooked rice and mix with the saffron liquid. Spoon the remaining rice onto a warm serving platter and mound into a pyramid. Sprinkle on the saffron rice followed by all the 'jewels'. Drizzle over a little of the reserved mandarin syrup, which will make the jewels shine. Serve the crunchy tah-deeg separately. **SERVES 6**

Albaloo polow
SOUR-CHERRY RICE WITH LAMB

Sour cherries are abundant in Iran where they are eaten fresh, dried or as sheets of fruit paste. They have an exquisite sour–sweet flavour that marries brilliantly with lamb and the warm spices in this polow. If you are unable to find dried sour cherries, then fresh morello cherries will do.

50 ml olive oil

1 small onion, finely chopped

1 clove garlic, finely chopped

sea salt

½ teaspoon freshly ground black pepper

½ teaspoon ground ginger

250 g lamb (from the leg), trimmed of fat and cut into 1 cm cubes

125 g dried sour cherries or 250 g fresh morello cherries, pitted

2 tablespoons caster sugar

300 g basmati rice

70 ml vegetable oil

40 g unsalted butter, melted

2 tablespoons Saffron Liquid (page 54)

2 tablespoons lightly toasted slivered almonds (optional)

Heat the olive oil in a medium saucepan over a low heat. Add the onion, garlic, ½ teaspoon salt, pepper and ginger and fry gently for 4 minutes. Add the meat and fry for 2 minutes, turning it around in the spices. Add enough water to cover and bring to a simmer. Cover the pan and simmer over a very low heat for 1 hour, or until the meat is tender. Remove from the heat and leave to cool.

Meanwhile, soak the dried cherries in cold water for 1 hour, then drain. Combine the cherries, sugar and 100 ml water in a medium saucepan and heat gently until the sugar dissolves. Simmer gently for a further 10 minutes, then remove from the heat and set aside. When cool, strain the cherries and reserve the syrup separately.

Wash, soak and parboil the rice as described on page 53.

Return the rice saucepan to a medium heat and add the vegetable oil and 2 tablespoons water. As soon as the oil begins to sizzle, spoon in enough rice to cover the base of the pan in a thin layer. Spoon on a layer of lamb and scatter with cherries. Continue to layer the rice, lamb and cherries, building them up into a pyramid. Use the handle of a wooden spoon to poke 5 or 6 holes down through the rice to the base of the pan to help it steam. Pour on any residual meat juices. Mix 2 tablespoons warm water with the melted butter and saffron liquid and drizzle this over the rice. Continue as described on page 53.

With 5 minutes of the cooking time to go, pour on the reserved cherry syrup and cover the pan again. When ready to serve, scatter on the almonds, if using.

SERVES 6

Maygoo polow

PERSIAN GULF-STYLE SHRIMP AND HERB RICE

The Indian influences on Persian Gulf cooking are obvious in this dish, which has more than a hint of heat and many more spices than you find elsewhere in Iran.

water

300 g basmati rice

2 tablespoons sea salt

1 teaspoon fenugreek seeds

80 ml vegetable oil

1 small onion, finely diced

1 teaspoon freshly ground black pepper

1 teaspoon ground turmeric

½ teaspoon ground ginger

1 large tomato, seeded and diced

200 g peeled prawns (tails intact)

⅓ cup finely snipped chives

⅓ cup finely shredded flat-leaf parsley leaves

⅓ cup finely shredded dill sprigs

⅓ cup finely shredded coriander leaves

40 g unsalted butter, melted

2 tablespoons Saffron Liquid (page 54)

Wash, soak and parboil the rice as described on page 53.

Meanwhile, soak the fenugreek for 10 minutes, then strain. Heat 1 tablespoon of the oil in a frying pan over a low heat. Add the onion and spices and fry gently for 5 minutes, or until the onion has softened. Add the tomato and cook for 1 minute. Add the prawns and stir them briefly in the spice mixture until they start to change colour. Remove the pan from the heat and stir in the herbs.

Return the rice saucepan to a medium heat and add the remaining oil and 2 tablespoons water. As soon as the oil begins to sizzle, spoon in enough rice to cover the base of the pan in a thin layer. Scatter a layer of the prawn mixture over the rice. Continue to layer the rice and the prawn mixture, building them up into a pyramid. Use the handle of a wooden spoon to poke 5 or 6 holes down through the rice to the base of the pan to help it steam. Mix 2 tablespoons warm water with the melted butter and saffron liquid and drizzle this over the rice. Continue as described on page 53. **SERVES 6**

Shirin polow

SWEET RICE WITH SAFFRON, NUTS AND ORANGE ZEST

There's no getting around the fact that this festive and exquisite golden polow is a bit of a palaver to make – but if you have a sweet tooth, you will find the combination of candied citrus zest, lightly toasted nuts and spices absolutely irresistible. The idea of candying carrot may seem a little strange at first, but of, course, it has an underlying sweetness all of its own and the bright colour adds to the amber glow of the dish.

Serve with grilled or roasted chicken or quail – or do as they do in Shiraz, and serve it with the earthy Khoresht-e Gheimeh (page 171), made from braised lamb and split peas.

water

zest of 2 oranges, cut into julienne strips

125 g unsalted butter

2 small carrots (about 200 g), peeled and cut into julienne strips

½ teaspoon ground cardamom

½ teaspoon ground cinnamon

pinch of ground cumin

150 g caster sugar

2 tablespoons Saffron Liquid (page 54)

50 g flaked almonds, lightly toasted

50 g slivered pistachios

300 g basmati rice

2 tablespoons sea salt

70 ml vegetable oil

2 tablespoons pomegranate seeds (optional)

Bring a small saucepan of water to a boil. Blanch the orange zest in the boiling water for 20 seconds. Drain and repeat twice more to remove any bitterness.

Melt 75 g of the butter in a medium saucepan over a low heat. Add the carrot and spices and sweat for 5 minutes, stirring constantly. Add the zest, sugar, half the saffron liquid and 250 ml water to the pan and bring to a boil, then reduce the heat and simmer gently for 10 minutes. Allow to cool, then strain off the syrup and reserve it and the zest and carrot separately.

Set aside a tablespoon each of the almonds and pistachios to use as a garnish and combine the rest with the orange and carrot mixture. Set aside.

Wash, soak and parboil the rice as described on page 53.

Return the rice saucepan to a medium heat and add the oil and 2 tablespoons water. As soon as the oil begins to sizzle, spoon in enough rice to cover the base of the pan in a thin layer. Scatter a layer of the carrot mixture over the rice. Continue to layer the rice and the carrot mixture, building them up into a pyramid. Use the handle of a wooden spoon to poke 5 or 6 holes down through the rice to the base of the pan to help it steam.

Melt the remaining butter and mix it with 2 tablespoons warm water, then drizzle this over the rice. Continue as described on page 53. After 20 minutes, quickly drizzle the reserved syrup over the rice, then replace the lid and cook for a further 20 minutes. You will need to keep an eye on the pan to make sure that the sugar syrup doesn't burn on the base.

Garnish with the reserved nuts and pomegranate seeds, if using. SERVES 6

Ìstambuli polow
TOMATO RICE

This is a favourite home-style rice dish, and one that we enjoyed several times in Iran. It is cooked using a more straightforward absorption method – which means no tah-deeg! The trade off is a really tasty, hearty meal that is particularly good on cold wintry days. Tomatoes and potatoes were introduced to Iran relatively recently, via Turkey – hence the name: Istambuli polow.

2 cloves garlic

50 ml olive oil

1 small onion, finely diced

½ teaspoon ground turmeric

½ teaspoon ground cumin

½ teaspoon ground coriander

pinch of cayenne pepper

sea salt

freshly ground black pepper

300 g lamb (from the leg), trimmed of fat and cut into 1 cm cubes

1 tablespoon tomato paste

300 g basmati rice

1 waxy potato, peeled and cut into 1 cm cubes

1 large tomato, seeded and cut into 1 cm cubes

Finely dice one of the garlic cloves. Heat the oil in a medium saucepan over a low heat, then add the onion, diced garlic and spices and season with salt and pepper and fry gently for 4 minutes. Add the lamb, tomato paste and enough water to cover and bring to a simmer. Cover the pan and simmer gently for 1 hour, or until the meat is tender.

While the lamb is cooking, put the rice into a large bowl and rinse well under cold running water, working your fingers through it to loosen the starch. Drain and repeat until the water runs clear. Cover the rice with cold water and leave to soak for 45 minutes. Drain and rinse for a final time.

Add the potato, tomato and rice to the lamb and pour in enough boiling water to cover by 1 cm. Stir gently and adjust the seasoning to taste. Lightly bash the remaining garlic clove and add it to the pan. Return to a boil, then cover with a tight-fitting lid and cook over a low heat for 10 minutes. Remove the pan from the heat, then slide a clean, folded tea towel under the lid and leave it to stand for 20 minutes without peeking.

To serve, tip the rice onto a warm serving platter and fluff the grains into a pyramid with a fork. **SERVES 6**

Tahcheen-e esfenaj
BAKED LAYERED RICE WITH SPINACH AND LAMB

'Tahcheen' means 'spread over the bottom' and the whole point of this dish is to end up with a lot of lovely golden crunch under the rice. Obviously, the wider and shallower the baking dish, the greater the crunch-to-rice ratio will be. On the other hand, if you bake the rice in a deeper, attractively curved or domed dish, it will look like a gorgeous golden cake when turned out, the secret filling revealed on cutting. The most important thing is that it be heavy duty to ensure even cooking all over – a Pyrex or heavy ovenproof porcelain dish would be ideal.

Tahcheen is a brilliant dish for entertaining, as once the preparation is done it just bakes away by itself for a couple of hours.

In this recipe the lamb needs to be slow-cooked first, and then marinated for a minimum of 8 hours for the flavours to develop. Omit the prunes, if you like, but somehow I think they contribute to the essential 'Persian-ness' of the dish.

3 tablespoons olive oil
2 large onions, finely sliced
1 clove garlic, roughly chopped
sea salt
1 teaspoon freshly ground black pepper
½ teaspoon ground turmeric
½ teaspoon ground ginger
½ teaspoon ground allspice
400 g lamb (from the shoulder), trimmed of fat and cut into 2 cm cubes
200 g thick natural yoghurt
2 egg yolks
80 ml Saffron Liquid (page 54)
250 g spinach leaves
400 g basmati rice
12 prunes, pitted and roughly chopped
60 g unsalted butter, plus extra for greasing
thick natural yoghurt and pickles, to serve

Heat half the oil in a medium saucepan over a low heat. Add one of the onions to the pan with the garlic, 1 teaspoon salt, pepper and spices and fry gently for 4 minutes. Add the meat and enough water to cover, then bring to a simmer. Cover the pan and simmer gently for 1 hour, or until the meat is tender. Remove from the heat and leave to cool.

Beat the yoghurt with the egg yolks and saffron liquid in a shallow dish. Drain the cooled meat well and add it to the yoghurt mixture. Cover and refrigerate for at least 8 hours, or up to 24 hours.

Heat the remaining oil in a large frying pan over a low heat. Add the remaining onion and fry gently until soft and lightly coloured. Add the spinach and turn it about in the pan until wilted. Cook over a medium heat to evaporate any excess liquid, then set aside. When cool, squeeze the spinach to remove any residual liquid and chop it roughly.

Wash, soak and parboil the rice as described on page 53.

Preheat the oven to 190°C and butter a 2 litre ovenproof dish. Remove the lamb from the yoghurt marinade. Mix half the parboiled rice with the marinade and spoon it into the base and up the sides of the ovenproof dish. Arrange the lamb on top of the rice, then cover with the spinach. Dot the prunes over the spinach, then spoon in the remaining rice to cover and smooth the surface. Cover tightly with a sheet of lightly buttered foil and bake for 1½ hours.

Remove the dish from the oven and dot the surface of the rice with bits of butter. Replace the foil and leave to rest for 10 minutes. Turn the rice out onto a warm serving platter and serve with a bowl of creamy yoghurt and a selection of relishes or pickles. SERVES 6

Tahcheen-e morgh
BAKED YOGHURT RICE WITH CHICKEN

Another attractive layered rice dish that is great for special occasions. It follows the same method as the previous baked rice recipe with lamb (page 67). If you have leftover cooked chicken from your Sunday roast, then by all means use it instead of the fresh chicken given here. Try to marinate the meat – whether raw or cooked – for at least 2 hours, as it really does develop the flavours.

250 g thick natural yoghurt

3 egg yolks

3 tablespoons Saffron Liquid (page 54)

1 teaspoon orange-flower water

finely grated zest of 1 orange

1 teaspoon sea salt

½ teaspoon freshly ground black pepper

500 g boneless free-range chicken
    breast and thighs, skin removed and
    cut into 2 cm cubes

400 g basmati rice

2 tablespoons sea salt

80 g unsalted butter, plus extra for
    greasing

thick natural yoghurt and fresh herbs,
    to serve

Beat the yoghurt with the egg yolks, saffron liquid, orange-flower water, zest, salt and pepper in a shallow dish. Add the chicken to the yoghurt mixture. Cover and refrigerate for at least 2 hours or up to 12 hours ahead of time.

Wash, soak and parboil the rice as described on page 53.

Preheat the oven to 190ºC and butter a 2 litre ovenproof dish. Remove the chicken pieces from the yoghurt marinade. Mix half the parboiled rice with the marinade and spoon it into the base of the ovenproof dish. Spread the rice over the bottom and up the sides of the dish. Arrange the chicken on top of the rice, then spoon in the rest of the rice to cover, and smooth the surface. Cover tightly with a sheet of lightly buttered foil and bake for 1½ hours.

Remove the dish from the oven and dot the surface of the rice with bits of butter. Replace the foil and leave to rest for 10 minutes. Turn the rice out onto a warm serving platter. Serve with a bowl of creamy yoghurt and a selection of fresh herbs – tarragon, basil, chives and parsley would be lovely. SERVES 6

LONG BEFORE WE TRAVEL TO IRAN I AM ENTRANCED BY THE NAME, BY THE VERY IDEA OF YAZD. For a start, the map shows it to be sited, rather pleasingly, slap-bang in the middle of the country, at the meeting point of its two vast deserts, the Dasht-e Kavir and Dasht-e Lut. Secondly, I know that this ancient town is home to Iran's largest community of Zoroastrians, followers of a rather mysterious faith that predates Islam by a thousand years or more. And thirdly, Yazd is famous all around Iran – and farther afield, too – for its silks and confectionery.

/

Marco Polo visited Yazd in 1272, describing it in his travel journals as, 'a very fine and splendid city and a centre of commerce'. In those days, most of this commerce revolved around a thriving cotton and silk trade. Mulberry trees grew in profusion around the city and Yazdi silk was spun with gold and silver threads into fine brocades that were exported across the Islamic world.

/

Seven-and-a-half centuries after Marco Polo's visit, the silk trade has largely vanished. But we have been invited to watch a different kind of silk being spun in a local confectionery workshop. We are visiting Haj Khalifeh Ali Rahbar's famous sweet emporium to see how pashmak – Persian fairy floss – is made. The business has been run by a partnership of three families for nearly a hundred years, and their sweets are considered to be some of the best in Iran.

/

As we wait in the factory office, nibbling on small lozenges of pistachio paste, Ali gives me a lesson in Persian names. 'Agha' and 'Khanum' I am already familiar with, being roughly the equivalent of 'sir' and 'madam'. 'Haj' is the honorific given to those Muslims, both men and women, who have made the pilgrimage to Mecca. Ali now explains to us that 'khalifeh' denotes a great master or expert. So, in his day, we surmise, Haj Khalifeh Ali Rahbar was both a devout Muslim and a master confectioner.

/

It is close to lunchtime, and by the time we are ushered into the workshop the morning shift is nearly over. There is an air of frantic energy and we watch a row of burly men with massively muscled forearms (and asbestos fingers) wrangle thick ropes of burnished amber toffee onto a long marble bench. To one side, another man stirs melted sheep's butter into flour to form a crumbly dough. We watch, transfixed, as the heavy toffee ropes are slapped and twisted on the marble. As they cool, the amber translucency gives way to an opaque, silvery-gold sheen. Next, the toffee is hoisted onto circular trays beneath the mechanical spider legs of a giant stretching machine. Two men stand at every station, throwing handfuls of buttery dough into the toffee as it is worked and stretched into ever-thinner strands.

/

'Is it hard work?', Greg asks. 'Ya Ali! We make around nine hundred kilos of pashmak a day and we used to do it by hand,' laughs one muscle-man. 'This is like playing.'

/

The toffee has been transformed by some strange alchemy into fluffy skeins of sugar silk and the two men gather up great armfuls of the stuff and drop it onto a large bench to be sprinkled with fragrant cardamom and packed into pretty pink boxes.

/

But now a loud siren sounds and within minutes the room empties. It's the signal for us all to leave for lunch.

/

Outside a small bakery we watch an old lady bend stiffly to pick up a piece of bread from the dusty ground. She brushes it off carefully and places it, almost reverently, on a nearby ledge. We are intrigued.

/

'This is some kind of tradition – or perhaps it is better to say superstition,' Ebi explains. 'Many older people believe that bread is sacred and should not be allowed to fall to the ground and wasted. So they pick it up and save it.'

/

'But for what?', he snorts disparagingly. 'In my country there are many kinds of pointless tradition like this.'

/

The next morning we wake early and wander through a twisting maze of sun-baked alleyways in the old town close to our hotel. We soon find ourselves standing beneath the lofty arched entrance of the Jameh Mosque. Jameh means 'Friday', and this is where Muslims congregate for the important weekly prayer service. The towering archway is topped by two slender minarets, and at nearly fifty metres it is the tallest portal in Iran. The entire façade is decorated in a dazzling pattern of blue and yellow tiles, and the early morning light washes it with a warm golden sheen.

/

We make our way up to the roof and gaze out at the old brown city stretched beneath us. From this vantage point it is easy to make out the distinctive wind-towers or badgirs that sprout from the skyline, cooling the city as they have for centuries. The caretaker has followed us, and he now produces a key from his trouser pocket and unlocks a small door at the base of one of the slender minarets. We troop in after him, feeling our way carefully up the cramped spiral interior. As we climb ever higher, I feel something crunching beneath my shoes on the rough stone steps, and when we emerge into a cramped chamber at the top I see that both steps and floor are strewn with crushed walnut shells. In the dim light we can also make out cushions propped around the walls. On a dusty rug a Koran lies open next to a few crumpled chadors and there are more scattered walnut shells. It seems a little sad, a little lonely.

/

'I think this is more superstition,' Ebi whispers in my ear.

/

The caretaker now adopts a serious expression. 'This is a special room only for young women,' he explains carefully. 'They come here on Fridays to pray for a husband. You must understand that these are girls who think they have no hope. Perhaps their families are poor or do not know any suitable boys.' He pauses awkwardly, '… or maybe they are not so pretty. So they come here and they scatter walnuts on the stairs. They break them open with their feet, and they pray that this will release good luck for them. Then they weep and they pray some more.'

/

It's not surprising that Iranian girls share the same preoccupations as young women the world over. They want security, they want family, they want love. They want a husband. But here in Iran there are no bars or pubs or clubs. In rural and remote areas and in conservative cities like Yazd, young men and women have few opportunities to socialise. For some, it is nigh on impossible to meet a mate. For some, it seems, the best they can do is to walk on walnuts.

/

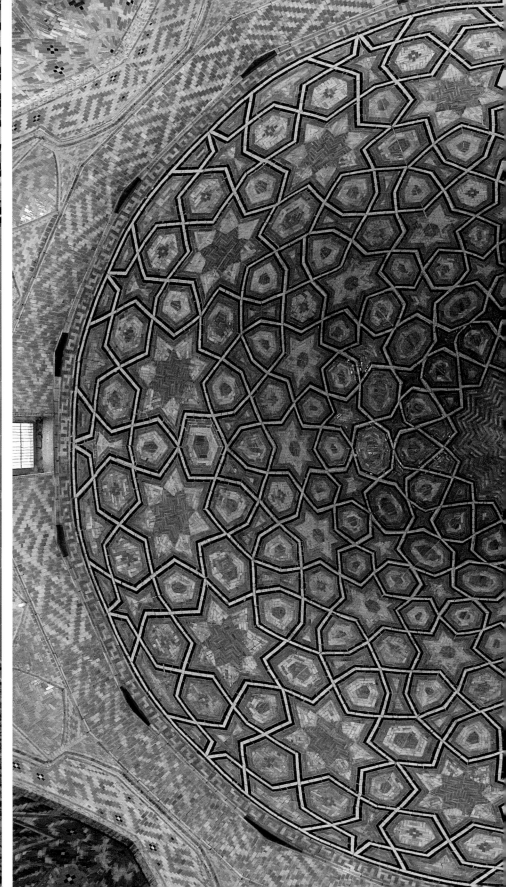

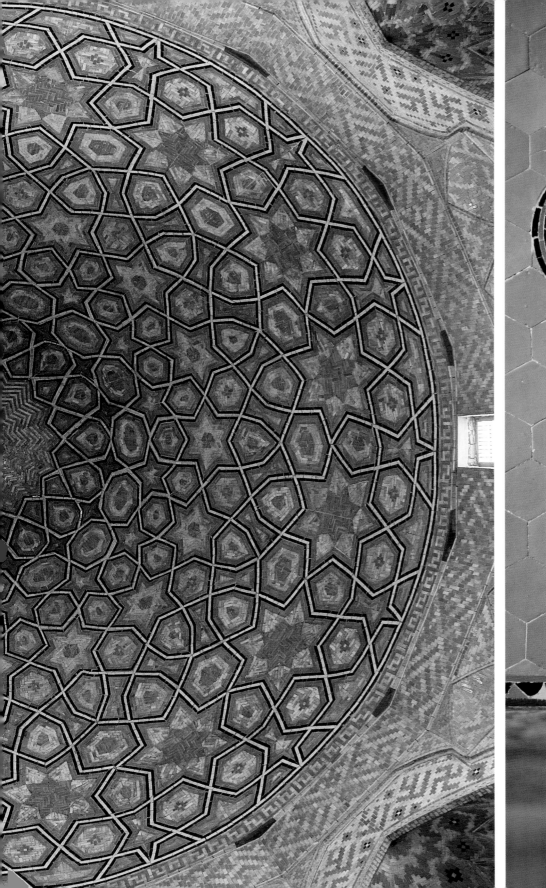

Here in yazd, summer temperatures soar into the high forties, and the city has an annual rainfall of only six centimetres. Even with modern-day urban comforts, this is a tough place to live.

/

Perhaps the fierce desert climate breeds a certain kind of fierce devoutness. As well as being traditionalists, we learn that the good citizens of Yazd are a religious lot, and dotted around the city we stumble across several takieh, ceremonial buildings used during Ashura, the important Shia anniversary of the 680 AD martyrdom of Imam Hossein. The grandest of these is the three-tiered Amir Chakhmaq complex, out the front of which stands a curious wooden contraption, a little like the frame of a massive pointed drum. Ali tells us that this is a nakhl, and is unique to this central desert region. Representing Hossein's coffin, the nakhl is carried through the streets during Ashura in an outpouring of public penitence and grief. It's the kind of ceremony, with its beating of breasts, thwacking of heads and lifting of heavy objects, that sends you spinning back to the Middle Ages.

/

But Yazd was also a capital of pre-Islamic Persia and is famous for its fire temples and its Towers of Silence – fascinating round buildings that sit on lonely hills beyond the city walls, where vultures once picked at the bones of the Zoroastrian dead, a neat way of dealing with decay and preventing disease. We visit Ateshkadeh, the most important of the fire temples, late in the afternoon, enjoying the peaceful atmosphere in the grounds. Above the entrance to the temple is an imposing bas-relief of Fravahar, the winged disc – half eagle, half man – that symbolises the soul's journey towards union with Ahura Mazda, the Zoroastrian supreme being.

/

When we enter the temple itself, I understand why it is so quiet outside. The dark interior is crowded with people pressing up against a glass window to catch a glimpse of the fire burning beyond. The central teaching of Zoroaster was of the eternal battle between forces of good and evil. In the crush a large man treads heavily on my foot, and I experience a brief internal battle between my own Vohu Mano (good mind) and Ahem Nan (bad mind). But thankfully good humour prevails, and we eventually reach the glass and gaze into the eternal flames.

/

But by now we've all just about had enough religion for one day.

/

IRAN'S VAST CENTRAL DESERT PLATEAU COVERS MANY THOUSANDS OF SQUARE kilometres and is one of the hottest and driest places on earth. It's not a landscape to enter lightly. And yet the fragile network of ancient tracks that criss-cross the barren expanse tells us that travellers have been braving it for many thousands of years. Aryan tribes first entered these lands in the second millennium BC, skirting a cautious route along the northern fringe of the Dasht-e Kavir desert. Next came merchants, carting goods to and from Asia in their caravan convoys. Today there are few signs of the ancient routes that made up the Silk Road, just the occasional crumbling caravanserai. But larger settlements gradually sprang up alongside the inhospitable desert, tucked in beneath the mountains that reach sheltering arms around the northern and western edges.

/

Iran's desert villages and cities appear strikingly similar, because the climate shapes not just the landscape, but also the architecture. From the beginning, these communities had to learn how to deal with extremes of temperature, aridity, salinity and wind. Above all, the people who lived here had to find shade, cool air and water. And so the buildings are low and squat, the walls made of thick mud bricks; the skyline is punctuated by wind-towers channelling cooling currents through the buildings; yakchal – ice houses – store blocks of ice brought from the mountains in the winter, and, most crucial of all, there are qanats, an underground system of pipes that deliver life-giving water from subterranean water sources in the foothills of the mountains to fields and villages.

/

THERE ARE ONLY A FEW ROADS THROUGH THE DESERT these days, carrying sparse traffic between Kerman, Yazd and Na'in and the distant pilgrim city of Mashhad. We seem to be the only car heading north-east towards Mashhad, although the occasional battered old truck comes from the other direction. Around us the stony ground seems to stretch to the edge of the world and the only other signs of life are little groups of dusty grey camels.

/

About an hour into our journey we stop at Kharanaq, a crumbling oasis village that is famous for its 'shaking' minaret. Much of the village is ruined, and we wander in and out of the higgledy-piggledy houses, built one on top of another up a hillside. When we reach the base of the minaret we gaze down onto a timeless rural scene. In the distance is an arid rocky expanse, back further a row of jagged brown mountains stabs the sky. But beneath our feet spreads a patchwork of vivid green, the first we have seen in this part of Iran, and it makes us laugh in delight. There are fields of cotton and sunflowers, tomatoes and eggplants, as well as small walled orchards of pomegranates. It is the qanat system in action!

/

JAVAR ROSE LONG BEFORE DAWN TO MAKE THE DOUGH FOR OUR BREAKFAST bread. Her son, yet another Ali, has been fuelling the fire for several hours and now we are summoned to watch. We gather sleepily around the old clay oven in the garden of the Moonlight House guesthouse, where we are staying. We are mesmerised by the tongues of orange fire that lick the rim hungrily, and then, before our eyes, the flames slowly retreat into the dark depths of the oven and vanish, leaving in their wake the required glowing embers.

/

Between the two of them, Javar and Ali have already prepared a tray of neat round balls of dough. Now Javar plunges her hands into a bag of flour, then she twists, turns and flattens each dough ball into a large oval. One by one she stretches them over a heavy padded cloth, then thrusts her hand into the hellishly hot depths of the oven. Moving briskly, she slaps the loaves against the wall and they bubble and blister before our eyes. Next, it's Ali's turn. He reaches in with a wooden paddle and peels the loaves away, holding them up triumphantly for our approval.

/

By now the sun is rising. The air is dense with wood smoke and the fragrant scent of warm bread, and we are silent in anticipation. Javar smiles at us kindly, gathers up the steaming flaps of bread and we follow her indoors for breakfast.

/

FINALLY WE HAVE LEFT THE DESERT AND WE ARE IN THE
Khorasan region in the north-east of Iran. When the
Arabs brought Islam into Persia in the seventh century
they knew of no lands beyond it so they named it 'the
land of the rising sun'.

/

It's a gentler climate and terrain, with pretty valleys
and hills and obvious signs of cultivation. Here we
meet Sami, who owns a fine orchard of zereshk trees.
Since arriving in Iran we've been enjoying sour–sweet
zereshk – barberries – in all kinds of rice dishes, and
we're delighted to discover that it is harvest time.
Yesterday we picked a basketful of the flame-red berries
from his trees, narrowly avoiding injury via the long
spiky thorns.

/

But now we are sitting round a table drinking chai
with Sami's uncle. He's a water controller, a mirab,
responsible for allocating this precious resource around
the village. It's an important job, especially at this time
of year as saffron is being planted and the fields need to
be flooded several times over the next few weeks.

/

Saffron is the real reason for our visit to Khorasan. That morning we watched the gnarled crocus bulbs being tucked into the rich brown soil. We are desperate to see the flowers themselves, but it seems that we are a month early. Saffron bulbs need cold weather in which to bloom, and although it is autumn, in this part of Khorasan the sun still holds too much heat. But Sami and his uncle tell us that we will almost certainly see the start of the harvest on our journey north to Mashhad. They have heard that the bulbs were planted several weeks ago and, of course, it is cooler there.

/

And so the saffron hunt begins in earnest. We drive steadily north, stopping at village after village to inspect the fields. Our hopes are briefly raised when we see a faint flash of green shimmer across the surface of one small plot, but there are still no flowers.

/

We drive for hours and eventually stop in Torbat-e Hedariyeh to buy some of the melons for which Mashhad is so famous. We slice them open greedily while Ali interrogates the stallholder about the saffron harvest. He directs us off the highway to a small village near by. And here, across a field, beneath an apple tree, next to a small stream, we find the very first fragile flowers of the season. Only a couple, mind, but for the moment, it's enough.

/

THERE IS MORE THAN ENOUGH saffron in Mashhad to make up for any disappointment with the harvest. We spot saffron cakes, cookies and candy and glittery saffron-hued sugar swizzle sticks. There's saffron ice-cream, saffron rice, saffron tea – and then there are shops selling a wide range of different forms, vintages and qualities of the spice itself. We are drawn to a mound of deep maroon-red strands secured beneath a heavy glass dome; when the shopkeeper lifts the lid, a complex acrid scent floods the air. Saffron is expensive even here, despite the fact that Iran is the largest producer in the world, accounting for around ninety percent of the total harvest. But when you consider that each delicate bloom contains only three fine stigmas, and that it takes seventy-five thousand flowers – that's about a hundred kilos – to make one kilogram of saffron, the cost somehow seems worth it.

‹ Our lovely friend and photographer, Ebi, could see how disappointed we were at missing the full splendour of the saffron harvest and so, unbeknownst to us, he returned to Khorasan a few weeks later with his camera.

OTHER THAN SAFFRON, THE FIRST THING ONE NOTICES IN Mashhad is that the streets are swarming with pilgrims. Around twenty million of them flock here every year, from all corners of the Shia world, to gather at the holy shrine of Imam Reza, a ninth-century martyr. Imam Reza was the eighth of the Twelver Shiite Imams, and to this day many Iranians believe that he was killed, on the order of the Caliph, by poisoned grapes. His mausoleum in Mashhad is one of the two key pilgrimage sites in Iran, and regular visits here are a crucial religious observation. We are quickly caught up in the crowd, which pulls us inexorably towards the entrance gates.

/

The shrine dominates the city. It is a vast, ever-expanding complex of courtyards and buildings and we are quite unprepared for the scale of the place. I am a little anxious when I realise that men and women must enter separately. I know that non-Muslims are not allowed inside the holiest inner buildings and I am worried about losing my way and straying off course. Ebi will walk through with Greg and he is determined to find someone to guide me. He explains my predicament to a young woman who is visiting the shrine with her mother. They smile at me sweetly and the older woman helps me adjust my chador, showing me how to tuck the cumbersome fabric under my arm and hold it tight with one hand. 'You welcome … you guest,' stutters the daughter.

/

Once inside, my new friends take me tenderly by the elbow and guide me through the crowds. Within minutes I have lost my bearings as we pass through large carpeted courtyards and small quadrangles, beneath archways and portals, in and out of shadow and light. I feel as if I am walking through a jewellery box. One chamber flashes turquoise tiles, another is lined with pure gold. Yet another is a kaleidoscope of tiny mirror mosaics: it's like being inside a diamond.

/

And now they lead me into another hall and we are suddenly swamped by a deafening roar of sound. I am in a sea of women chanting prayers, rocking and sobbing. In a great wailing wave the crowd moves forward, arms reaching out to touch the gilded cage of the tomb that rises up in the centre of the room. On the other side of the barrier an ocean of roaring men surges towards us. My friends urge me ever onwards. But I am overcome by the sudden sense that I have come too far and I let go of their hands and drop back. I watch for a moment as they are sucked into the crowd and vanish, then I turn and walk quietly away.

/

small dishes

THIS SECTION BEGINS – AS DOES every Iranian meal – with fresh herbs. Together with bread and rice, herbs are the defining characteristic of the Persian table.

/

The Persian way of eating is rather more free-form than the two- or three-course model that we are used to in the West. At mealtimes, at the most humble as well as the most elaborate tables, dishes of food gradually accumulate and are left for the duration of the meal for people to pick at in their own time and way.

/

Small dishes are first – these are intended to excite the eye and the palate and to balance and complement the more substantial rice and meat dishes that follow. It's a very similar idea to the Middle Eastern mezze spread – in fact the word 'mezze' derives from the Persian word 'mazeh', which means 'to taste'. A basket of mixed fresh herbs or sabzi is always the

first thing to arrive, and sometimes a few crunchy vegetables, such as radishes and spring onions. These are eaten with soft white cheese and flatbread to sharpen the appetite for subsequent dishes.

/

Small salads, cold or stuffed vegetables and pickles also appear, and yoghurt features in various forms. Sometimes it is thin and soupy, for slurping up with a spoon, or it can be thick and creamy and come with dates for dipping. Yoghurt is also mixed with vegetables, such as cucumber, spinach, beetroot or eggplant, to create borani, another kind of salad.

/

Slightly more substantial dishes might be egg-based omelettes, called kuku, or fried meat or vegetable patties. Kukus are often served cold, cut into bite-sized pieces, but also make a wonderful light meal in their own right.

/

Finally, Iranians are inveterate nibblers of nuts, seeds and dried fruit, often combined in mixtures that are stored in the pantry for a quick and easy snack or to have on hand to offer guests. Freshly roasted and salted nuts will nearly always be offered before a meal, accompanied by little cups of refreshing chai or a long glass of chilled sherbet – cordial – in the summer.

/

Each of the following recipes is intended to serve six people as part of a selection. Offer a few of these small dishes for a simpler meal, assuming you have larger dishes to follow, or put together a spread for more elaborate entertaining. The kuku recipes are slightly heartier, and could easily serve six people as a light lunch or supper dish, with just a green leaf salad as accompaniment.

/

Sabzi khordan
SOFT HERB SALAD

Iranians have an entirely different relationship with herbs than we do in the West. Not only do herbs feature heavily in stews and soups, but almost every Persian meal begins with a basket of fresh, unadorned herbs that are eaten with tangy, feta-like white cheese and flaps of soft flatbread. It's a totally addictive way of starting a meal, as the fresh, vital flavours sharpen the appetite and you can't help but feel somewhat virtuous, munching on all that greenery.

Needless to say, this approach to eating depends entirely on the freshness and quality of the herbs – straight from the garden is best! Failing that, try to buy herbs in big, hearty bunches from the market or a good greengrocer, and avoid at all costs the mean little plastic packets on offer on most supermarket shelves.

The leaves or sprigs of fresh herbs should be picked from their stalks (and any manky leaves discarded), then gently washed and left to soak in a bowl of cold water for 20 minutes or so to allow any sand or dirt to sink to the bottom. They should then be allowed to drain and air-dry in a colander before being wrapped loosely in a clean tea towel and stored in the fridge. Prepared this way herbs should keep for around a week.

This is hardly a recipe but, rather, a list of popular herbs that feature regularly on the Persian table, depending on the season. We've included two of the more unusual ones –costmary and summer savory – for those who are keen gardeners as it's simple enough to grow them yourself.

The idea is to choose four or five herbs that you fancy, and toss them together on a serving platter or in a basket. You'll need about a cup of herbs per person to be really Iranian – and you'll be surprised how quickly you want to eat more and more of them. At first it may seem strange to eat this sort of salad without a dressing, but doing so really allows the flavour of each herb to shine through.

baby beetroot leaves
basil (all the varieties, including Asian)
chives (usual and garlic)
coriander
costmary
dill
flat-leaf parsley
French tarragon
mint (all the varieties)
radishes
spring onions
summer savory
turnip leaves
watercress
fresh white cheese, to serve
warm flatbread, to serve

Serve a platter of herbs with your favourite fresh white cheese – a creamy feta is ideal – and a pile of warm flatbread, so that everyone can wrap or roll to their heart's content.

Salad-e Shirazi
SHIRAZ SALAD

Even though it's called Shiraz salad, this dish is popular all around Iran. Once again, the freshness and quality of the ingredients is all-important. The tomatoes, in particular, must be really tasty – vine-ripened, if possible. In some versions, the vegetables are cut into tiny dice and left to stand in the dressing to allow the flavours to develop. My preference is for a chunkier style, dressed just before serving, for a crisper and fresher result.

Shiraz is the city of roses, so I like to further strengthen the association by garnishing the salad with an exotic sprinkling of edible flowers.

4 vine-ripened tomatoes, roughly chopped
2 Lebanese cucumbers, peeled, seeded and roughly chopped
3 shallots, finely sliced
6 radishes, cut into small wedges
2 tablespoons shredded flat-leaf parsley leaves
2 tablespoons chopped dill sprigs
¼ teaspoon dried mint
juice of 1 lime
2 tablespoons extra-virgin olive oil
sea salt
freshly ground pepper
edible flower petals (rose, nasturtium, chrysanthemum), to garnish

Combine the vegetables and herbs in a large mixing bowl. Whisk the lime juice and oil together and pour over the salad. Season with salt and pepper and toss everything together gently. Scatter with petals, if using. SERVES 6

Kahoo sekanjebeen
BABY COS WEDGES WITH
APPLE VINEGAR–MINT DRESSING

Utterly simple; utterly brilliant. Crisp little lettuces served with a sweetly sour and minty dressing for drizzling or dipping are blissfully reviving on a baking hot summer's day. The dressing is based on sekanjebeen, an ancient Persian sherbet recipe, which is most often diluted with chilled water and ice to make a refreshing summer cordial. Cut the baby lettuces into wedges or, if you prefer, separate the leaves out and arrange them artfully on a platter.

3 baby cos lettuce

APPLE VINEGAR–MINT DRESSING
175 g caster sugar
250 ml water
80 ml apple vinegar
juice of ½ lemon
12 sprigs mint

To make the dressing, combine the sugar and water in a small heavy-based saucepan over a low heat until the sugar dissolves, then increase the heat and simmer for 10 minutes. Add the vinegar, lemon juice and mint leaves and simmer for a further 5 minutes. Remove from the heat and leave to cool. When cold, fish out the mint leaves, then transfer the dressing to a jar with a lid and refrigerate.

Leaving them whole, remove any blemished outer leaves from the lettuce and trim their bottoms neatly. Wash each lettuce thoroughly, then sit them upside-down in a deep bowl or saucepan so they fit snugly. Fill with cold water, two-thirds of the way up the lettuce, and leave for 10 minutes, then drain. Shake the lettuce thoroughly, then sit them in the same bowl, lined with a tea towel, to drain for 10 minutes. Wrap loosely in a damp tea towel and refrigerate until ready to eat. You can do this up to a few hours ahead of time for a super-crisp result.

To serve, cut each lettuce lengthwise into 4 wedges, keeping each wedge intact at the bottom. Serve with a bowl of the dressing for everyone to dunk into or drizzle on to taste. Alternatively, separate the leaves out and arrange them on a platter before drizzling over the dressing.

SERVES 6

Shaved cucumber and pomegranate salad

Cucumber and pomegranate is a popular combination in Iran, and in this recipe I've taken the idea and run with it. Creamy white cheese and a toasty crunch of almonds make this is a refreshing salad or side dish, and it is especially good with spicier meat dishes.

Sometimes you can find lovely little curled cucumbers, which somehow seem extra tasty. But the run-of-the-mill Lebanese ones obviously work just as well.

6 Lebanese cucumbers, peeled
3 tablespoons vegetable oil
60 g flaked almonds
seeds from ½ pomegranate
2 tablespoons shredded mint
  leaves
2 tablespoons shredded
  chervil sprigs

2 tablespoons snipped chives
  in 2 cm lengths
juice of ½ lemon
2 tablespoons extra-virgin
  olive oil
80 g creamy feta, crumbled
sea salt
freshly ground black pepper

Using a vegetable peeler, shave the cucumber flesh into long strips, being careful not to include any seeds. Discard the seedy core. Tip the shavings into a colander set on a plate and refrigerate for 10 minutes.

Meanwhile, heat the vegetable oil in a frying pan over a low heat and fry the almonds until golden brown. Drain briefly on paper towels.

Combine the shaved cucumber with the pomegranate seeds and herbs in a large mixing bowl. Whisk the lemon juice and extra-virgin olive oil together and pour over the salad. Scatter on the feta and crisp almonds, then season with salt and pepper and toss everything together gently. SERVES 6

Olive and pomegranate salad with grated walnut

Olives are especially popular in the north-western provinces of Iran. In Gilan, on the shores of the Caspian Sea, they are often marinated in a thick sludge of finely ground walnuts and a very sour pomegranate paste. Interestingly, this sweet–sour–salty combination is also popular in the neighbouring southern provinces of Turkey, and it's one of my favourites for salads. The flavours are rather intense, so you'll only need a small serve.

80 g shelled walnuts
80 g black olives, pitted and cut into
    quarters
3 shallots, finely sliced
¾ cup pomegranate seeds
¼ cup slivered pistachios
2 tablespoons shredded coriander leaves
2 tablespoons shredded flat-leaf parsley
    leaves

DRESSING

1 tablespoon olive oil
1 tablespoon walnut oil
juice of ½ lemon
1 teaspoon pomegranate molasses
sea salt
freshly ground black pepper

Preheat the oven to 180°C. Roast the walnuts on a baking tray for 5–10 minutes until a deep golden brown. Tip the nuts into a tea towel and rub well to remove as much skin as possible. Set aside.

Mix the olives, shallots, pomegranate seeds, pistachios and herbs in a large bowl. To make the dressing, whisk the oils with the lemon juice and pomegranate molasses and season to taste with salt and pepper. Drizzle over the salad and toss gently to combine. Leave to stand for 5 minutes or so, to allow the flavours to meld.

Just before serving, grate the walnuts over the salad in a delicate dust – a fine Microplane grater is ideal for this. **SERVES 6**

Salad-e olivieh
PERSIAN-STYLE RUSSIAN SALAD WITH TARRAGON MAYONNAISE

We were surprised to see interpretations of this old-fashioned favourite on buffet tables at restaurants and hotels around Iran. Russia's history with neighbouring Iran is colourful, to say the least, including as it does numerous wars, occupation and the deposition of Reza Shah in 1943. We found it heartening in a way – another reminder that food crosses all barriers.

The success of this salad rests on the quality of the ingredients, so please use young, tender freshly cooked vegetables. I think the addition of chicken is entirely Iranian, but leave it out altogether if you prefer. Adding chicken makes for a heartier dish, and you can even use leftover roast chicken. Ironically, I suggest French tarragon, rather than its Russian cousin, as it has a much more intense aniseed flavour.

I've provided a recipe for a generous amount of mayonnaise, as it's hard to make in small amounts – and it's always good to have some in the fridge anyway! If you really can't face making it yourself, then please use a good-quality bought one.

250 g peas in the pod or 100 g frozen peas
400 g waxy potatoes
6 baby carrots, lightly scraped
260 g cooked free-range chicken breast
   (on the bone, ideally), cut into small
   chunks
½ cup finely diced cornichons
3 hard-boiled eggs, finely chopped
2 tablespoons thick natural yoghurt
   or sour cream

MAYONNAISE
1 large egg yolk
1 teaspoon Dijon mustard
1 teaspoon white-wine vinegar
250 ml olive oil
juice of ½ lemon
sea salt
freshly ground black pepper
2 tablespoons chopped tarragon leaves,
   or to taste

To make the mayonnaise, whisk the egg yolk with the mustard and vinegar until light and creamy. Gradually whisk in the oil, drop by drop, ensuring it has been incorporated before adding more. When you have added about half the oil you should have a thick, glossy paste. Loosen the mixture with the lemon juice, then continue to add the oil in a slow trickle, whisking all the while. Season with salt and pepper and stir in the chopped tarragon, adding more or less to taste. Refrigerate until ready to use.

Shell the peas, if using fresh ones. Cook the potatoes, carrots and peas, separately, until tender. Peel the potatoes and cut into 1 cm dice. Cut the carrots into 1 cm chunks. Toss the vegetables together in a large mixing bowl and allow to cool.

Add the chicken, cornichons and egg to the cooled vegetables and toss gently.

In a separate bowl, mix the yoghurt with 3 tablespoons mayonnaise. Add to the salad and toss so that everything is lightly coated. Add a little more mayonnaise if necessary. Taste and adjust the seasoning to your liking. **SERVES 6**

Corn on the cob with sumac and lime-zest butter

Charcoal-grilled corn cobs are a popular street snack in Iran, and corn is very well suited to the barbecue on summer days. But for those times you don't want to set a fire or wait for the barbecue to heat up, this method of boiling sweetcorn until it is tender and then frying it in spicy butter is a real treat. Serve the cobs as a snack, quick supper or side dish.

sea salt

4 corn cobs

80 g unsalted butter

grated zest of 2 limes

2 teaspoons ground sumac

1 teaspoon freshly ground
  black pepper

juice of 1 lime

Bring a large saucepan of salted water to a boil. Meanwhile, peel the husks and trim the 'silk' away from the cobs, then cut each cob into thirds. Simmer the corn until tender – this can take up to 20 minutes, depending on how fresh (or unfresh!) the corn is. Drain thoroughly and allow to steam dry for a few moments.

Melt the butter in a large frying pan. Add the lime zest, sumac and pepper and allow to sizzle for 10–20 seconds, swirling the pan gently. Once the zest has released its volatile oils, add the corn to the pan with the lime juice. Toss to coat and serve hot from the pan, adding salt to taste. SERVES 6

Kashk-e badenjan
FRIED EGGPLANT WITH CREAMY SOUR SAUCE

This distinctively Persian dish combines the rich flavour of baked eggplant with tangy, sour kashk, one of those unusual ingredients that can initially be a little challenging for Western palates. But I urge you to give this dish a go – anyone who loves the lusciousness of eggplant will enjoy the combination.

A bit like an intense and rather cheesy sour cream, kashk is made from whey – the liquid that remains after making butter, yoghurt or soft cheese – that is then sun-dried and rolled into hard little white chalky balls that can last for years. Kashk is pounded to a powder and dissolved in water before use. Outside Iran, depending on where you live, it is possible to find liquid kashk in specialist Iranian stores, and this is what we use in the following recipe.

If you can't find kashk, make a simple sauce by heating half a cup each of thick yoghurt and sour cream with the garlic over a very low heat. Don't allow the sauce to boil, though, or it will split.

2 eggplants, peeled and sliced lengthwise

sea salt

100 ml olive oil

1 clove garlic, sliced

1 onion, finely sliced

½ teaspoon dried mint

½ teaspoon freshly ground black pepper

80 ml liquid kashk

100 ml water

Sprinkle the eggplant slices with salt and put them into a colander. After 20 minutes, rinse under cold water and pat dry.

Preheat the oven to 160°C. Heat the oil in a small saucepan until warm, then add the garlic and swirl over the heat for 30 seconds to release some of the flavour. Strain the oil into a bowl and reserve the garlic for making the sauce.

Heat a few tablespoons of the garlic-infused oil in a large frying pan over a medium-high heat. Brown the eggplant slices in batches until lightly coloured, then transfer to a baking dish. Heat a little more garlic oil in the same frying pan and fry the onion over a gentle heat until it starts to soften. Add the mint and pepper and fry for a further 2 minutes. Tip the onion onto the eggplant and toss together gently. Bake for 20 minutes, or until the eggplant is very tender.

Meanwhile, make the sauce. Mix the liquid kashk and water in a saucepan with the reserved garlic and bring to a boil. Lower the heat and simmer for 20 minutes, stirring from time to time.

To serve, use a fork to mash the eggplant mixture roughly – you don't want it to be too smooth – then adjust the seasoning and tip into a warm serving dish. Pour on the sauce and serve warm or at room temperature. SERVES 6

Whipped yoghurt with feta and soft herbs

In Iran, yoghurt – mast – makes an appearance at every meal. It can be thin and runny for slurping, or strained and mixed with vegetables or herbs to make 'salads' called borani (pages 104 – 106). Yoghurt with cucumber and mint is an ever-popular combination, as is yoghurt and shallot or spring garlic.

This is my version of a great all-purpose thick, herby yoghurt dip. In fact the addition of feta makes it thick enough to use as a spread on warm or toasted bread, but it is just as good with raw vegetables or as an accompaniment to grilled lamb dishes. Vary the herbs depending on the season or personal preference.

For this dish you need to strain the yoghurt to thicken it. It's easy enough to do at home yourself, and the longer you strain it, the thicker the result.

500 g thick natural yoghurt
220 g creamy feta
1 generous teaspoon Dijon mustard
½ cup shredded flat-leaf parsley leaves
2 tablespoons chopped tarragon leaves
2 tablespoons snipped chives
2 tablespoons chopped chervil sprigs
sea salt
freshly ground black pepper
pomegranate seeds, to garnish (optional)

To strain the yoghurt, spoon it into a clean muslin or cheesecloth square or tea towel. Tie the corners together and suspend the bundle from a wooden spoon over a deep bowl. Refrigerate overnight to drain.

To remove excess salt from the feta, soak it in cold water for around 10 minutes, changing the water twice. Crumble the feta roughly into a food processor and purée for a minute, pushing the mixture down from the sides once or twice. Add the strained yoghurt and mustard and purée again until very smooth and creamy.

Tip the mixture into a large bowl and stir in the fresh herbs. Taste and adjust seasoning if necessary. Chill, covered, until ready to eat, then transfer to a serving bowl or plate and garnish with pomegranate seeds, if using. SERVES 6

Borani-ye esfenaj
SPINACH, TURMERIC AND GOLDEN-RAISIN DIP

Borani are a kind of yoghurt 'salad' or side dish and they are made with endless different vegetables and herbs. This is a particularly brilliant combination – serve it as an accompaniment to grilled or roast lamb, spread it onto little toasts or flatbread as a pre-dinner nibble or serve it as a dip with fresh vegetables.

2 scant tablespoons golden	sea salt
raisins, roughly chopped	250 g spinach leaves
1 tablespoon olive oil	200 g thick natural yoghurt
2 large shallots, finely chopped	freshly ground black pepper
¼ teaspoon ground turmeric	squeeze of lemon juice

Soak the golden raisins in a little warm water for 15 minutes, then drain.

Heat the oil in a heavy-based frying pan over a medium heat. Fry the shallots until soft and translucent. Stir in the turmeric and golden raisins and fry for another 2–3 minutes. Remove from the heat and leave to cool.

Bring a large saucepan of salted water to a boil and blanch the spinach for 20 seconds. Refresh in cold water, then squeeze firmly to extract as much liquid as you can. Chop the spinach finely, then mix into the yogurt. Season with salt and pepper to taste and add lemon juice.

Mound the spinach and yoghurt into a small bowl and spoon the turmeric, shallot and golden raisin mixture over the top. Alternatively, mix it all together. **SERVES 6**

Borani badenjan
EGGPLANT AND CRUSHED WALNUT DIP

As with Lebanese baba ghanoush, smokiness is the essence of this borani. If you can char the eggplants over a direct flame, all the better. If you don't have a barbecue or gas stove, you can always bake the eggplants in the oven until very soft, but you won't get the same distinctive smoky flavour.

1–2 eggplants (about 650 g)	175 g thick natural yoghurt
1 small clove garlic	juice of ½ lemon
1 teaspoon sea salt	50 g shelled walnuts
1 teaspoon extra-virgin olive oil	

Prick the eggplants all over with a fork and sit them directly on the naked flame of your stove top or barbecue. Set the flame to low–medium and cook for at least 10 minutes, turning constantly until the whole eggplant is charred. Remove from the flame and place on a cake rack in a plastic bag so the juices can drain off and the skins loosen. Allow the eggplants to cool for about 10 minutes.

When the eggplants are cool, gently peel away the skin from the flesh, taking care to remove every little bit or the dip will have a bitter, burnt flavour. Tip the flesh into a colander, then press gently and leave to drain for 5–10 minutes.

Tip the drained eggplant into a bowl, then crush the garlic with the salt and beat into the eggplant with the oil, yoghurt and lemon juice. Chill, covered, until ready to eat.

Preheat the oven to 180°C. Roast the walnuts on a small baking tray for 5–10 minutes until a deep golden brown. Tip into a tea towel and rub well to remove as much skin as possible. Chop the walnuts coarsely and toss in a sieve to remove any remaining skin or dust.

Transfer the eggplant to a serving bowl or plate, then sprinkle on the walnuts and serve. **SERVES 6**

Borani-ye laboo
CANDIED BEETROOT AND YOGHURT SALAD

Nothing would induce me to buy the lurid pink gloop that passes for beetroot dip in supermarkets. Which is a shame, because beetroot has a lovely earthy sweetness that complements the creamy sourness of yoghurt brilliantly.

Think of this borani as more of a deconstructed salad than a dip, and keep the components separate as you serve.

I prefer the sweetness of baby beets, but you can also use larger beetroot here. Whichever you use, I like to toss the cooked beetroot in a little sugary butter to candy it lightly and accentuate the sweetness.

200 g beetroot, trimmed
sea salt
25 g unsalted butter
2 teaspoons caster sugar
freshly ground black pepper
squeeze of lemon juice
1 small clove garlic
250 g thick natural yoghurt
¾ teaspoon dried mint

Cook the beetroot in salted boiling water for 20 minutes, or until tender. Slip them out of their skins while still warm and cut into chunky wedges if using baby beets or into rough 2 cm cubes if using larger ones.

Heat the butter in a heavy-based frying pan over a low heat and add the beetroot. Fry for a few minutes, then sprinkle on the sugar and season with salt and pepper. Increase the heat and cook until the beetroot begins to caramelise, tossing it around in the buttery syrup from time to time. Add the lemon juice and remove from the heat. Leave to cool completely.

Crush the garlic clove with ½ teaspoon salt to form a paste and mix into the yoghurt with the dried mint, then adjust the seasoning to taste. Spoon into a serving bowl and when ready to serve mound on the cold candied beetroot. SERVES 6

Kuku-ye sabzi
SOFT HERB OMELETTE

It's an omelette, but not as we know it! This is the most famous of the Persian kukus – thick, tortilla-style egg dishes – and it is always served at Persian New Year to symbolise spring and new life. Kuku-ye sabzi is made with a startling quantity of soft herbs – you cut through the golden exterior to a soft, dense, green interior. Strictly speaking, the barberries are optional – they're usually reserved for special occasions (sometimes combined with chopped walnuts) – but I love the little bursts of zing they add. Use any combination of fresh herbs that you fancy, and add chopped spring onion or garlic, as you like. Omit the fenugreek if you don't like its slight curry flavour, but it is a traditional component of this particular kuku.

A non-stick, ovenproof frying pan – no more than 24 centimetres in diameter – is ideal for making kuku.

2 tablespoons barberries, stems
   removed
1 cup chopped flat-leaf parsley leaves
1 cup chopped coriander leaves
½ cup chopped dill sprigs
½ cup snipped chives
50 ml olive oil
6 eggs
2 tablespoons Saffron Liquid
   (page 54 optional)
1 tablespoon self-raising flour
⅓ cup fresh fenugreek leaves or
½ teaspoon fenugreek seeds, lightly
   crushed (optional)
1 teaspoon sea salt
1 teaspoon freshly ground black pepper

Preheat the oven to 180ºC. Soak the barberries in cold water for 2 minutes, then drain and dry. Toss the herbs together and use paper towels or a clean tea towel to pat out as much moisture as you can.

Pour the oil into a non-stick ovenproof frying pan and heat in the oven for 5–10 minutes.

Whisk the eggs and saffron liquid, if using, until frothy. Whisk in the flour, fenugreek, salt and pepper, followed by the herbs and barberries.

Pour the egg mixture into the hot oil. Cover the pan with a lid or foil and bake in the oven for 15 minutes or until nearly set. Remove the cover and cook for a further 15 minutes to brown the surface.

Cut into wedges and serve hot from the pan. Alternatively, drain on paper towels and cut into wedges when cold. Cold kuku is particularly good as a sandwich filling. SERVES 6

Kuku-ye kadoo
WHITE ZUCCHINI OMELETTE WITH MINT AND MELTING CHEESE

Although Kuku-ye Sabzi (page 107) is the most famous Iranian omelette, it can, of course, be made with almost any combination of fresh vegetables and herbs. Other popular fillings are lamb's brains or leftover cooked chicken and there are even sweet kukus (page 264).

I love white zucchini, which are more delicate and less bitter than the dark-green variety, but obviously either will do. Adding provolone is a deviation from the purist Iranian kuku, but hot from the oven, its melting softness is irresistible.

A non-stick, ovenproof frying pan – no more than 24 centimetres in diameter – is ideal for this sort of kuku.

100 ml olive oil
1 onion, finely diced
1 teaspoon freshly grated nutmeg
1 teaspoon dried mint
4 white zucchini (about 350 g), coarsely grated
6 eggs
2 tablespoons self-raising flour
grated zest of 1 lemon
½ teaspoon sea salt
½ teaspoon freshly ground black pepper
200 g provolone or any other melting cheese, grated
herbs to garnish (optional)
thick natural yoghurt, to serve (optional)

Preheat the oven to 180°C.

Heat half the oil in a frying pan over a low heat and fry the onion until it softens. Stir in the nutmeg and mint and fry for another minute. Remove from the heat and leave to cool.

Pour the remaining oil into a non-stick ovenproof frying pan and heat in the oven for 5–10 minutes.

Squeeze the grated zucchini firmly to remove as much moisture as possible. Whisk the eggs until frothy. Whisk in the flour, lemon zest, salt and pepper, followed by the zucchini and cheese. The mixture will be quite sloppy.

Pour the mixture into the hot oil. Cover the pan with a lid or foil and bake in the oven for 15 minutes or until nearly set. Remove the lid and cook for a further 15 minutes to brown the surface.

Cut into wedges and serve hot from the pan with a sprinkling of herbs and thick yoghurt. Alternatively, drain on paper towels and cut into wedges when cold to serve with pickles or relish. **SERVES 6**

Kuku-ye sibzamini
PERSIAN POTATO PATTIES WITH GARLIC CHIVES

Another variation on the Persian kuku, these potato patties are light, fluffy and incredibly tasty. You can also make the mix into one big tortilla-like pancake and serve it in wedges – although you have to be careful flipping it over when cooking. If you have two frying pans, then you can cook the patties all at the same time. Otherwise you'll have to cook them in batches and keep the cooked patties in a warm oven.

2 desiree potatoes, peeled

sea salt

olive oil

30 g unsalted butter

1 large onion, diced

1 teaspoon ground turmeric

2 teaspoons ground cumin

½ teaspoon freshly ground black pepper

2 tablespoons self-raising flour

¾ cup shredded coriander leaves

¾ cup snipped garlic chives

5 eggs

thick natural yoghurt and pickles,
    to serve

Boil the potatoes in generously salted water until tender, then mash them coarsely and allow to cool. It's nice to leave a bit of texture – you don't want the potato too smooth.

Heat 2 tablespoons oil with the butter in a frying pan over a low heat and fry the onion until it softens. Stir in the turmeric and cumin and fry for another minute. Remove from the heat and leave to cool.

Combine the potato and onion and mix in 1 teaspoon salt and the pepper, flour and herbs. Whisk the eggs until frothy, then stir them into the potato so that everything is well combined. The mixture will be quite sloppy.

Heat a shallow layer of oil in a large non-stick frying pan over a low–medium heat. Drop in large spoonfuls of the potato mixture and flatten gently. Cook for about 5 minutes, checking from time to time to make sure the patties are not burning. Turn them over and cook for another 5 minutes. Transfer to a warm oven while you cook more patties, adding more oil if needed. If you make one big pancake it will take about 8 minutes on each side.

Serve piping hot with thick yoghurt and your choice of pickles. MAKES 12

Kuku-ye badenjan
SMOKY EGGPLANT FRITTERS

This is my very loose interpretation of an Iranian eggplant kuku, and in truth what I've come up with is really a bit closer to a fritter. They have an irresistibly delicate, soft texture and the smoky eggplant combines brilliantly with the slight aniseed flavour of chervil and tarragon.

2 large eggplants
2 eggs, lightly whisked
2 tablespoons self-raising flour
2 teaspoons rice flour
1 teaspoon ground turmeric
¼ cup finely chopped chervil sprigs
¼ cup finely chopped tarragon leaves
sea salt
freshly ground black pepper
olive oil
thick natural yoghurt or sour cream,
   to serve

Prick the eggplants all over with a fork and sit them directly on the naked flame of your stove top or barbecue. Set the flame to low–medium and cook for at least 10 minutes, turning constantly until the whole eggplant is charred. Remove from the flame and place on a cake rack in a plastic bag so the juices can drain off and the skins loosen. Allow the eggplants to cool for about 10 minutes.

When the eggplants are cool, gently peel away the skin from the flesh, taking care to remove every little bit or the dip will have a bitter burnt flavour. Tip the flesh into a colander, then press gently and leave to drain for 5–10 minutes.

Roughly chop the eggplants, then mix the flesh in a bowl with the eggs, flours, turmeric and herbs and season with salt and pepper. Stir to combine thoroughly.

Heat a shallow layer of oil in a non-stick frying pan over a medium heat until sizzling. Drop in small tablespoons of the eggplant mixture and flatten gently. Cook for 1–2 minutes on each side, or until golden brown. Drain on paper towels and serve piping hot with thick yoghurt or sour cream. MAKES 12

Persian-spiced seeds and nuts

Iranians are big nibblers of all kinds of nuts and seeds – both fresh and roasted, singly and in mixtures. Most households will have a tub to offer to guests or for day-long snacking. This particular spice mix is wonderfully addictive, so it's worth making a reasonable batch. If you can resist scoffing them down too quickly, the nuts store well for several weeks in an airtight container.

For the sake of freshness, it's a good idea to purchase nuts and seeds from a specialist nut store or any store with a high turnover. Middle Eastern food stores do a brisk trade in nuts and seeds, and would be a good bet.

400 g can chickpeas or 250 g cooked chickpeas
3 tablespoons olive oil
250 g unsalted peanuts
250 g unsalted cashew nuts
250 g blanched almonds
200 g unsalted shelled pistachios
100 g sunflower seeds
100 g hulled pumpkin seeds

SPICE MIX

2 teaspoons sweet paprika
½ teaspoon ground cardamom
1 teaspoon ground cinnamon
1 teaspoon ground cumin
½ teaspoon freshly ground black pepper
1 teaspoon ground turmeric
½ teaspoon cayenne pepper
2 tablespoons sea salt, or to taste

Preheat the oven to 220°C and line a large baking tray with baking paper.

To make the spice mix, toss all the spices in a bowl.

If using canned chickpeas, rinse them thoroughly, then drain. Spread the chickpeas out on the baking tray and roast for 10 minutes, shaking the tray from time to time so they colour evenly.

Tip the chickpeas into another bowl and add 1 teaspoon of the oil and ¼ teaspoon of the spice mix. Toss to coat evenly, then tip the chickpeas back onto the baking tray and return to the oven for another 10 minutes. Shake every now and then. Remove from the oven and tip back into the bowl to cool.

Reduce the oven temperature to 160°C. Mix the peanuts, cashews, almonds and pistachios in another large bowl. Add the remaining oil and spice mix and toss well so the nuts are evenly coated. Transfer to the baking tray and roast for 30 minutes, shaking the tray from time to time so the nuts colour evenly. Add the seeds to the tray and stir them in thoroughly, then roast for 5 minutes. Set aside to cool.

When the chickpeas, nuts and seeds are cold, mix them together thoroughly. Serve straight away or store in an airtight container. **MAKES 1 KG**

Pesteh-ye zafaran
SAFFRON-TOASTED PISTACHIOS

We were taught this method in Rafsanjan, the pistachio capital of Iran. Mr Mahmud Hassani, the owner of a pistachio orchard, invited us to an impromptu lunch, and on our departure his wife loaded us up with a big bag of these tasty nuts to see us through our long journey. The saffron turns the nuts a glorious and exotic gold, and fresh lime juice and salt give them an irresistible tang. Once you start snacking, it's hard to stop!

1 kg raw pistachios in the shell
juice of 1 lime
2 tablespoons Saffron Liquid (page 54)
1 tablespoon sea salt, or more to taste

Heat a large, heavy-based frying pan over a medium heat. Tip in the pistachios and toss them over the heat to warm. Mix the lime juice with the saffron liquid and sprinkle over the nuts. Cook, shaking the pan continuously, so that the nuts absorb the liquid and colour evenly. When most of the liquid has been absorbed or has evaporated, and the nuts are golden brown, sprinkle on the salt. Toss for a few more minutes, then remove the pan from the heat. Tip the pistachios into a serving bowl and serve hot, or allow to cool and store in an airtight container. MAKES 1 KG

Ajeel-e shab-chera
LONGEST-NIGHT GRAZING MIX

Ajeel is the generic name for mixtures of dried fruit, nuts and seeds, and the varieties are virtually infinite in Iran. Make your own mix, depending on what you think goes together well. Some particular combinations are reserved for special festivals, such as Persian New Year or Yalda, the ancient winter solstice festival. On this longest night of the year, families and friends gather to read the poetry of the legendary Persian poet, Hafez, while they snack on fresh pomegranates, watermelon and ajeel into the early hours. As with so many Persian things, the number seven is all-important to this mixture, as is the inclusion of watermelon seeds, which represent the warmth of summer in the midst of winter. You can find watermelon seeds in Middle Eastern food stores, otherwise use pumpkin seeds instead.

3 tablespoons olive oil

300 g blanched almonds,

150 g unsalted shelled pistachios

100 g watermelon or pumpkin seeds

100 g sunflower seeds

1 tablespoon sea salt, or to taste

150 g dried sour cherries, diced

150 g sultanas

150 g small dried wild figs, diced

Heat the oil in a large, heavy-based frying pan over a medium heat. Tip in the almonds and stir until an even golden brown. Remove with a slotted spoon and drain on paper towels. Wipe out the pan and fry the pistachios until they begin to colour and smell toasty. Shake the pan continuously so they colour evenly. Combine the almonds and pistachios in a large bowl and set aside.

Add the watermelon and sunflower seeds to the pan and cook until lightly coloured, shaking the pan continuously. Tip into the nuts, then toss with the salt and leave to cool.

Toss the dried fruit with the cool nuts. Serve straight away or store in an airtight container. MAKES 1 KG

zendegi

WE LEAVE TEHRAN IN THE DIM LIGHT OF A NEW DAY, CREEPING THROUGH AN ENDLESS sprawl of outer suburbs that are choked with traffic even at this hour. The road takes us north-west and after a while we begin to climb the scrubby slopes of the Alburz Mountains. Further north beyond their peaks, hidden in a series of deep folds and densely forested slopes, lies the fabled Valley of the Assassins. The Nizari or Hashhashins, to use the name given them by their enemies, were secretive mercenary members of an eleventh-century heretical Shia Ismaeli sect whose goal was to overthrow the newly arrived Sunni Seljuk rulers by a gradual and highly effective campaign of kidnap and murder. The Assassins' war of terror lasted for nearly two hundred years, and their tiny fortified kingdom remained impregnable until the Mongols swept through the region in the thirteenth century, destroying everything and everybody in their path.

But our journey is taking us to the Caspian Sea, and as we pass over the mountains, the smog of the city and the dun dustiness of the Tehran plateau falls away and we cross into a very different world. Now the road winds steadily downward through craggy gorges and wooded ravines. We sink into shadow and when I wind down the car window and reach out my hand I feel a fine mist of cool rain – the first we have seen or felt for several weeks. As we drive on, the thin cloud seems to evaporate. The road twists around a bend and we enter a narrow valley filled with sunlight.

Eventually, we emerge into gently rolling hills of dazzling, eye-hurting green. 'Rice,' says Ali, as we hurtle along. This is the Caspian littoral, a narrow stretch of land that fringes the sea shore and is effectively cut off from the rest of Iran by the impenetrable ridge of the Alburz Mountains. Thus isolated, it has its own distinctive micro-climate that is leafy, fertile and wet. These are the perfect conditions for the region's two major crops: tea and rice. The rice harvest is nearly finished for the year and the threshed sheaves are stacked in tidy mounds waiting to be carried away for processing. 'Iranian rice is the best in the world,' says Ali. 'You have never smelled a perfume like it.'

WE ARE IN A BIT OF A PREDICAMENT. ALI HAS INVITED US FOR DINNER AND TO spend a night with his family at their villa near the Caspian. By now we are used to being invited into people's homes for refreshments and meals – it's all part of the extraordinary level of Iranian hospitality. But this will be a far greater intrusion and we are unsure how to respond.

/

The problem is that many social interactions in Iran are wrapped in an elaborate protocol of polite, self-deprecating, back-and-forth exchanges known as ta'arouf: it's a kind of one-upmanship of flattery and good manners. But there are rules to this game, and after a few desperate exchanges with Ali we are none the wiser. Is he just being polite, or does he really want us to come and stay? Does he want us to accept his offer, or should we decline gracefully? The worst possible outcome will be to offend.

/

Eventually I can bear it no longer and decide that the only way out of the dilemma is to ask Ali directly. His face falls at my question and he looks hurt. 'No, this is not ta'arouf,' he says quietly. 'You are my friends and I invite you from my heart.'

/

Well that seems to be that then, and we accept his invitation in a flurry of embarrassed gratitude. He seems greatly cheered by our enthusiasm and whips out his mobile phone to call his wife with the good news. 'Now you will taste the best cooking in Iran,' he says proudly.

/

ALI'S VILLA IS CLOSE TO RASHT, THE capital of Gilan Province, and he takes us to see its impressive fresh produce market before dinner. Here we find stalls stocked with fish from the nearby Caspian Sea – including some monster sturgeon and couli, a tiny local delicacy that the Gilani eat, head and all (earning them the moniker 'fish-head-eaters'). Even more popular with shoppers are smoked and salted fish and long wedges of pinkish-brown roe. Needless to say, there is no Iranian caviar to be found. This is an expensive delicacy, reserved for the export market.

/

But there are endless other delights and we are tempted by fresh walnuts, plump olives and all manner of fresh and pickled fruits and vegetables. We're especially pleased to spot the famous Persian sweet lemons (limonshirin) and sour oranges (naranj).

/

Ali lingers by a rice merchant's stall, scooping up handful after handful from each sack and offering it to us for inspection. We can see fine distinctions in the length and girth of the different grains, and Ali tells us that the best costs around two US dollars per kilogram. It doesn't seem like much, until you remember that the average monthly salary ranges between four- and six-hundred US dollars (for some it is much less) and Iranian families such as Ali's will get through around three hundred kilograms of rice every year. The best rice on offer is called 'hashemi' or 'ambar-boo' – which translates rather lyrically as amber-scented – and is grown in only a few very small areas. As we run our hands through the long, fine, translucent grains they leave a light oily film on our fingers. 'The most important thing is the perfume,' says Ali, and we all inhale deeply, enjoying the delicate nutty fragrance.

/

We are distracted from our rice reverie by another aroma of cooking and we head toward a neighbouring pancake stall. These are reshteh khoshkar, a sort of lacy pancake made, logically enough for this part of the world, from rice flour. They are filled with a mixture of ground walnuts and sugar and folded into neat parcels to be fried in sugar syrup. Naturally we can't resist buying some for tomorrow's breakfast.

/

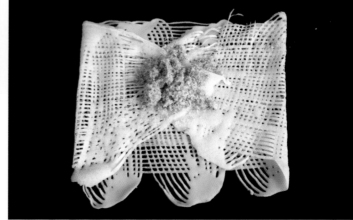

We arrive at ali's home in time to watch his wife, farrah, tip a huge mound of rice onto a serving platter. She carefully lifts the precious tah-deeg – the delectable crisp golden layer from the bottom of the pot – onto a separate plate. Iranian family members fight over tah-deeg in the same way that Westerners fight over roast pork crackling, but I also know that as honoured guests we have the advantage of being served first. A vast array of local Gilan delicacies are already set out on the table and we can't wait to tuck in.

/

We are already familiar with sabzi, the mixture of fresh green herbs that grace every Iranian table and are eaten with soft white cheese and warm flatbread, but here we also find a bowl of peppery radish leaves and plump green olives in a paste of chopped walnuts and pomegranate molasses.

/

Greg and I are both pleased to discover that garlic features heavily in Gilan cooking; as well as a dish of black pickled garlic, Farrah has prepared garlic shoots fried with egg, and mizra ghasemi, a glorious mixture of puréed eggplant, tomato and, naturally, plenty of garlic. The star of the meal is the local interpretation of fesenjun, one of Iran's most popular dishes. Fesenjun combines chicken (or sometimes duck) with a sauce of crushed walnuts and pomegranate, but in Gilan they favour mouth-puckeringly sour pomegranate sauce, making it quite different from sweeter versions we have sampled elsewhere.

/

There is genuine warmth around the table. Farrah beams throughout the whole meal, clearly delighted by our appetites, and Amin, Farrah and Ali's teenage son, peppers us with questions about our incomes, families, work and education. The conversation rambles around movies, television, politics (of course) and religion. Finally he stammers out the question that, sooner or later, all Iranians ask us. 'Do people in your country really think that Iranians are all terrorists? Or is it just our government that they don't like?'

/

It's a genuine question that requires a truthful answer. Greg begins cautiously: 'I think that there will always be people who are influenced by what they see on the television or read in the papers,' he says. 'I'm afraid that there are Australians who think they don't like Iranian people, just as there are Iranians who think they don't like Westerners. But this comes from ignorance.'

/

Amin and Ali are nodding in agreement and Greg is warming to his theme. 'Underneath of course, we are all the same. It doesn't matter what religion you have or where you live.' A smile breaks over Ali's face and he smacks his hand on the table. 'Of course you are right, my friend! And do you know who said this first? A Persian man! It was Cyrus the Great, the first king of Persia, who wrote the very first charter of human rights on the Cyrus Stone. When he captured Babylon in the sixth century he freed the Jewish people from captivity and declared that all people would be free under his rule. You can find his words even today in the United Nations.'

/

It seems a bold assertion, and we wonder whether this is an example of the by-now-familiar Persian pride. Later that evening we read up on Cyrus and his Stone in our guide books and are humbled to find that Ali is quite right.

/

It's a day of rushing clouds and flashing sunshine, but even the sun can't make the Caspian Sea lovely. It's a disappointing expanse of polluted steely-grey and the beach is littered with rubble and all manner of rubbish. Proving themselves to be the most determined picnickers in a country of determined picnickers, a young couple has parked their car at the water's edge and sit together contentedly, apparently oblivious to their grim surroundings. I'm not sure whether this cheers me up, or depresses me.

WE SPEND THE MORNING FIGHTING THE TRAFFIC ALONG the narrow coast road, but, thankfully, at Astara many of the roaring juggernauts cross over the border into neighbouring Azerbaijan. We turn onto a more peaceful road that curves up into the forested hinterland, and, before long, we are crossing the mountains and emerge into rolling highlands.

/

Gone is the lush, wet, green vegetation of the Caspian littoral and we are back in a wild, wide landscape that feels more recognisably Iranian. The car speeds along a high plateau that disappears into a ridge of snow-capped mountains; the air has a sharp clarity and above us a brilliant blue sky seems to stretch forever.

/

We pass tiny villages and small holdings and in the brown fields women wearing brightly coloured headscarves, dresses and sturdy boots bend over crops of potatoes and onions. Here and there we spy a flock of scruffy sheep, and rough-looking men on horseback stare silently as we pass.

/

It's all too easy to imagine Mongol hordes riding across this landscape, which might not have been all that different from their home in the broad steppes of Central Asia. The Mongol invaders came thundering out of the East in the thirteenth century in two terrible, unstoppable waves, leaving much of northern and central Iran in flaming ruins. The destruction swept as far as China in the east, to Poland and Moscow in the north and extinguished the Islamic seat of power in the great Persian capital, Baghdad, to the west.

/

In the wake of this carnage, many Iranians turned to Sufism, a different, more spiritual kind of Islam that flourished in the north-western part of the empire, especially in Ardabil, an old trading city that sits in the middle of this lonely plateau. We are here to visit the shrine of Sheikh Safi al-Din, a mystic Dervish, but, first, Ali ducks into a nearby sweet shop to buy a tub of the city's famous black helva. This turns out to be a dense, sticky, sweet black sort of pudding, flavoured with cinnamon, cloves and nutmeg, and a little goes a long way to reviving us after the drive.

/

The shrine has a timeless, ancient quality, with three tower-like tombs clad in a graceful counterpoint of baked brickwork and glazed blue and turquoise tiles. Ali explains that Sheikh al-Din came from a clan called the Safavids, and within 150 years his descendants had converted to Shia Islam, reunified the empire and become one of Persia's most successful and glorious dynasties.

/

At a livestock market outside Tabriz we stop and watch wiry horsemen test-riding sturdy little horses. 'This is the first time they have seen a woman in a place like this,' laughs Ali, and I realise that intense black eyes are following our every step. We buy a watermelon with vivid orange flesh and the seller refuses to accept payment. 'Ta'arouf?', I whisper to Ali. The two men engage in a brief, energetic exchange, but eventually Ali turns to me and laughs, 'No. I think he just likes you!'.

/

Most of the guide books – and some family and friends – have been warning us that Tabriz will disappoint, and on approach it seems they could be right. We arrive in the afternoon to discover a sprawling concrete city, surrounded by power plants and factories and shrouded in a vile yellow smog. There seem to be few obvious signs of its earlier splendour as an impressive Mongol Ilkhanid capital, under Genghis Kahn's grandson, Hulegu – 'Il Khan' – with extravagant palaces, observatories, mosques, a dazzling jewellery bazaar and a thriving silk trade.

/

Wracked by regular earthquakes over the centuries, and occupied in between times, Tabriz's wealth seemed destined for ruin. In the eighteenth century, most of Tabriz's former glories – along with more than eighty thousand of its citizens – were buried in one of the world's worst earthquakes, leaving behind little more than a few patches of tile on a formerly blue mosque and several miles of brick-vaulted bazaar.

/

The rubble from the Blue Mosque has been laboriously reconstructed and it is still possible to get a sense of its former splendour. While the grand entrance portal is a mere ultramarine patchwork of its former self, within the main hall the towering vaulted arches and thick, square columns are covered with friezes of azure, turquoise, sky-blue, teal, indigo and cobalt.

/

More impressive still, is the bazaar, and we spend a long, happy morning wandering its atmospheric passageways. It is bustling with customers and we quickly lose our way, but that proves to be half the fun. We stumble into two different carpet bazaars (one for old carpets and one for modern) where there are more carpets than I've seen in my life. They are strung about the walls, rolled into massive pyramids and stacked flat into towering piles. Old men sit with needle and thread, tilting the carpets towards golden spotlights of sunshine that stream in through the domed roof. These carpets are luscious shades of deep plum, oxblood red and velvety blues – but we are well aware that our lack of knowledge will make us easy prey for these wily bazari, and so we hold back from buying.

/

A pleasant surprise is the friendliness of the Tabrizi themselves. There's the taxi driver, who, upon hearing of our interest in food, jumped out of his battered old Paykan and rushed ahead of us into the restaurant to introduce us to the owner personally. There's the mullah in a tiny tea house who insisted on paying for our chai, with a nod of the head and a hand pressed to his heart, and there's the kindly lady who walked twenty minutes out of her way to steer us back to the main part of the bazaar. These people all contributed to the glow of well-being that washes over us as we dine in a flashy revolving restaurant atop a grand hotel at the city's edge.

/

Our fancy dinner is nice enough, with its expansive buffet of soup and salads and an excellent dish of locally caught freshwater trout, but Greg and I agree that one of the best things about the journey so far is the impromptu meals we've enjoyed along the way.

/

Like all good Iranians, Ali has a rug tucked into the boot of his car, ready to be whisked out whenever there's the slightest chance of a picnic. Yesterday, before leaving for Ardabil, he conjured up an al fresco breakfast of warm turmeric-tinted naan sonetti with local buffalo-milk butter, sheep's cheese from the nearby mountains and a thick clotted cream called gheymak.

/

It seems that in these pastoral reaches of Iran the roadsides are cluttered with stalls selling local produce, and we've been sampling and stocking up as we go. On the road to Kandovan, a disappointingly touristy troglodyte village near the foothills of Mount Sahand, we stop to buy lavashak, sheets of dried mulberry and apricot paste. A little further on, we spy a husband and wife puffing smoke into a stack of beehives and we come away with an impressive comb dripping with clear, dark honey. In the sleepy village of Osuko we roam among sacks of new-season's walnuts, their milky-white flesh as crisp as apples.

/

Outside the village we climb over a stone wall into a small apricot orchard and Ali spreads the faithful rug beneath one of the trees. We feast on golden watermelon, honey and walnuts in the warm autumn sunshine. We must make the most of the solitude and enjoy these last moments with Ali, for tomorrow we must say farewell to our saraban – and great new friend – and head back to the city.

/

soups and ash

Soup – generally called ash – plays a huge role in the Iranian diet; it's eaten for breakfast, lunch and dinner, and all through the day, too. On freezing winter mornings people queue up to buy steaming bowls of thick, sustaining ash from street stands and hole-in-the-wall kitchens; it's served as part of a meal and as a meal in its own right, and certain ash are an important feature on the table during festive occasions.

In fact, ash is far more than just a meal; it also plays a vital symbolic role in many Iranian social traditions, and there is pretty much a different ash to suit every occasion. There is an ash to celebrate a child's first tooth and one to sustain women during pregnancy. Another ash – ash-e pusht-e pa – is served at farewell celebrations (it translates as 'thick soup behind the foot'). Ash-e isfandi is a use-it-all-up soup, made as you clear out the pantry during the last month of the old year, while ash-e reshteh is served on the first workday of a New Year to celebrate new beginnings. Abu dard ash (which means 'father of pain') uses seven different types of bean you collect from your neighbours, and is made to help disperse pain and suffering in times of ill-health. Ash-e nazri – charity soup – is part of an age-old tradition of community and sharing. Nazri soups are made by families – usually by many families together – to give thanks for significant events, or to mark occasions of sadness. They are nearly always made in vast quantities and distributed throughout the neighbourhood, so they serve not only as a nourishing meal, but as a reminder that someone else is in need of care or that others are aware of your situation – a quiet communal hug, if you like.

There are various fine distinctions between the vast repertoire of ash dishes, but they are nearly all thick and hearty – a far cry from the thin consommés and broths of other cuisines. Some ash are meat-based (although meat is usually only added in small quantities), others are made solely from vegetables or sometimes even fruit. They are nearly all thick with herbs, and some are distinguished by their sour flavour. Some ash are based on rice, others on grains and pulses, yet others on pasta. In fact, many are so thick that they are almost stew-like, and the only thing that differentiates them from khoresht (pages 170–0188) is that they are not eaten with rice, but on their own or with bread.

Abgoosht – and its widely represented derivative dizi, which is what we experienced mostly on our travels – is another distinct and incredibly popular category of meat-based soup that is really two meals in one. A slow-cooked combination of meat on the bone, vegetables, pulses, tomatoes and meat stock, it is defined by the way it is served and eaten. The translation of 'abgoosht' – 'meat-water', or perhaps more kindly 'meat juices' – provides some clues. The tasty broth is strained off and eaten first, and the remaining solid ingredients are pounded to a coarse paste to be eaten with bread and strongly flavoured accompaniments. It's filling, nutritious and very tasty.

A final word about soups: the Persian word for cook is 'ashpaz', which means, literally, 'soupmaker'. It gives a pretty clear message about how important these dishes are in the Iranian diet.

Abdugh khiar
CHILLED YOGHURT SOUP WITH SUMMER HERBS

Wonderfully refreshing on a hot summer's day, icy-cold yoghurt and herb soups are popular all around the Middle East, with slight variations from country to country. Iranian versions often include chopped walnuts and raisins, which make the soup richer and more filling; a little goes a surprisingly long way. Serve with plenty of warm flatbread.

3 Lebanese cucumbers, peeled

1 small clove garlic

sea salt

800 g thick natural yoghurt

2 tablespoons chopped tarragon leaves

2 tablespoons finely snipped chives

1 tablespoon chopped chervil sprigs

1 teaspoon dried mint

¼ teaspoon freshly ground white pepper

⅓ cup finely chopped walnuts

2 tablespoons currants

up to 300 ml icy-cold water

squeeze of lemon juice

slivered pistachios, fresh or dried rose
    petals or 1 small radish, thinly shaved,
    to garnish

Split the cucumbers lengthwise and scoop out and discard the seeds. Grate the cucumber coarsely into a colander set on a plate and refrigerate for 30 minutes.

Crush the garlic with 1 teaspoon salt to make a smooth paste. Whisk the garlic paste into the yoghurt until evenly distributed, then whisk in the herbs. Squeeze the grated cucumber firmly to remove as much moisture as you can, then stir into the yoghurt. Season with the pepper and salt and refrigerate for at least 1 hour to let the flavours develop.

Just before serving, stir the walnuts and currants into the yoghurt and whisk in enough of the icy-cold water to achieve a soupy consistency – you may not need it all. Add a big squeeze of lemon juice, then taste and adjust the seasonings to your liking once more.

Sprinkle with pistachios, rose petals or radish as you please, and serve straight away. SERVES 6

Hot yoghurt soup with apricots and sizzling mint butter

I was raised on yoghurt soups, both hot and cold, so, for me, their comforting creamy tang sings of childhood. I can't pretend that this one is truly Persian (or Lebanese for that matter!), but I like to think that combining sweet— sour dried apricots with the bland smoothness of rice and chickpeas in a rich yoghurty broth is at the very least a nod in the right culinary direction. It's also a good recipe to make if you have leftover rice.

1 litre good-quality chicken stock

140 g cooked basmati rice

170 g cooked or canned chickpeas

500 g thick natural yoghurt

3 tablespoons thickened cream

2 teaspoons cornflour

50 ml water

1 egg, lightly beaten

80 g dried apricots, finely diced

sea salt

freshly ground black pepper

squeeze of lemon juice

¼ cup snipped chives

¼ cup chopped chervil sprigs

1 tablespoon chopped flat-leaf parsley leaves

SIZZLING MINT BUTTER

60 g unsalted butter

1 teaspoon dried mint

pinch of cayenne pepper

Bring the stock, rice and chickpeas to a gentle boil in a large saucepan over a medium heat, then lower the heat and simmer for 2–3 minutes.

While the soup is simmering, whisk the yoghurt and cream in a bowl until very smooth. Mix the cornflour with the water and add to the yoghurt with the egg. Stir well to combine, then whisk in a few tablespoons of the hot stock. Pour this back into the just-simmering soup. Add the apricots and cook at a bare simmer for about 10 minutes, stirring in one direction only from time to time. Be sure not to let the soup boil or it will curdle.

When ready to serve, prepare the mint butter. Melt the butter in a small saucepan over a medium heat until it sizzles. Add the mint and cayenne and swirl over the heat for a minute. Meanwhile, season the soup with salt and pepper, add a squeeze of lemon juice and stir in the fresh herbs, then ladle the soup into serving bowls. Swirl on a little sizzling butter and serve straight away. **SERVES 6**

Soop-e jo
CREAMY PEARL BARLEY SOUP WITH CANDIED CARROT

This, as we discovered, is 'soup of the day' all around Iran. It's served up everywhere, from tiny diners to city restaurants and big hotels. But it often comes straight out of a tin, which is a shame, as that bland slop bears little resemblance to the homemade stuff, which is creamy comfort food par-excellence. This recipe borrows heavily from a soop-e jo we tried in a restaurant in Tabriz. The soup itself was extra creamy – surely from the addition of a good dollop of sour cream? – and was topped with a sweet tangle of orange-scented carrot.

50 ml oil

2 onions, finely chopped

1 leek, finely chopped

2 sticks celery, finely chopped

2 cloves garlic, finely chopped

1 teaspoon ground ginger

150 g pearl barley, soaked for 1 hour and drained

1 bay leaf

few sprigs of thyme

1 long strip lemon peel, all pith removed

1 teaspoon sea salt

½ teaspoon freshly ground black pepper

1.75 litres good-quality chicken stock

30 g unsalted butter

2 carrots, finely grated or shredded

finely grated or shredded zest of 1 orange

1 tablespoon caster sugar

splash of white-wine vinegar

juice of 2 limes

120 ml sour cream

Heat the oil in a large, heavy-based saucepan over a low heat. Add the onion, leek, celery and garlic and fry gently until soft and translucent. Stir in the ground ginger and cook for another minute.

Add the soaked barley to the saucepan with the bay leaf, thyme and lemon peel. Stir well and season with salt and pepper. Add the stock and bring to a boil. Lower the heat and simmer gently, covered, for 2 hours, stirring from time to time. After 2 hours, check to see if the barley is tender. It might need another 30 minutes or so.

Towards the end of the cooking time, melt the butter in a large frying pan over a low heat and add the carrot and orange zest. Fry for 3–4 minutes until they start to soften. Sprinkle on the sugar and cook for a further 2–3 minutes, until the carrot and zest are sticky and translucent. Stir in the vinegar and remove from the heat.

Just before serving, remove the lemon peel and stir the lime juice and sour cream into the soup. Scatter on the candied carrot and serve straight away. SERVES 6

Eshkeneh

This is my twist on a simple, rustic onion soup we ate on a chilly spring evening at the Apadana Hotel at Persepolis. Eshkeneh is an ancient dish thought to date back several thousand years. Onions traditionally give courage and strength in battle and legend has it that eshkeneh was the daily diet of Persian soldiers under the Parthian King Arsaces back in the third century. It was bulked up with pieces of dry bread that would soften in the soup – similar to the way that croutons are used in French onion soup. In some eshkeneh recipes the eggs are whisked into the hot broth, where they create long eggy strands. Poaching them, as I've done here, makes this a more elegant dish, and I can't resist the way the creamy yolks ooze into the warming, golden broth.

Serve with a small jug of verjuice or mild vinegar, and perhaps a few tiny sour grapes as an extra tangy garnish.

2 tablespoons olive oil
20 g unsalted butter
2 onions, finely sliced
2 cloves garlic, finely sliced
½ teaspoon ground turmeric
½ teaspoon fenugreek seeds, lightly crushed
1 teaspoon freshly ground black pepper
250 g kipfler or other waxy potatoes, peeled and cubed
1.25 litres good-quality chicken stock
few sprigs of thyme
1 bay leaf
1 long strip peel from ½ orange, all pith removed
sea salt
2 tablespoons verjuice
juice of ½ lemon
6 small eggs, at room temperature
freshly ground black pepper
verjuice, tiny sour grapes (optional), flatbread and lemon wedges, to serve

Heat the oil and butter in a large, heavy-based saucepan over a low heat. Add the onion and garlic and fry gently until soft and translucent. Stir in the spices and cook for another couple of minutes.

Add the potato and cook for a minute, stirring to coat well with the onion mixture. Add the stock, herbs, and orange peel. Add salt to taste and simmer gently for 30 minutes.

Just as you are ready to serve, fish out the bay leaf and orange peel, then stir in the verjuice and lemon juice. Crack the eggs and carefully slip them into the simmering soup and poach gently for 3–4 minutes or until the yolks are barely set – they will continue to cook in the broth after you remove the pan from the heat.

Ladle the soup straight from the pan at the table, ensuring everyone has an egg. Season with salt and pepper and serve with flatbread and lemon wedges or verjuice, and a few tiny sour grapes, if you like, as garnish. **SERVES 6**

Soop-e pesteh
PISTACHIO SOUP WITH BARBERRIES AND
A SOUR-CREAM SWIRL

This is an unashamedly rich, creamy and luxurious soup for when you want to pull out all the stops. It's an extraordinary golden–green hue, and it looks stunning with a garnish of deep-crimson barberries and bright-green pistachio slivers.

Use unsalted, shelled pistachios for this soup. They should be blanched and peeled, which is a fiddly job, but results in a much more vibrant colour.

1 tablespoon olive oil
40 g unsalted butter
1 small leek, white part only, diced
2 shallots, diced
1 small clove garlic, finely diced
½ teaspoon ground ginger
½ teaspoon freshly ground black pepper
¼ teaspoon ground cumin
¼ teaspoon ground turmeric
50 g basmati rice
1.25 litres good-quality chicken stock
sea salt
160 g unsalted pistachios, blanched
   and peeled
juice of 1 orange
juice of ½ lime
1 tablespoon dried barberries, stems
   removed
100 ml sour cream
1 tablespoon slivered pistachios

Heat the oil and half the butter in a large, heavy-based saucepan over a low heat. Add the leek, shallots and garlic and fry gently until soft and translucent. Stir in the spices and cook for another couple of minutes.

Add the rice and cook for a few seconds, stirring to coat it with the onion mixture. Add the stock and salt to taste and simmer gently for 30 minutes.

Towards the end of the cooking time, tip the blanched pistachios into a food processor with a generous ladleful of the hot soup. Blitz until as smooth as possible, then pour back into the soup. Add the orange and lime juice, then taste and adjust the seasonings to your liking.

When nearly ready to serve, prepare the garnish. Soak the barberries for 2 minutes in cold water, then drain and dry well. Melt the remaining butter in a small saucepan over a low heat, then add the barberries and fry for 4–5 minutes, stirring constantly. Remove from the heat.

Ladle the soup into bowls and top each serve with a swirl of sour cream. Scatter on the barberries and slivered pistachios and serve straight away. SERVES 6

Ash-e sak
SPINACH SOUP WITH LITTLE BEEF KOOFTEH

A bowlful of irony, green goodness! Who knew that the English word 'spinach' derives from the Farsi word 'esfenaj'? In this dish, though, it is called sak, an Indian word. It suggests that the dish might have come to Persia from India, a reversal of the trend that saw Persian recipes taken with Zoroastrian exiles who became Parsis in their new homeland back in the seventh century.

Koofteh are very popular in Persian cooking, and the word itself derives from the Farsi verb 'to pound', which describes the paste-like consistency needed to make these tender little meatballs. The secret is to mince the meat twice; ask your butcher to do this for you, or do it yourself at home. The mince must then be energetically and thoroughly kneaded so that the fat is evenly distributed throughout the meat and it turns into a soft, sticky paste. You can do this quickly in a food processor if you like, but chill the bowl and blade in the fridge first.

2 tablespoons olive oil
1 small onion, finely diced
1 clove garlic, finely chopped
½ teaspoon ground turmeric
½ teaspoon freshly ground black pepper
1.5 litres good-quality chicken stock
sea salt
250 g spinach leaves, finely shredded
½ cup coriander leaves
2 eggs, lightly whisked
3 tablespoons verjuice
generous squeeze of lime juice

BEEF KOOFTEH
300 g lean beef, minced twice
1 small onion, grated
1 clove garlic, grated
½ teaspoon dried mint
½ teaspoon freshly ground black pepper
½ teaspoon ground turmeric
½ teaspoon sea salt
splash of extra-virgin olive oil

To make the koofteh, combine all the ingredients in a large bowl and knead thoroughly for at least a minute (alternatively, pulse in a chilled food processor). When everything is well combined, cover and refrigerate for 30 minutes.

Heat the oil in a very large, heavy-based saucepan over a low heat. Add the onion and garlic and fry gently until soft and translucent. Stir in the turmeric and pepper and cook for another couple of minutes. Add the stock and salt to taste, then simmer gently for 10 minutes.

While the soup is simmering, use wet hands to roll the beef koofteh mixture into smooth, even dumplings, about the size of a small walnut. You should get 24 dumplings from the mixture.

Pop the dumplings into the soup and bring to a boil. Lower the heat and simmer gently for 12 minutes, skimming away any impurities that rise to the surface.

Add the spinach to the pan and increase the heat to a rolling boil. Cook for 2 minutes, then stir in the coriander and eggs. Stir gently to distribute the egg threads. Add the verjuice and lime juice and season to taste. Serve immediately, making sure that everyone gets 4 koofteh. **SERVES 6**

Goosh bareh

Simmering pasta dumplings in a tasty broth is an idea that dates back more than fifteen hundred years in Persian cooking. The name of this dish refers to the crescent shape of the dumplings, which are said to resemble lamb's ears. The broth itself is a little spicy, reflecting its origins in Azerbaijan to the north-west.

It might seem tedious to poach the dumplings separately from the soup, but as starch inevitably leaches out of pasta dough, doing it this way results in a much clearer broth and finer flavour.

Dried-lime powder is available from Middle Eastern food stores and some good providores.

4 vine-ripened tomatoes, peeled and
    seeded
1 generous teaspoon tomato paste
2 tablespoons Saffron Liquid (page 54)
1 litre good-quality chicken stock
1 teaspoon dried-lime powder or juice
    of ½ lime
½ teaspoon dried oregano
¼ teaspoon cayenne pepper
sea salt
freshly ground black pepper
splash of verjuice (optional)
¼ cup snipped chives
sumac, to garnish

DOUGH

150 g self-raising flour
pinch of sea salt
2 small eggs
2 tablespoons cold water

STUFFING

100 g lean minced lamb
1 shallot, finely diced
1 small clove garlic, finely chopped
½ teaspoon ground coriander
pinch of ground allspice
pinch of freshly ground black pepper
½ teaspoon sea salt
splash of extra-virgin olive oil

To make the dough, sift the flour and salt into a bowl and make a well in the centre. Crack in the eggs and add the water, then use your hands to bring the dough together. Knead for a few minutes on a work surface, just until the dough is smooth. Cover the dough and refrigerate for 30 minutes.

To make the stuffing, combine all the ingredients in a large bowl and knead thoroughly for at least a minute. When everything is well combined, cover and refrigerate for 30 minutes.

Roughly chop the tomatoes, then blitz them to a very smooth purée in a food processor. Pour into a large heavy-based saucepan and stir in the tomato paste and saffron liquid. Add the stock, dried-lime powder (if using), oregano and cayenne and season with salt and pepper. Bring to a boil over a medium heat, then lower the heat and simmer for 30 minutes.

When ready to make the lamb's ear dumplings, divide the dough into 2 portions. Working with one portion at a time, roll the dough out as thinly as you can. Use a 9 cm pastry cutter to cut out 12 rounds from each piece of dough. Place a spoonful of filling across the centre of each round and brush the edges with a little water. Fold one side edge in, just to cover the end of the filling. Now fold the edge in front of you over the filling to create a lopped-off crescent – the lamb's ear – and press gently to seal. Cover the dumplings with a damp tea towel as they are completed. You should make 24 dumplings in total.

Bring a very large saucepan of lightly salted water to a boil over a high heat. Add the dumplings and cook at a fairly vigorous simmer for 10 minutes, or until the dough is tender. Scoop out the dumplings with a slotted spoon, and drain briefly.

When ready to serve, add a splash of verjuice (or lime juice, if you didn't use the lime powder) to the soup and adjust the seasoning to your liking. Slip 4 dumplings into each bowl and ladle on the hot soup. Sprinkle on the snipped chives and sumac and serve straight away. SERVES 6

Ash-e ordak

DUCK ASH WITH QUINCE, SAFFRON AND NOODLES

To be honest, we didn't see a huge number of duck dishes on our travels around Iran, although it is often served as a fancy fesenjun, in a rich and tangy pomegranate–walnut sauce. But duck meat does have a wonderfully rich flavour, and I think it's the perfect candidate for a thick, hearty ash, full of noodles, white beans and chunks of golden quince.

50 ml olive oil

1 small onion, finely diced

2 cloves garlic, finely chopped

1 teaspoon ground cumin

½ teaspoon ground coriander

½ teaspoon ground cardamom

½ teaspoon freshly ground black pepper

¼ teaspoon freshly grated nutmeg

2 duck legs, boned, trimmed of excess
    fat and cut into 2 cm cubes

150 g dried white beans, soaked
    overnight and drained

2 long strips orange peel, all pith removed

8 sprigs thyme

1.5–2 litres good-quality chicken stock

2 tablespoons Saffron Liquid (page 54)

2 quinces, washed and dried

1 small tomato, seeded and finely diced

60 g vermicelli noodles

sea salt

juice of ½ lemon

2 tablespoons finely shredded flat-leaf
    parsley leaves

Heat the oil in a large, heavy-based saucepan over a low heat. Add the onion and garlic and fry gently until soft and translucent. Stir in the spices and fry for another couple of minutes.

Add the duck to the pan and cook over a highish heat for a minute until coloured, stirring to coat with the spice mixture. Add the beans to the pan with the orange peel and thyme. Pour in the stock and saffron liquid and bring to a boil. Lower the heat and simmer gently for 20 minutes, skimming away any impurities that rise to the surface.

Meanwhile, core and peel the quinces. Cut into small chunks, putting them into acidulated water to prevent discoloration as you go.

Add the quince to the soup and simmer for 15 minutes, or until the quince and duck are tender. Towards the end of the cooking time, stir in the diced tomato. Add the noodles and cook for 4–5 minutes. Remove the orange peel. Season the soup to taste with salt and stir in the lemon juice, then sprinkle on the parsley and serve straight away. **SERVES 6**

Ash-e reshteh
NEW YEAR NOODLE SOUP

Thick with beans, pulses and fresh herbs, this soup feels full of enough healthy goodness to see you through an entire year. But the real point of it is the noodles. Any New Year is inevitably associated with new beginnings, and in Persia it is seen as a good time to take control of the 'threads' of your life and forge a fresh direction for the year ahead.

In traditional recipes for ash-e reshteh the herbs are added at the start of the cooking time. I've tweaked things a tad by adding them at the end, which preserves the vibrant green colour and makes for a fresher, albeit slightly less intense, flavour.

Liquid kashk is available in specialist Iranian stores.

2 tablespoons olive oil
1 onion, thinly sliced
1 long red chilli, finely chopped
½ teaspoon ground turmeric
1 teaspoon ground cumin
½ teaspoon freshly ground black pepper
120 g dried chickpeas, soaked overnight and drained
2 litres good-quality chicken stock
250 g borlotti beans in the pod
100 g brown lentils
sea salt
80 g fresh thin egg noodles
250 g spinach leaves, finely shredded
½ cup finely shredded coriander leaves
2 tablespoons chopped dill sprigs
juice of 1 lime

GARNISH

1 tablespoon olive oil
25 g unsalted butter
1 large onion, thinly sliced
100 ml liquid kashk or sour cream
50 g shelled walnuts, finely chopped

Heat the oil in a large, heavy-based saucepan or casserole dish over a low heat. Add the onion and chilli and fry for a few minutes until they soften. Add the spices and fry for another minute, then stir in the chickpeas and stock. Bring to a boil, then lower the heat and simmer for 40 minutes, or until the chickpeas are tender. If they are old, it may take a little longer.

Pod the borlotti beans and add to the pan with the lentils and simmer for a further 30 minutes, until the lentils are tender. Once the pulses are cooked, season to taste with salt.

Towards the end of the cooking time, prepare the garnish. Heat the oil and butter in a frying pan over a medium heat and fry the onion for 8–10 minutes, or until golden and caramelised. Set aside until ready to serve.

Add the noodles to the soup and cook for 3–4 minutes until they are just al dente. Add the spinach to the pan in handfuls, mixing it into the soup as it wilts. Stir in the coriander and dill and add a big squeeze of lime juice. Taste and adjust the seasoning to your liking.

Serve straight away, topped with a mound of caramelised onion, a dollop of kashk or sour cream and a sprinkling of walnuts. SERVES 6

Dizi
MORTAR AND PESTLE SOUP WITH CHICKPEAS, LAMB AND FLATBREAD

Dizi became one of our favourite quick-and-easy lunch dishes during our travels, and we would actively seek out specialist restaurants, with their large ovens full of neat rows of individual stoneware dizi pots.

It's a simple enough idea: small chunks of meat-on-the-bone are simmered slowly over several hours with potato, tomatoes, beans and a piece of lamb tail fat, which releases an unctuous richness during the cooking. To serve, the broth is poured into a bowl onto pieces of flatbread and slurped up with a squeeze of sour orange or lemon. The bone is then fished out of the dizi pot and discarded, and the remaining meat, fat and vegetables are pounded to a coarse paste using a special dizi pestle. This tasty mush (for want of a better word) is eaten with plenty more flatbread, pickles, onion, sour orange (or any citrus, really) and fresh herbs (try tarragon, mint and basil). It's far from refined, but unspeakably delicious.

This version omits the scary lamb tail fat to suit Western palates and health concerns, and it is probably a tad more spiced than authentic dizi. The longer you can simmer the lamb, the better the result.

3 tablespoons olive oil

3 lamb shanks

1 teaspoon sea salt

8 small shallots, peeled

6 cloves garlic, peeled

1½ teaspoons ground turmeric

1 teaspoon ground cinnamon

1 teaspoon freshly ground black pepper

1 tablespoon tomato paste

250 g dried chickpeas, soaked overnight and drained

8 sprigs thyme

2 bay leaves

2 litres water

2 potatoes, peeled and cut into chunks

12 small tomatoes

fresh herbs, onion wedges, citrus wedges and flatbread, to serve

Preheat the oven to 160ºC.

Heat the oil in a large, heavy-based casserole dish over a high heat. Add the lamb shanks and season with salt, then brown all over and remove from the pan.

Add the shallots, garlic and spices to the pan and fry over a medium heat for a few minutes until the vegetables soften. Stir in the tomato paste and fry for a minute, then stir in the chickpeas. Return the lamb shanks to the pan with the thyme and bay leaves and pour in the water. Cover the pan and cook in the oven for 2–3 hours, or until the meat is falling away from the bones.

Tuck the potato and tomatoes in among the lamb shanks and return the pan to the oven for another 30 minutes, or until the potato is tender.

Lift the lamb shanks from the soup and remove the meat from the bones. Break the meat roughly into smallish chunks and return it to the pan.

Encourage everyone to eat the dizi the authentic Iranian way. You may not have a dizi pestle at home, but after you've drunk the soup, you could use a mortar and pestle, or just mash the meat and vegetables in your bowl with a fork. Scoop it all up with flatbread, add herbs and onion and squeeze on citrus juice – delicious! **SERVES 6**

jaan

WE ARE BACK IN THE CAPITAL AND STUCK IN A traffic JAM. IN THE FRONT SEAT, EBI IS HAVING a heated discussion over directions with our taxi driver, a wizened man in a flat cap who looks to be about ninety years old. Greg and I sit mutely in the back, stunned into silence by the surrounding mayhem. All around us cars are honking, flashing their lights and pushing through the gridlock like bumper cars at a fairground. Motorcyclists, usually with one, two, three or more passengers, weave in and out of the crush like angry wasps, and pedestrians launch themselves into the fray with an apparent total disregard for their own safety.

/

Our driver mutters a vicious curse, winds down his window and shakes an angry fist at a car that is nudging through the skinniest of openings ahead of us. 'He says he has been driving in this stinking city for thirty years and it is has all turned to shit!', Ebi says over his shoulder. The taxi driver rants on as Ebi translates. 'In the Shah's time it used to be a good place. But now it's full of thieves, drug addicts and other sons-of-bitches who would sell their mothers for a few lousy tomans.'

/

It's true that Tehran is a hard city to love. It was made Iran's capital relatively recently, by the first of the Qajar kings at the end of the late eighteenth century. Whatever charms it may once have had, as a small town tucked into the foothills of the Alburz Mountains, have long disappeared under the weight of concrete and metal and the relentless thundering traffic.

/

Despite its relative youth, in just over two centuries Tehran's population has exploded a thousand-fold and today nearly fifteen million souls cram into its ever-expanding suburbs. And the population goes a long way to explaining the volume of traffic. The problem is that there are just too many cars here – and in the main they are old cars, most of them dating back long before today's emission standards. The pollution is terrible. Since we've been in Tehran, we've barely seen the mountains as they've been shrouded in a yellowish-grey haze, the same poisonous haze that reportedly kills a staggering twenty-seven people here every day.

/

At last we break free of the traffic impasse and our driver flicks the gears, thumps his foot down on the accelerator and takes off at a terrifying pace, careering along a series of narrow alleyways with blatant disregard to the no-entry signs. 'If he's been driving for thirty years I suppose he must know the city well,' I gasp. 'It's impossible to know Tehran well!', the driver retorts. 'It changes every five minutes when they tear something down and put up another monstrosity in its place.'

By now we are in Ebi's neighbourhood, an old suburb in the east of the city. It's where he grew up and still lives, and now he joins in with the driver's tirade. 'Look around you here! When I was a boy there used to be more than a hundred garden squares in this area. There were old houses with beautiful walled gardens. It was *green* here!' He gesticulates angrily at the charmless, densely packed apartment buildings that line the streets on either side of us.

/

The driver gives a snort of disgust. 'See, I'm right,' he says. 'It's all gone to shit!'

/

A FEW DAYS LATER, WE'RE EXPERIENCING A VERY DIFFERENT TEHRAN. WE have been invited to dinner by a Zoroastrian family who live in in a leafy suburb north of the city. Out of politeness, as we enter I ask if may take off my hijab and bend down to remove my shoes. Shirin laughs at me. 'Take your scarf *off* darling, take it *off*! But leave on your shoes, I insist. You must feel at home in my house.' I like her immediately!

/

Like many privileged Iranians, Shirin and her daughter, Laleh, spend part of the year abroad and part of the year in Tehran and they speak flawless, slightly inflected English. Both are elegantly coiffed and made-up, and although they are dressed casually, they are immaculate. They welcome us warmly and I try hard not to feel self-conscious about our own scruffy travel attire. They usher us into their spacious, exquisitely appointed house and through to a lovely salon where a tempting array of biscuits and sweets is arranged on a low table. Laleh is a keen cook and tells us that she had been busy in the kitchen testing sweets for Nowruz, the Persian New Year. Within minutes we are sitting down, nibbling on dainty shortbread and sipping glasses of chilled orange-flower cordial.

/

Unlike many other houses we've visited on our journey so far, their home is decorated in a Western style, with elegant modern furnishings and exquisite ornaments. They come from a family of artists, and the walls are hung with bold modern paintings. A display cabinet is filled with row-upon-row of antique stone heads, and I long to reach up and stroke their worn, fragile contours. Apart from the odd Persian touch, we could be in a fine apartment in Paris, London or New York.

/

We dine on velvety eggplant soup, delicately spiced rice with lamb and green beans, and a salad of finely diced cucumber, tomato and spring onion. Despite the usual Iranian protestations about the humbleness of the offerings, it is beautifully presented, perfectly balanced and quite delicious. We retire to a cosy seating area and the meal is rounded off with fresh fruit salad and homemade blackberry ice-cream. Shirin and Laleh are charming hostesses and we feel ourselves sinking into their world of effortless good manners and easy sophistication.

/

The conversation roams pleasantly from cooking to art, poetry and philosophy, and eventually I can't resist asking the inevitable question. 'Does it get you down, living here?' Shirin leans in towards me. 'Listen darling,' she says. 'What you must understand is that in Iran we live two completely different lives.' She waves a dismissive hand towards the window. 'Out there is one world, with the traffic and the stupid rules about what you can and can't wear or do. That's the world the government worries about – the visible world. But they know that they can't touch us here, inside our homes. Here we do what we like.'

/

This mantra of a double life, a hidden life, is one that we've heard for several weeks now, from men and women, the young and old, wealthy and poor. And here in this lovely home, with these warm, generous people, I am almost convinced. This is a Tehran I think I could grow to like.

/

We've put in a solid morning sightseeing. We've been to the Golestan Palace, admired carpets and glass in their respective museums, and whirled through Persian history – pre-and post-Islam – at the National Museum. But now we need a break from culture and we're tired of rushing around. 'Take us somewhere great for lunch,' we say to Ebi.

/

A few minutes later we are tucked around a table in a small subterranean dizi restaurant near Tehran's heaving bazaar. The busy traffic noise and the shouts of the stallholders fade away, and now all we can hear is the dull thud of the dizi pestle and the slurp of satisfied diners.

/

Somewhere between a soup and stew, dizi is not gourmet fare by any stretch of the imagination, but it has become one of our favourite meals, and it's the perfect restorative after a hard morning of museums. Dizi is also known as abgoosht – which literally means 'meat-water' – and is a category of thick soups that often have meat as a main ingredient. Dizi is usually made from lamb, chickpeas, potatoes and broth in individual clay or aluminium pots, and we can see dozens of them simmering away on a massive slow oven at the rear of the restaurant.

/

The tables are already crowded and our fellow customers seem to be shopkeepers and businessmen from the nearby bazaar. As we wait, a delivery man heads out the door with a tray of lunchtime orders. Finally our dizi arrives, accompanied by folds of hot, blistered flatbread, wedges of raw onion and sour orange, and our own distinctive dizi pestles. The technique is to pour off most of the rich, meaty stock and to load it up with bits of torn-up bread. The soup being slurped, we take a lead from Ebi and our fellow diners and tip the vegetables and meat back into our soup bowls and pound them to a paste with the pestle. This is fun! But keeping track of a chunk of slippery lamb fat keeps us busy. It's not for the fainthearted, but no self-respecting Iranian would remove this fat – it adds flavour and a rich sheen to the entire dish – and we don't either. We munch on onion and sour orange in between mouthfuls of this rich brew, and we leave feeling both sated and refreshed.

/

IT IS ALMOST IMPOSSIBLE TO VISIT TEHRAN AND NOT TACKLE VALIASR STREET AT SOME POINT. This twenty-kilometre stretch of traffic-clogged road bisects the entire city, running from the working-class south to the privileged northern suburbs. Near its end it climbs steeply into the foothills of the snowcapped Alburz Mountains, and in the late afternoon sunshine we find ourselves here, clambering along the Darband walking track. It feels more like northern Europe than Iran, with its waterfalls and rushing streams, dense plantings of spruce and silver birch, and the mountain peaks as a backdrop.

/

The start of the walking track is lined with gaudy, neon-lit restaurants and stalls selling drinks and snack foods. We pass vendors with trays of hot broad beans sprinkled with cumin, jewel-like boiled turnips, pickled walnuts and endless varieties of dried fruit pastes. We pause to buy a tub of candied sour cherries and a glass of pomegranate juice – the first of the season.

/

'It's quiet today,' says Ebi, 'but on Fridays it can be so busy here.' In a nearby tea house we stop to chat with a group of young men and women who are sprawled on daybeds, drinking tea and smoking water pipes. The men sport leather jackets and gelled hair; the young women are doe-eyed beauties, and instead of the all-enveloping black chadors that are a common sight in country areas, they wear skin-tight manteaus (a kind of belted overcoat) and headscarves that barely contain their tumbling black locks. One sports a sticking plaster over her nose, the tell-tale sign of Iran's most popular surgical operation. At least three of them have mobile phones pressed to their ears. It reminds us that this is, above all, a young country, and that around two-thirds of the population (which totals some seventy million) are under the age of thirty.

/

I tell Ebi that I'm surprised to see young people mixing so freely. I had thought that under the current regime unmarried men and women were not meant to socialise – not in public at least. Ebi is amused. 'I think it's the same as any place there are rules,' he says. 'People will always find a way to break them. This is also the Iranian double life.'

/

EBI INSISTS THAT WE LEAVE TEHRAN at night to avoid the worst of the traffic, so when we load up the car a slim crescent moon hangs low in the sky. We stop for petrol and I am childishly excited that it costs a mere four dollars to fill the tank.

/

I am sleepy and it feels strange to be starting a journey so late at night, when others are already tucked up in bed. And then it occurs to me that this is the way it has always been done in this part of the world. Pilgrims, armies, merchants on the Silk Road – they all travelled under the cool mantle of darkness to avoid the heat of the day. My lagging spirits are revived by this sense that even here on our small journey we are in some way re-living history and it feels good to be on the road again.

/

And then we're off, leaving the choking city behind and speeding south along the Qom highway into darkness – and towards another world.

/

I'M SITTING ON A CARPETED PLATFORM IN THE COURTYARD OF OUR traditional hotel, eating breakfast of warm flatbread and honey in the open air. The sun is warm on my shoulders and I can smell orange blossom. It's a relief to be out of the city again and I realise that the hard little knot of anxiety I've felt for the last few days in Tehran has disappeared.

/

Kashan is an oasis town on the edge of Iran's northern desert and is most famous for a collection of fine traditional houses built by wealthy merchants in the nineteenth century. I read in my guidebook that, like all oasis settlements, a great deal of its charm lies in the contrast between the parched desert surroundings and the greenery within the city walls – although as yet we've seen nothing of the countryside because of our middle-of-the-night arrival. As we set off to explore, Ebi reminds me that this theme of contrast is also found in traditional Persian architecture.

/

And so it proves to be. The houses are hidden behind high walls at the end of narrow, twisting alleyways and the simplicity of the exteriors gives little clue to the delights within. All that is visible from the street are massive wooden front doors, each with two different door knockers – a heavy one for male visitors, and a lighter one for women. Each has a small octagonal vestibule where visitors are received; from there, separate passageways lead to public entertaining areas or to the private, internal quarters where the family lives. 'You see,' says Ebi, 'It's not so hard for Iranian people to live a double life. It's something that's bred into us. Even our architecture has taught us that we must have a public and a private face.'

/

Each house – or grand mansion, as they really are – seems more gorgeous than the one before. We wander languidly through large sunny courtyards with long reflection pools that magnify and double the surroundings. They are fringed by delicate, two-storeyed façades, some embellished with exquisite carvings or elaborate stucco work. Every now and then we stumble into secret gardens containing fig, orange and pomegranate trees or flowerbeds of Kashan's famous roses.

Inside one house, I stand in a cooling draught at the base of a wind-tower and laugh in surprise. It really does work! Large airy spaces are flooded with coloured light from stained-glass windows. Elsewhere, the walls – in soft shades of pearl, pink or alabaster – are illuminated from above by pierced domed ceilings. I crane my neck in another lofty chamber to admire the intricately carved niches – muqarnas – that glitter with a million tiny fragments of mirror.

A serious young woman with feathery eyebrows and wide eyes points us towards Boroujerdi House. There I sit for a while in the reception hall and watch in fascination as an architecture student struggles to capture the proportions of the central courtyard in a sketchbook. When I look up, I discover that I am surrounded by a group of teenage schoolgirls. They have identified me as a foreigner and pepper me with questions. 'What is your name?' 'Aahh, Khanum Lucy!' 'Where are you from?' 'Sydney or Melbourne?' 'Do you like Iran?' 'Why are you visiting?' 'Can we have your email address?' 'Your phone number?' 'Please go back to your country and tell them we are not terrorists.'

The girls are bouncing around excitedly, all flashing eyes and high spirits, despite the gloomy black of their chadors. 'They must wear this type of chador because they are on a school trip,' says Ebi, who is listening to their chatter and trying not to smile. 'I think if hijab is abolished, tomorrow this lot will be dancing in the streets in bikinis!'

We make a pleasant diversion to the Bagh-e Fin. These lovely sixteenth-century gardens are fed by water from a mountain qanat, ingeniously supplied via underground pipes, and are laid out in the typical Persian design of squares edged with avenues of trees and bisected by long turquoise-tiled canals of rippling water. In the centre is a pretty pavilion, where we nearly trip over a young couple canoodling in the shadows. As the sun filters through the ancient cypresses onto basins of overflowing water, it's easy to appreciate the blissful respite these gardens offer from the blistering summer heat. And here I learn that this is indeed the intent: Persian walled gardens or pairidaeza (from 'pairi', meaning 'around' and 'daiza', meaning 'wall') are creations of paradise here on earth. A few glasses of chai perfumed with rosewater revive us further, and we gather our strength for the onward journey.

/

We drive out of town in the fragrant wake of a truck loaded with a vast container of rosewater. Abyaneh lies eighty kilometres south of Kashan and soon we find ourselves winding through wide valleys and sweeping hills, their shadowy slopes tinged with pretty shades of mauve and lilac. The village is nestled on the side of a valley, and glows pink in the spring sunshine. It is reputed to be nearly two thousand years old, and its twisting lanes and red mud-brick buildings have earned it UNESCO World Heritage listing. After the Persian New Year it will be packed with Iranian tourists, but today it is quiet and we are the only visitors.

/

A few old men sit in doorways, rattling their worry beads, but otherwise the village seems to be populated by toothless crones swathed in floral shawls who try to sell us bags of dried apple and borage-flower tea. This sleepy backwater has been all but abandoned by the younger generation, who seek better prospects in Tehran. We walk out of the village to a better vantage point across the valley, and clamber around happily on the rocky hillside where spring wildflowers are starting to push their way up through the scrubby ground. The sky is a bright clear turquoise and as we gaze back at Abyaneh, through a cloud of almond blossom, the world is utterly silent.

/

We return to the village through a maze of miniature walled orchards and stumble across a group of elderly farm workers enjoying a late breakfast of carrot jam and white cheese with wholewheat flatbread. They invite us to join them for a glass of cinnamon-infused chai, and we crouch down for a few moments, enjoying their company and the warm sunshine. As we listen to the soft hiss of the lunchtime dizi pot, simmering in the embers of the fire, and watch them eat their simple meal, I feel time and space slipping away.

/

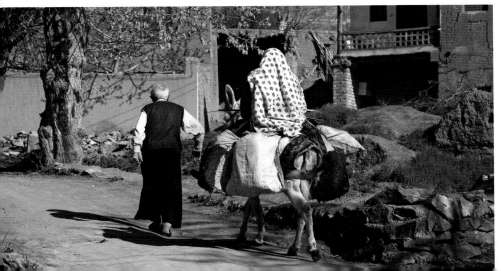

stews and sauces

Together with polow rice, khoresht is the dish that is most distinctively and uniquely Persian. Iranians think of khoresht as sauces that accompany rice (or occasionally bread), but in reality they are thicker and more substantial – closer to a stew.

However, neither sauce nor stew comes close to describing the exotic reality of many khoresht, which are imaginative and often unusual combinations of meat, chicken or fish with vegetables, fruit, nuts, spices and herbs. While they are slow-cooked so the flavours develop and intensify, khoresht are, in fact, about subtlety and refinement and are rarely strongly spiced or chilli-hot. Many have a sour – or sour–sweet – edge through the use of dried limes or lime powder, tamarind, verjuice or pomegranate juice. And nearly all khoresht are thick with varying combinations of fresh herbs that are often purchased ready-mixed from the market.

Every region has its own khoresht specialities based upon locally grown produce. In the northern provinces around the Caspian Sea, sour oranges are popular. The central provinces of Iran favour pairings of lamb with fresh and dried fruits such as quince, apricot, peach and apple or pomegranate, barberries and even rhubarb. Khoresht from the Persian Gulf make good use of fish and seafood, and are some of the few that use hot spices, as they are influenced by nearby India and Pakistan.

Traditionally khoresht only used a small ratio of meat to vegetables, and this is still the case in many rural areas of Iran. In more affluent urban quarters – and among the Iranian diaspora in the West – meat is eaten in greater quantities, and the recipes that follow reflect this preference. Meat for khoresht (which is nearly always lamb or chicken) is often cooked on the bone, but even if it is diced and trimmed the bones are usually added to the cooking pot for extra flavour, and are removed before serving.

Khoresht dishes should be fairly thick, a consistency achieved by adding minimal water or stock and long, slow cooking. And this is one of the chief virtues of the khoresht: after the initial preparation, you can leave it to simmer away on its own, entirely unattended. Some cooks even suggest preparing khoresht a day ahead of time, for the flavours to meld and develop, although others feel that the dish tastes fresher if served on the same day. Either way, a khoresht should be served with plain white or saffron rice (page 52-54), and accompanied by torshi – pickles and relishes (pages 306–308), various yoghurt dishes such as borani (page 104–106) and mounds of fresh herbs by way of a salad.

There are seemingly endless khoresht recipes. I've selected some of my favourite Persian classics, while others included here have been inspired by dishes we ate on our travels. I've also included a few meat-free khoresht, which are not strictly authentic but are good for vegetarians or lighter meals.

For family dinners one khoresht served with rice makes a really satisfying meal. For special occasions, choose a couple of dishes that you feel will complement each other. Iranian cooks will, of course, always make sure there is an appropriate balance between 'hot' and 'cold' ingredients at any mealtime, to ensure a happy and healthy home (page 12).

Khoresht-e ghormeh sabzi
FRESH HERB STEW WITH LAMB AND DRIED LIMES

When made well, this dish is a stunner, and the definition of everything a khoresht stands for. It combines sweet, slow-cooked lamb with tangy dried limes, creamy kidney beans and a veritable mountain of fragrant fresh herbs. Although every part of my body screams 'add the herbs at the last minute', this is, of course, an entirely cheffy instinct to preserve their bright-green colour.

But ghormeh sabzi is not about the colour – and to be honest, it is not the world's most beautiful dish. Instead it is about the richness of texture, aroma and flavour. Part of the distinctive flavour comes from fenugreek, which in the summer months can sometimes be found fresh at Middle Eastern stores. You can substitute crushed fenugreek seeds quite happily all year round, but use them cautiously as they have a tendency to overwhelm if you use too heavy a hand.

3 tablespoons olive oil
1 onion, finely diced
1 leek, finely diced
1 teaspoon ground turmeric
½ teaspoon freshly ground black pepper
450 g lamb (from the shoulder),
    cut into 2 cm cubes
1 cup coriander leaves
1 cup flat-leaf parsley leaves
½ cup chervil sprigs
⅓ cup dill sprigs
⅓ cup fresh fenugreek leaves or
½ teaspoon fenugreek seeds, lightly
    crushed
100 g dried kidney beans, soaked
    overnight and drained
2 large dried limes, lightly cracked
1 litre good-quality chicken stock
100 g spinach leaves
juice of ½ lemon
1 teaspoon sea salt, or to taste
Chelow Rice (page 53) and thick
    natural yoghurt, to serve

Heat the oil in a large, heavy-based saucepan or casserole dish over a low heat. Add the onion and leek and fry gently until soft and translucent. Stir in the spices and fry for another couple of minutes.

Add the lamb to the pan and brown over a high-ish heat for a minute. Add the herbs and fenugreek leaves or seeds and stir well. Stir in the kidney beans, dried limes and stock and bring to a boil. Lower the heat and cook, covered, for 1½ hours, or until the beans and lamb are very tender. As the limes soften, squeeze them against the side of the pan to extract the juice.

Towards the end of the cooking time, bring a saucepan of water to a boil and blanch the spinach briefly. Refresh in cold water, then squeeze very firmly to extract as much liquid as you can. Chop the spinach finely, and stir it into the stew to revive the rich green colour (and make my chef's heart happy!). Bubble vigorously for 5 minutes until the sauce is lovely and thick. Add lemon juice and salt to taste and serve with plain chelow rice and plenty of yoghurt. SERVES 6

Khoresht-e gheimeh
LAMB AND SPLIT PEA STEW

This is one of Lucy's favourite khoresht dishes, and not just because of the crunchy matchstick potatoes that are an essential garnish! We ate this dish several times in Iran, and it has to be said that a few restaurants used the kind of potato straws that come in a packet. If you must, you must, but the kind made at home using real potatoes are so much better.

The lamb and split peas cook down to a lovely earthy braise that is absolutely delicious with orange-scented, sweetly-spiced shirin polow; this is the way they serve it in Shiraz.

The spice mix given here makes twice as much as you need, but it's a really good all-purpose khoresht mix that you could, in fact, use to add a touch of Oriental magic to any lamb casserole.

3 tablespoons olive oil
600 g lamb (from the shoulder),
    cut into 2 cm cubes
2 onions, diced
½ teaspoon ground turmeric
3 tablespoons tomato paste
200 g yellow split peas
2 dried limes, lightly cracked
2 bay leaves
8 sprigs thyme
1 litre good-quality chicken stock
    or water
juice of 1 lime
1½–2 teaspoons sea salt
Shirin Polow (page 64), to serve

KHORESHT SPICE MIX
1 teaspoon ground dried rose
    petals (optional)
1 teaspoon ground cinnamon
1 teaspoon ground cumin
1 teaspoon ground coriander
1 teaspoon ground ginger
½ teaspoon ground cardamom
½ teaspoon freshly ground black
    pepper
½ teaspoon freshly grated nutmeg

POTATO STRAWS
vegetable oil for deep-frying
3 starchy potatoes, peeled and
    cut into matchsticks
sea salt

To make the spice mix, combine all the ingredients thoroughly in a bowl, then transfer to an airtight jar.

Heat the oil in a large, heavy-based saucepan or casserole dish over a medium–high heat. Brown the lamb in batches, turning to colour it evenly, then remove from the pan.

Add the onion, 3 teaspoons of the spice mix and the turmeric to the pan and fry for a couple of minutes until the onion softens. Stir in the tomato paste and cook for a minute, then return the browned meat to the pan. Add the split peas, dried limes, bay leaves and thyme, then pour on the stock and bring to a boil. Lower the heat and cook, covered, for 1½ hours, or until the split peas and lamb are very tender. As the limes soften, squeeze them against the side of the pan to extract the juice. Add the fresh lime juice and season to taste with salt.

About 20 minutes before the end of the cooking time, prepare the potato straws. Heat a reasonable amount of oil in a deep saucepan and deep-fry the potato straws in batches until crisp and golden. Drain them on paper towels and season lightly with salt.

Serve the khoresht with a sprinkle of potato straws and shirin polow. **SERVES 6**

Khoresht-e aloo
LAMB WITH PRUNES AND HONEY

Versions of this dish also pop up as a favourite Moroccan tagine, brought to North Africa from Persia courtesy of the Arabs, of course. It's a lovely sweet-and-mildly-sour combination of lamb and fruit, which cooks down to form a luscious, thick sauce. We use forequarter lamb chops – it's a great dish for this rather fatty cut – but you could, of course, use shoulder or leg meat, cut into large chunks, if you prefer.

3 tablespoons olive oil

1.2 kg lamb forequarter chops, cut into medium pieces

2 onions, cut into quarters

2 cloves garlic, roughly chopped

1 teaspoon ground ginger

1 teaspoon ground cinnamon

1 teaspoon sweet paprika

1 teaspoon sea salt

1 teaspoon freshly ground black pepper

1 litre good-quality chicken stock

1 cinnamon stick

1 long strip orange peel, all pith removed

2 bay leaves

2 tablespoons Saffron Liquid (page 54)

3 tablespoons honey

300 g pitted prunes

Saffron Chelow Rice (page 54) and thick natural yoghurt, to serve

Heat 2 tablespoons of the oil in a large, heavy-based frying pan. Brown the lamb in batches over a medium heat, then transfer to a large, heavy-based saucepan or casserole.

Pulse the onion and garlic to a coarse paste in a food processor. Add the remaining oil to the frying pan and tip in the onion mixture. Fry over a medium heat for 3–4 minutes, or until soft and translucent. Stir in the spices, salt and pepper and cook for a further 2 minutes, then add to the casserole. Pour in the chicken stock, stir well, then add the cinnamon stick, orange peel, bay leaves, saffron liquid and honey. Stir again and bring to a boil. Lower the heat and simmer, uncovered, for 1¼ hours, topping up with a little water if the mixture becomes too dry.

Add the prunes and cook for a further 30–45 minutes, squishing them into the sauce as they soften. At the end of the cooking time, the sauce should be thick and rich and the meat falling away from the bones. When ready to serve, taste and adjust the seasoning to your liking. Serve with plain or saffron chelow rice and plenty of creamy yoghurt. **SERVES 6**

Khoresht-e naranj
BEEF RIBS BRAISED WITH ORANGE

Although lamb is far and away the most readily available meat in Iran, beef is used occasionally. For this dish I use beef short ribs that, in true khoresht fashion, are ideal for long, slow cooking. The meat shreds softly away from the bone into an intense orange-scented sauce. You could do this for your diners, and present the dish as a casserole, or you could serve each person with a rib, to attack themselves, which would be the more satisfying option! Sour oranges are a commonplace ingredient in Persian cooking, and I find Seville oranges a good alternative.

2 Seville oranges

2 tablespoons olive oil

6 x 400 g beef short ribs

sea salt

freshly ground black pepper

12 shallots, peeled

3 carrots, peeled and cut into chunks

3 tablespoons red-wine vinegar

2 teaspoons sugar

2 bay leaves

few sprigs of thyme

1 litre good-quality rich beef stock

2 tablespoons Saffron Liquid (page 54)
  (optional)

2 tablespoons shredded flat-leaf parsley
  leaves

Preheat the oven to 120°C. Remove strips of peel from the oranges with a vegetable peeler and cut any clinging pith from the peel. Dry the orange peel on a baking tray in the oven for 15–20 minutes. Reserve both the dried peel and the oranges.

Increase the oven temperature to 160°C. Heat the oil in a large heavy-based frying pan over a medium heat. Season the beef ribs generously with salt and pepper, then brown them really well all over. Transfer to an ovenproof casserole dish.

Add the shallots and carrot to the frying pan and fry for 4–5 minutes over a medium–high heat until they begin to colour a deep golden brown, then tip into the casserole dish. Deglaze the pan with the vinegar and let it bubble vigorously. Add ½ teaspoon freshly ground black pepper, the sugar, herbs and dried orange

peel, then add the stock and saffron liquid, if using. Stir well, then transfer to the oven and cook for 2½–3 hours, or until the meat is very tender. Check every 30 minutes or so and skim away any fat.

When cooked, remove from the oven and lift out the beef ribs and vegetables. Simmer the braising liquid briskly over a high heat, skimming frequently, until reduced to a thicker sauce, then return the beef ribs and vegetables to the pan.

When nearly ready to serve, squeeze the reserved oranges and simmer the juice in a small saucepan until reduced to a thick, intense syrup. Stir into the khoresht, then taste and adjust the seasoning to your liking. Sprinkle on the parsley and serve straight away. SERVES 6

Khoresht-e mast

CHICKEN WITH SAFFRON, YOGHURT, RAISINS AND PISTACHIOS

Not strictly authentic, however this delectable, creamy dish is based on yoghurt khoresht that are sometimes made with lamb, sometimes with chicken. The sauce is delicate, mildly spicy and a little sour and reminds me, once again, of the culinary connections between Persia and India.

Feel free, by all means, to use chicken thighs on the bone, if you can find them.

3 tablespoons vegetable oil
2 onions, finely sliced
4 sticks celery, finely sliced
1 teaspoon ground cumin
½ teaspoon ground ginger
½ teaspoon ground cardamom
¼ teaspoon cayenne pepper
½ teaspoon freshly ground black pepper
1 kg boneless free-range chicken thighs,
    cut into bite-sized pieces
1 bay leaf
500 ml good-quality chicken stock
3 tablespoons Saffron Liquid (page 54)
zest and juice of 1 lime
juice of 1 orange
1 teaspoon sea salt
350 g thick natural yoghurt
1 teaspoon cornflour
1 tablespoon water
1 egg, lightly beaten
2 tablespoons roughly chopped
    golden raisins
1 tablespoon slivered pistachios
Chelow Rice (page 54), fresh herbs and
    flatbread, to serve

Heat the oil in a large, heavy-based saucepan or casserole dish over a low heat. Add the onion and celery and fry gently until soft and translucent. Stir in the spices and fry for another couple of minutes.

Add the chicken pieces to the pan and brown over a high-ish heat for a minute, stirring to coat with the spice mixture. Add the bay leaf, stock, saffron liquid, citrus juices and zest and bring to a boil. Add the salt, then lower the heat and simmer gently for 50–60 minutes, skimming away any impurities that rise to the surface.

While the stew is simmering, whisk the yoghurt in a bowl until very smooth. Mix the cornflour with the water and add to the yoghurt with the egg. Stir well to combine, then whisk in a few tablespoons of the hot broth from the pan. Pour this back into the barely simmering stew. Add the raisins and pistachios and cook at a bare simmer for about 5 minutes, stirring in one direction only from time to time. Be sure not to let the sauce boil or it will curdle.

When ready to serve, taste and adjust the seasoning to your liking. Serve with buttery plain chelow rice, fresh herbs and flatbread. SERVES 6

Duck with pumpkin and cinnamon

This is a lovely combination for a khoresht, albeit entirely my own invention. Pumpkin has a natural earthy flavour that complements the sweet richness of duck meat. Personally, I think you could add a touch more heat – perhaps a second long green chilli or a pinch of cayenne – although I do know that too much spice is frowned upon by Iranians.

1 teaspoon ground cinnamon
1 teaspoon ground cumin
1 teaspoon ground coriander
½ teaspoon ground turmeric
½ teaspoon freshly ground
  black pepper
3 tablespoons olive oil
6 duck marylands, separated
  through the joint and
  trimmed of excess fat
4 shallots, finely sliced
1 long green chilli, seeded
  and finely shredded
2 tablespoons tomato paste

2 tablespoons pomegranate
  molasses
1 litre good-quality chicken
  stock
200 g dried white beans, soaked
  overnight and drained
2 large tomatoes, seeded and
  finely diced
1 teaspoon sea salt, or to taste
500 g peeled pumpkin, cut into
  wedges
generous squeeze of lime juice
coriander leaves, to garnish
  (optional)

Combine the spices in a small bowl and add 1 tablespoon of the oil to make a paste. Massage the spice paste into the duck pieces, coating each thoroughly. Cover and refrigerate for 1 hour.

Heat the remaining oil in a large, heavy-based saucepan or casserole dish over a medium–high heat. Brown the duck pieces, turning so they colour evenly. Lower the heat and add the shallots, chilli and tomato paste. Cook gently until the shallots begin to soften. Stir in the pomegranate molasses and stock, then add the drained beans. Bring to a boil, then lower the heat, cover, and simmer gently for 1–1½ hours, or until the duck is very tender. From time to time, skim away any impurities that rise to the surface.

Stir in the tomato and salt. Tuck in the pumpkin pieces and squeeze in the lime juice. Cover the pan and cook for a further 20–25 minutes, or until the pumpkin is very tender, but not so long that it disintegrates.

Garnish with coriander leaves, if using, and serve straight away. SERVES 6

Duck breast with 'fesenjun' sauce

Fesenjun, one of the celebrated classics of Persian cuisine, is always brought out for special occasions or to honour invited guests. There's no denying the appeal of this exotic sweet–sour– earthy sauce, traditionally served with strongly flavoured game birds, such as duck or pheasant. These days, in truth, most Iranians make fesenjun with a humble chicken, but the combination also works surprisingly well with firm white fish, and it is often served this way in the Caspian Sea area.

In classic fesenjun recipes the bird is cooked in the sauce itself, but I like the firmer consistency of roasted whole duck or, as here, pan-fried duck breasts. Either way, the dish is extremely rich, and needs only plain chelow rice (page 53) and perhaps a few peppery herbs by way of accompaniment.

6 x 200 g duck breasts

sea salt

freshly ground black pepper

1 tablespoon honey

generous splash of boiling water

½ teaspoon pomegranate molasses

¼ teaspoon freshly ground black pepper

¼ teaspoon cardamom seeds, crushed

2 tablespoons olive oil

seeds of 1 pomegranate, to garnish

FESENJUN SAUCE

200 g shelled walnuts

3 tablespoons olive oil

1 onion, finely diced

1 teaspoon ground cinnamon

½ teaspoon ground turmeric

½ teaspoon freshly ground black pepper

1 tablespoon tomato paste

1 tablespoon pomegranate molasses

250 ml pomegranate juice (freshly squeezed, if available)

55 g sugar

1 bay leaf

400 ml good-quality chicken stock

1 teaspoon sea salt

juice of ½ lemon

Preheat the oven to 180ºC. To make the sauce, roast the walnuts on a baking tray for 5–10 minutes until a deep golden brown. Tip the nuts into a tea towel and rub well to remove as much skin as possible, then set aside until cool. Pulse the cooled nuts in a food processor until coarsely ground – you want to maintain some texture and a few chunky bits, so be careful not to overdo it.

Heat the oil in a large, heavy-based saucepan over a low heat. Add the onion and fry gently until soft and translucent. Stir in the spices and tomato paste and fry for another couple of minutes. Add the walnuts to the pan with the pomegranate molasses and juice, the sugar, bay leaf and stock. Bring to a boil, then add the salt, lower the heat and simmer gently for 1 hour, stirring regularly, until rich, thick and a little oily.

Meanwhile, score the duck skin in a criss-cross pattern with a sharp knife and season generously with salt and pepper. In a small saucepan, warm the honey over a gentle heat with the water and the pomegranate molasses, then stir in the pepper and cardamom seeds to make a glaze.

Heat the oil in a heavy-based roasting pan over a medium–high heat until hot. Add the duck breasts, skin-side down, then lower the heat and cook for about 5 minutes until the skin turns golden brown and the fat starts to render. Turn the breasts over and cook for a further 4 minutes. Tip the rendered fat from the pan and brush the skin with the glaze. Turn the breasts, skin-side down again, and cook over a low–medium heat for a final 4 minutes; at this stage it's really important not to have the heat too high or the glaze will burn. Remove from the heat and rest in a warm place for several minutes – when carved the duck breasts should be medium–rare.

When ready to serve, add the lemon juice to the sauce, then taste and adjust the seasoning to achieve a good sweet–sour–earthy balance. Spoon a generous amount of sauce onto each plate. Slice each duck breast into chunks and stack on top. Scatter on the pomegranate seeds and serve straight away. **SERVES 6**

Quail stewed with melting onions, saffron and chickpeas

I love these plump little game birds, and their succulent flesh is ideal for slow-braising in a fragrant, herby sauce such as this. The carrots and currants combine to add an enticing sweetness. Easy to make, it's an impressive dinner-party dish.

3 tablespoons olive oil

2 large purple onions, thinly sliced

4 cloves garlic, thinly sliced

½ teaspoon cardamom seeds, lightly crushed

½ teaspoon dried oregano

6 quail, legs tied

sea salt

freshly ground black pepper

150 g chickpeas, soaked overnight or 200 g canned chickpeas

4 baby carrots, trimmed and cut in half

⅓ cup oregano leaves

8 sprigs thyme

1 bay leaf

300 ml good-quality chicken stock

2–3 tablespoons Saffron Liquid (page 54)

2 tablespoons currants

squeeze of lemon juice

Heat the oil in a large, heavy-based saucepan or casserole dish over a low heat. Add the onion and garlic and fry gently until soft and translucent. Stir in the cardamom seeds and dried oregano and cook for another couple of minutes. Lift the mixture out of the pan with a slotted spoon and set aside.

Season the quail with salt and pepper. Add a little more oil to the pan, if need be, and brown the quail thoroughly. Drain the soaked chickpeas (rinse and drain the canned ones, if using). Return the onion mixture to the pan and add the chickpeas, carrot and fresh herbs. Pour in the stock and saffron liquid. Bring to a boil, then lower the heat, cover the pan, and simmer gently for 1–1½ hours, or until the quail and onions are very tender and the chickpeas are cooked. From time to time, skim away any impurities that rise to the surface.

Towards the end of the cooking time, add the currants to the pan. Simmer for a further 4–5 minutes, then season with salt to your liking and stir in the lemon juice. Serve straight away. SERVES 6

Koofteh Tabrizi
GIANT MEATBALLS STUFFED WITH FRUIT AND NUTS

There is something vaguely comical about these over-sized meatballs, a speciality of the north-western city of Tabriz. In some cases they are made large enough to encase a small chicken, while other popular versions have a hard-boiled egg at the centre, similar to Scotch eggs. What follows is slightly less ambitious – although the number of ingredients may look somewhat daunting. But please don't let that put you off – this dish is a stunner! The koofteh themselves are herby and moistly tender and have a delicious stuffing of dried fruit and crunchy walnuts. As they are about the size of a tennis ball, one per person should be ample. Serve with lots of creamy yoghurt and warm flatbread to scoop everything up.

One of the secrets to making these koofteh is to mince the lamb twice; ask your butcher to do this for you, or do it yourself at home. The mince must then be energetically and thoroughly kneaded so that the fat is evenly distributed throughout the meat and it turns into a soft, smooth, sticky paste. You can do this quickly in a food processor, if you like, but chill the bowl and blade in the fridge first.

50 ml olive oil
1 large onion, sliced
2 cloves garlic, chopped
1 teaspoon dried mint
2 tablespoons sugar
1 tablespoon tomato paste
250 ml crushed tomatoes
2 tablespoons Saffron Liquid
   (page 54)
1 litre good-quality chicken stock
sea salt
freshly ground black pepper
2 tablespoons finely snipped chives
flatbread, thick natural yoghurt
   and fresh herbs, to serve

GIANT KOOFTEH

400 ml good-quality chicken stock
100 g yellow split peas, soaked
   overnight and drained
125 g short-grain rice, soaked
   overnight and drained
1 teaspoon sea salt
450 g lamb (from the shoulder),
   minced twice
2 shallots, finely diced
2 eggs
1 tablespoon rice flour
1 tablespoon Saffron Liquid
   (page 54)
½ teaspoon ground turmeric
1½ cups shredded tarragon leaves
1½ cups shredded mint leaves
1½ cups shredded flat-leaf parsley
   leaves
½ teaspoon freshly ground black
   pepper

STUFFING

30 ml olive oil
1 small purple onion, finely diced
60 g dried apricots, diced
50 g shelled walnuts, roughly
   chopped
2 tablespoons roughly chopped
   currants
⅓ cup shredded flat-leaf parsley
   leaves
sea salt
freshly ground black pepper

To make the koofteh, bring the stock to a boil in a medium saucepan over a medium heat, then remove from the stove and add the drained split peas and rice. Return to a boil, then lower the heat, cover, and simmer for 20–30 minutes, or until all the stock has been absorbed. Season with the salt, then tip into a large bowl and leave to cool completely

Add the remaining ingredients to the cold rice mixture and knead thoroughly for 5 minutes until combined, then refrigerate while you make the stuffing (alternatively, pulse in a chilled food processor).

To make the stuffing, heat the oil in a small saucepan over a low heat. Add the onion and fry gently until soft and translucent. Stir in the apricots, walnuts and currants and cook for another couple of minutes. Stir in the parsley, season lightly, then set aside.

Heat the oil in a large, heavy-based saucepan or casserole dish over a low heat. Add the onion and garlic and fry gently until soft and translucent. Stir in the dried mint, sugar, tomato paste,

crushed tomatoes, saffron liquid and stock and season lightly. Bring to a boil, then lower the heat and simmer gently while you make the koofteh.

Divide the koofteh mixture into 6 portions. With wet hands, roll a portion into a smooth, round ball about the size of a tennis ball. Use your thumb to make a cavity and wiggle it around a bit – the cavity needs to take a sixth of the stuffing mixture – then cram in the stuffing. Pinch the koofteh mixture to seal it over the stuffing, then roll the dumpling between your hands again to re-form. Repeat with the remaining mixture and stuffing. Lower the dumplings into the simmering broth, then cover and simmer for 1 hour, turning them occasionally so they cook evenly.

Just before serving, sprinkle on the chives. Serve the koofteh and broth in wide, shallow bowls with plenty of flatbread, yoghurt and extra sprigs of fresh herbs. **SERVES 6**

koofteh sholleh
LITTLE LAMB DUMPLINGS WITH OREGANO AND RICE

This is the ultimate in comfort food: soft, soupy, tomatoey rice with tender little dumplings – koofteh. Both the sauce and koofteh are scented with oregano (fresh and dried), and as with other dishes from the north-west of Iran, this one has a hint of peppery spice.

One of the secrets to making these koofteh is to mince the lamb twice; ask your butcher to do this for you, or do it yourself at home. The mince must then be energetically and thoroughly kneaded so that the fat is evenly distributed throughout the meat and it turns into a soft, smooth, sticky paste. You can do this quickly in a food processor, if you like, but chill the bowl and blade in the fridge first.

120 g short-grain rice
50 ml olive oil
1 large onion, finely sliced
sea salt
2 litres good-quality chicken stock
2 tablespoons tomato paste
3–4 vine-ripened tomatoes, roughly chopped
1 teaspoon sweet paprika
½ teaspoon dried oregano
½ teaspoon dried mint
2 tablespoons oregano leaves
300 g lamb (from the shoulder), minced twice
1 egg
½ cup finely snipped chives
freshly ground black pepper
2 tablespoons Saffron Liquid (page 54)
juice of ½ lime
flatbread, to serve

Soak the rice in cold water for 5 minutes.

Heat the oil in a heavy-based saucepan or casserole dish over a low–medium heat. Fry the onion until soft and starting to colour. Drain the rice and stir it into the onion. Add 1 teaspoon salt and pour on enough stock to cover and reserve the rest. Bring to a boil, then lower the heat and simmer for 10 minutes, or until the rice is just cooked and the stock has been absorbed.

Take out 4 tablespoons of the rice and set aside to cool. When cool, refrigerate until well chilled.

Meanwhile, add the remaining stock to the saucepan. Stir in the tomato paste, then add the tomato, paprika, dried herbs and half the oregano leaves. Bring to a boil, then remove the pan from the heat and set aside.

To make the koofteh, mix the reserved chilled rice with the lamb mince, egg, chives and the remaining oregano leaves and season with salt and pepper. Knead thoroughly for at least a minute until everything is well combined (alternatively, pulse in a chilled food processor). Use wet hands to roll the koofteh mixture into smooth, even dumplings, about the size of a small walnut. You should get 24 koofteh from the mixture.

Stir the saffron liquid into the rice, then add the koofteh and bring to a boil over a medium heat. Lower the heat and simmer gently for 12 minutes, skimming away any impurities that rise to the surface and stirring from time to time to ensure the rice doesn't stick to the bottom of pan. By the end of the cooking time the rice should have become a soft, gloopy liquid. Freshen with lime juice and adjust the seasonings to taste. Serve with warm thick flatbread. SERVES 6

Khoresht-e esfenaj
SPINACH WITH CHICKEN-AND-ORANGE KOOFTEH

Spinach is one of my favourite vegetables and it cooks down to a most satisfying thick green sauce, the ideal vehicle for meatballs! These koofteh are mild and orangey, which complements the strong, vital earthiness of spinach. Serve on Saffron Chelow Rice (page 54).

3 tablespoons olive oil

12 shallots, peeled

2 cloves garlic, finely chopped

½ teaspoon ground allspice

½ teaspoon freshly grated nutmeg

½ teaspoon freshly ground black pepper

250 ml good-quality chicken stock

2 tablespoons Saffron Liquid (page 54)

juice of 2 oranges

juice of ½ lime

1 tablespoon rice flour

1 long strip dried orange peel (page 309)

500 g spinach leaves, very finely chopped

100 ml vegetable oil

½ cup flaked almonds

CHICKEN-AND-ORANGE KOOFTEH

300 g minced chicken (preferably leg meat)

1 large shallot, finely diced

1 small clove garlic, grated

finely grated zest of 1 orange

⅓ cup shredded coriander leaves

1 teaspoon ground ginger

½ teaspoon freshly ground black pepper

1 teaspoon sea salt

To make the koofteh, combine all the ingredients in a large bowl and knead thoroughly for at least a minute. When everything is well combined, cover and refrigerate for 30 minutes.

Use wet hands to roll the cold koofteh mixture into smooth, even dumplings, about the size of a small walnut. You should get 24 koofteh from the mixture.

Heat the olive oil in a very large, heavy-based saucepan or casserole dish over a medium heat. Add the shallots and toss gently until they start to colour. Stir in the garlic and spices and fry for another couple of minutes. Add the stock and saffron liquid and bring to a boil. Whisk the citrus juices with the rice flour, then add to the stock with the dried orange peel. Return to a boil, then add the koofteh to the pan. Lower the heat, cover the pan and simmer gently for 45 minutes.

Add the spinach to the pan and simmer for a further 15 minutes until reduced to form a thick sauce.

Meanwhile, heat the vegetable oil in a small frying pan over a medium heat. Add the almonds and stir briskly until they start to colour. Tip into a sieve and discard the oil, then drain the almonds on paper towels.

Taste the spinach sauce and adjust the seasoning to your liking. Serve the sauce and koofteh topped with a sprinkling of golden flaked almonds. SERVES 6

Golden seafood stew with Bandari spices

The Persian Gulf is teeming with prawns of all sizes, including my all-time favourite, king prawns. I find that smaller prawns can sometimes be a little mushy, but these whoppers are always meaty and firm and have a fabulous sweet flavour. They combine really well with molluscs, such as clams or mussels, to make this lovely stew. It would make a great dinner-party dish, or could just as easily be served as a simple supper dish with warm flatbread and perhaps a few extra fresh herbs. There's no need for rice, as the potatoes and chickpeas are pretty filling.

The spice mix given here makes more than you need for this dish. It is hard to make in smaller quantities, though, and it will keep reasonably fresh if stored in an airtight jar. It's a brilliant all-purpose spice mix for any seafood.

3 tablespoons olive oil

1 purple onion, finely chopped

200 g cooked chickpeas or 400 g can chickpeas, drained and rinsed

300 g waxy potatoes, peeled and cut into 1 cm cubes

6 baby carrots, trimmed and cut in half lengthwise

200 g tomatoes, seeded and diced

zest of ½ orange

3 tablespoons Saffron Liquid (page 54)

500 ml water

500 g clams, scrubbed

12 king prawns, peeled (heads and tails intact)

sea salt

freshly ground black pepper

⅓ cup chopped flat-leaf parsley leaves

¼ cup chopped tarragon leaves

¼ cup chopped chervil sprigs

flatbread, to serve

BANDARI SPICE MIX

1½ teaspoons ground cumin

1 teaspoon ground coriander

1 teaspoon ground turmeric

½ teaspoon caraway seeds, finely ground

½ teaspoon cardamom seeds, finely ground

½ teaspoon freshly ground black pepper

½ teaspoon freshly grated nutmeg

To make the spice mix, combine all the ingredients, then transfer to an airtight jar.

Heat the oil in a large, heavy-based saucepan or casserole dish over a low heat. Add the onion and fry gently until soft and translucent. Stir in the 3 teaspoons of the spice mix and cook for another couple of minutes. Add the chickpeas, potato, carrot, tomato, zest, saffron liquid and water. Bring to a boil, then lower the heat and simmer gently for 8 minutes, or until the potato is just tender. Turn up the heat and add the clams and prawns. Cover and cook for 1–2 minutes until the clams open. Season to taste with salt and pepper, then stir in the fresh herbs and serve straight away with warm flatbread. SERVES 6

Ghaliyeh maygoo
PRAWNS BRAISED IN A TAMARIND-HERB SAUCE

'Ghaliyeh' is the Arab word for khoresht, or stew, and its usage in the Persian Gulf region of Iran reflects the influence of the Arabic language on Old Persian, after the arrival of Islam in the seventh century.

Both Arab and Indian influences are also strongly evident in the cooking here – in part because of the proximity to the Arab states over the water, and also because of the long history of trading with Arabia and the Indian subcontinent. The complex layers of spicing in dishes from this part of Iran set them apart from other Persian food, which tends to be herb based and fairly subtle.

This is my interpretation of a dish we enjoyed on Qeshm Island, using prawns from the Persian Gulf. Substitute a firm white fish, such as rockling, blue-eye, hapuka or sea bass, if you like, to make ghaliyeh mahi – fish stew, and if you really don't have the energy to make the curry spice mix given here, substitute a good-quality purchased curry powder. This mix is more than you need for the recipe, but keeps well, and is a good all-purpose curry powder.

80 ml olive oil

3 cloves garlic

2 onions, finely sliced

1 tablespoon tamarind paste

200 g tomatoes, diced

300 ml water

sea salt

1 kg king prawns, peeled (to yield 600 g)

freshly ground black pepper

½ cup shredded coriander leaves

½ cup shredded flat-leaf parsley leaves

CURRY SPICE MIX

2 teaspoons fennel seeds

1½ teaspoons fenugreek seeds

1 tablespoon ground turmeric

2 teaspoons ground cumin

2 teaspoons ground coriander

1 teaspoon ground ginger

1 teaspoon freshly ground black pepper

To make the spice mix, lightly toast the fennel and fenugreek seeds in a dry frying pan over a low heat. Tip them into a mortar and grind as finely as you can. Sieve to remove the husks – you will end up with about half the original quantity. Combine with all the other spices. If not using straight away, store in an airtight jar.

Heat 50 ml of the oil in a large, heavy-based saucepan or casserole dish over a low heat. Finely slice 2 of the garlic cloves and fry gently with the onion until soft and translucent. Stir in 1 tablespoon of the curry spice mix and cook for another couple of minutes. Add the tamarind paste, tomato and water and season with salt. Bring to a boil, then lower the heat and simmer gently for 40 minutes, adding a splash more water if need be.

Towards the end of the cooking time, finely chop the remaining garlic clove. Heat the remaining oil in a large heavy-based frying pan over a high heat. Season the prawns with salt and pepper and cook for a minute only, tossing so they colour evenly. Stir in the chopped garlic and stir well, then tip into the pan with the sauce. Throw in the fresh herbs, stir to combine and serve straight away. **SERVES 6**

Steamed John Dory with saffron–potato stew

Although Iran is a huge saffron-producing country, we didn't find quite the variety of saffron-flavoured seafood dishes you do on the Mediterranean. The preference seemed to be for turmeric, perhaps because it's cheaper or maybe because it's closer to the Indian tradition that's influenced some Iranian food. I think it's a bit of a shame, given that saffron has a natural affinity with seafood, so I've given it a starring role in this stew.

Fish tastes so much sweeter when cooked on the bone, and steaming is a great way to cook a delicate fish like John Dory. To steam more than one fish at a time, you'll either need a big collection of steamer baskets or a fish kettle, or, simplest of all, a rack set into a large water-filled baking tray that you then cover with aluminium foil.

6 x 280 g John Dory, heads removed (known as 'trunks')
a few coriander stalks
1 lemon, cut into wedges
sea salt
freshly ground black pepper
extra-virgin olive oil
2 tablespoons shredded coriander leaves
lime wedges, to serve

SAFFRON–POTATO STEW

50 ml olive oil
1 large purple onion, diced
1 teaspoon Bandari Spice Mix (page 184)
1 teaspoon tomato paste
400 g waxy potatoes, peeled and cut into 2 cm cubes
6 sprigs thyme
1 bay leaf
500 ml water
2 tablespoons extra-virgin olive oil
1 teaspoon sea salt
1 tablespoon Saffron Liquid (page 54)
juice of 1 lime
¼ cup shredded coriander leaves

To prepare the saffron–potato stew, heat the olive oil in a large, heavy-based saucepan or casserole dish over a low heat. Add the onion and fry gently until soft and translucent. Stir in the spice mix and cook for another couple of minutes. Add the tomato paste and cook, stirring constantly, for a minute, then add the potato, thyme, bay leaf, water, extra-virgin olive oil, salt and saffron liquid and bring to a boil. Lower the heat, and simmer, covered, for 30–40 minutes, or until the potato is tender and beginning to break down. Stir in the lime juice and coriander leaves.

Halfway through the cooking time, start preparing the fish. Preheat the oven to 200°C. Score the skin of the John Dory in long slashes, from head to tail, being careful not to cut too deeply into the flesh.

Pour boiling water into a large baking tray to a depth of 1 cm. Toss in the coriander stalks and lemon wedges (squeeze the juice into the water first). Sit a wire rack in the tray – make sure the top is clear of the water – then put a large sheet of wet baking paper on top. Arrange the fish on the baking paper, then season lightly with salt and pepper and brush lightly with olive oil. Cover the baking tray with a large sheet of foil, tucking it in tightly around the edges but making sure it billows loosely around the fish. Lift the tray carefully into the oven, then bake for 10–12 minutes. Check to see if the fish is cooked through by piercing the thickest part with the tip of a knife – the flesh should be opaque.

Serve the fish on top of a generous spoonful of saffron–potato stew. Scatter on the coriander, drizzle with extra-virgin olive oil and serve with wedges of lime. SERVES 6

Khoresht-e badenjan
SILKY BRAISED EGGPLANT

Iranian khoresht dishes tend to include meat, even when they are primarily vegetable based. This eggplant khoresht is meatless, so Iranians may not consider it authentic, but the principles of the dish are the same – slow-cooked ingredients that result in lots of delicious sauce. It's actually a very versatile dish and is equally delicious served hot, warm or cold, with rice or plenty of warm bread.

6 small long eggplants

sea salt

1 leek, cut in half lengthwise and washed

2 tablespoons olive oil

12 small shallots, peeled

1 long red chilli, seeded and finely shredded

1 teaspoon ground turmeric

½ teaspoon freshly ground black pepper

1 teaspoon coriander seeds, lightly toasted and roughly crushed

400 g can crushed tomatoes

450 ml vegetable stock or water

1 teaspoon honey

thick natural yoghurt, to serve

Peel the eggplants from stem to base, keeping them whole and the stems intact. Arrange them on a tray, and sprinkle generously with salt. Leave them to sit for 1 hour, then rinse thoroughly and pat dry.

Preheat the oven to 180°C. Arrange the eggplants in an ovenproof dish, just large enough for them to fit snugly. Cut the leek into 5 cm lengths.

Heat the oil in a large, heavy-based saucepan or casserole dish over a medium heat. Add the shallots and toss gently until they start to colour. Add the leek and chilli, then gently stir in the spices and cook for another couple of minutes. Add the crushed tomatoes and stock, then gently stir in the honey. Pour the sauce over the eggplants and cover the surface with a sheet of baking paper cut to fit. Cover the dish tightly with foil and bake for 1½ hours, or until the eggplants are very tender. Serve hot, warm or cold with lots of creamy yoghurt. SERVES 6

Mixed summer vegetable khoresht

This is a vegetable stew to make when summer ingredients are at their tender best. Cook until the vegetables are just done to maintain their flavour and texture. I've taken a bit of a liberty – no extra-slow cooking or meat involved – just great ingredients that combine wonderfully with Iranian flavourings.

3 artichoke hearts

225 g peeled pumpkin, cut into wedges

200 g kipfler potatoes, scraped and cut into chunky discs

6 baby turnips, peeled, trimmed and cut into wedges

3 baby carrots, trimmed and cut in half

3 shallots, peeled and cut in half

1 teaspoon coriander seeds, lightly crushed

½ teaspoon freshly ground black pepper

½ teaspoon dried mint

3 tablespoons olive oil

1 teaspoon sea salt

500 ml water

2 tablespoons Saffron Liquid (page 54)

juice of 1 lemon

½ cup tarragon leaves

400 g broad beans in the pod, shelled

150 g peas in the pod, shelled or 60 g frozen peas

120 g flat green beans, trimmed and sliced on an angle

flatbread, to serve

Trim the artichoke hearts, then quarter each one and put into a bowl of acidulated water.

Toss the artichoke hearts, pumpkin, potato, turnip, carrot and shallots in a large bowl with the spices, dried mint and oil. Heat a large, heavy-based frying pan over a medium heat and cook the vegetables in batches, turning so they colour evenly. As they are done, transfer them to a large casserole dish, then add the salt, water, saffron liquid, lemon juice and tarragon. Stir gently and bring to a boil. Lower the heat, cover, and simmer gently for 25–30 minutes, or until the vegetables are barely tender.

Meanwhile, bring a saucepan of water to a boil, then blanch the broad beans briefly and refresh quickly under cold water. When cool enough to handle, peel off the skins. Add the broad beans, peas and green beans to the casserole and cook for a further 10 minutes. Taste and adjust the seasonings to your liking and serve hot, warm or cold with plenty of flatbread for mopping up the juices. SERVES 6

mohj

OUR PLANE LEAVES TEHRAN BEFORE DAWN. WE FLY SOUTH TRACKING THE ENDLESS FOLDS and furrows of the Zagros Mountains to the west, and through my window the rising sun spills a rosy wash over the dun-coloured desert. It's a heavy, humid kind of a day when we land in Bandar Abbas at the other end of Iran, and we are relieved to meet up with Yas, who will be our saraban for the rest of our journey. She is petite and pretty and bursting with energy, and before long we find ourselves whisked away to the waterfront.

Stretched before us is the Persian Gulf, one of the most significant and busiest inland seas in the world – and its largest single source of crude oil. Massive tankers plough these waters day and night, edging through the narrow Hormuz Strait with their cargoes of black gold.

But many centuries before oil was struck, the Gulf – and its towns, villages and islands – was inextricably entwined with trade. From the days of Marco Polo, Alexander the Great and as far back as Darius I, the southern ports of Persia were a natural maritime hub along the Silk Road that transported goods between the East and West. The warehouses that fringed these waters were stuffed with spices, silks, wine jars, precious jewels, porcelain and all the riches of the known world.

Today nearly all cargo ships to and from Iran are offloaded here at Bandar Abbas – and the town is a notorious smuggling centre, with a never-ending relay of small boats bringing in all manner of more prosaic household goods from the Gulf States.

The Persian Gulf is also teeming with fish and the seafood industry provides much of the local population with employment. As we make our way along the waterfront, we can see that the harbour is clogged with large, brightly painted wooden fishing boats that rise and fall lazily on the slow swell of the Gulf tide and that lithe, barefoot men are hurling the morning's catch ashore with brisk efficiency. From there, the tubs of fish are loaded onto trolleys for porters to wheel to the nearby market.

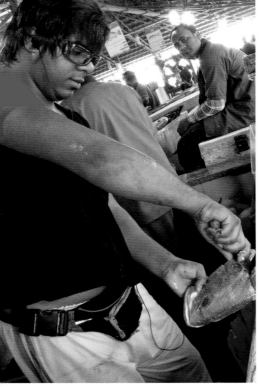

Inside the shuttered, airy market hall the action is just getting started and stallholders and customers are engaging in plenty of tough, loud bargaining. Things seem to be a model of organisation, though, and at either end of the room teams of fishmongers are scaling, skinning, gutting and filleting to order with murderous-looking knives. There is a huge variety of seafood on offer, including several types of crab and prawn, both tiny and huge. Greg is delighted to spot pomfret and sand whiting as well as massive bonito tuna, barracouta and mackerel and countless unidentifiable others. The gently whirring fans and hard-working air-conditioners are keeping the air cool, but back outside the temperature and humidity is rising. Yas tells us that in the summer the temperature here reaches nearly 50°C, and that when the deadly local wind, the tash abat – wind of fire, blows, it's like standing behind a jet aeroplane.

/

Despite the early hour, the passenger terminal is clogged with porters and waiting passengers and a constant stream of ferries and speedboats churns the green waters of the Gulf. As we queue for tickets Yas explains that most of our fellow travellers are heading to the nearby islands to shop. These are free-trade zones and Iranians flock there in their droves to stock up on duty-free goods.

/

As we inch our way forward in the queue, a ferry docks and within seconds jostling passengers spew out onto the walkway and begin to push and shove their way back towards the shore. Some people have mounds of blankets, bed linen and pillows piled upon their heads, others are dragging their spoils along behind them – microwave ovens and flat-screen televisions seem to be particularly popular – and all are arguing loudly with each other. It's complete and utter chaos.

/

Our destination this morning is Qeshm, the largest of the Gulf islands, and eventually we clamber into a tiny speedboat and our luggage is hurled in behind us. Our fellow passengers are all local women and small children and there is a bit of hasty shuffling around so that Ebi and Greg can sit next to each other, and separate from them. We're jammed in like sardines, and the smell of petrol is overwhelming, but the journey is mercifully quick.

/

Over the centuries, traders from Africa, India and the Arab countries across the Gulf have all left their mark on the features and culture of the Bandari people – the people of the ports – and as a result their clothing is highly distinctive. Women wear floral chadors and wrap themselves, sari-style, in lengths of gauzy, colourful fabric. Beneath these layers they wear loose embroidered pants that tighten and button around the ankles like glittering leggings. Many wear burkhas and some older women have tattoos on their faces and hands. The men wear tunics and sandals, and long Arab headscarves or twisty white turbans.

/

On qeshm island we are met off the boat by another Ali, a friend of Yas. This one is a cheerful, handsome Bandari man in his mid-thirties. There's no traditional dress for him, though, and his shiny black curls fall over the collar of a fashionable leather jacket. By now our early morning start is beginning to catch up with us, and we stretch out gratefully in his shiny new-model Toyota Hilux. Here on Qeshm, cars are much cheaper than on the mainland, and this is a pleasant and comfortable change from the assortment of run-down Iranian Paykans, Kia Prides and old-model Peugeots to which we've become accustomed.

/

We collect a hot picnic lunch of chicken khoresht and rice with yoghurt and flatbread that Ali has ordered from a nearby restaurant, then head inland through an arid, sun-bleached landscape of rocky hills and mountains. Although Qeshm is a large island, most of the population lives in the main town or in fishing villages around the coast, leaving the starkly beautiful interior eerily empty. We stop in a nature reserve next to a broad, still river and after lunch we spend a blissful hour puttering through the lagoons in a boat, looking for turtles and trailing our fingers in the jade-green waters.

/

Later that afternoon we drive along the coast, passing tiny fishing villages and boatyards where the traditional wooden cargo boats that plough up and down the Gulf are made. At one yard Yas introduces us to the owner, Abdul Rachman, who proudly shows us around, pointing out how the massive, ark-shaped lenges are still built entirely by hand. The techniques have remained unchanged over the centuries, and the skills are passed down from father to son. Although this boatyard seems busy, with twenty-odd men clambering about the giant wooden frames – like the skeletons of ancient whales, Abdul Rachman seems subdued. 'This industry is dying,' he tells us matter-of-factly. 'Each boat takes between eighteen and twenty-four months to complete, so they are expensive. And anyway, the younger generation are not interested in this kind of work.'

/

We accept his invitation to have tea with his family at their home in a nearby village, where Greg and Ebi are shunted off with the menfolk, and I am whisked away to cool interior rooms by a gaggle of women and children. They wear colourful, flowing dresses over pretty embroidered leggings and the soles of their feet and tips of their fingers are stained with henna. They seem delighted by the intrusion and feed me tangerines, show off their embroidery and laughingly dress me up in traditional Bandari clothes.

/

By the time we drag ourselves away from the happy chatter, the heat of the day is beginning to fade and the shadows are lengthening. Ali drives us to the picture-perfect fishing village of Laft, and we sit up on a hillside and look out through the wind-towers as the sun sinks into the sea.

/

ALI'S FAMILY HAS ALLOWED US TO disrupt their lives for a few days. We park in a quiet area of Qeshm Town and he leads us along a twisting alleyway to a low, white-washed house behind a high wall. The rooms are set around a large courtyard and even in the moonlight we can see a large vegetable patch densely planted with tomatoes and herbs.

/

Ali retreats gracefully to the main part of the house, leaving us to take over his own bachelor quarters. We slip off our shoes and enter a spacious, pleasant room. As is traditional there is no furniture, but the floor is covered entirely with bright tribal rugs, and generous, soft cushions are propped around the walls. In pride of place at one end of the room is a gigantic wide-screen television, and we sprawl in front of it happily.

/

Before long Ali's family troops in to meet us. We are introduced to two of his brothers and their wives and children, who all welcome us warmly and ply us with chilled melon and oranges. Soon, on some unseen cue, the women disappear to the kitchen and Ali and his brothers start grilling dainty chicken kebabs on a manqal – a small charcoal brazier – in the courtyard. We are ravenously hungry and the smell is intoxicating in the soft night air. In the glow of a few small lanterns, we help Ali spread a large sofreh – tablecloth – out on the ground and soon an astonishing array of dishes is being ferried out from the kitchen.

/

Many Iranian families eat their main meal in the middle of the day, so we know that we are being treated as honoured guests with this feast. As well as the chicken skewers, there are two big platters of rice with dill and black-eyed peas. There are baskets of soft warm bread, fresh herbs from the garden and several salads. Gulf cooking, unsurprisingly, makes ample use of locally caught seafood, and is spiced more generously than in other parts of the country. We enjoy tiny fried sand whiting; tender strips of octopus in a thick tomato sauce flavoured with turmeric, black pepper, fennel, caraway and cumin; and a wonderful dish of razor clams in a rich, slightly sweet, cinnamon-spiced sauce. To drink there is dugh, a thin, minty yoghurt drink, which Ebi tells us is good for the digestion and will help us sleep.

/

Later, Ali arranges mattresses and bedding on the floor of our room and the four of us lie down in a chaste little row. Before long, the dugh starts to work its magic and I am surrounded by a fug of peaceful breathing. It's curiously reassuring being bedded down with Yas, Ebi and Greg – like being on a camping trip or a school outing as a child. I lie awake for a while, and watch a crescent moon shining through the window, then I, too, fall sound asleep.

/

FROM THE TENTH TO THE SEVENTEENTH CENTURIES THIS PART OF THE Persian Gulf was the location of the ancient kingdom of Hormuz, one of the most important trading hubs in the Middle East. Originally located on the mainland, a secondary settlement was established on Jarun Island – now Hormuz Island – in the late thirteenth century. These two ports grew into a small but powerful state that controlled all sea trade to and from the Gulf. In its heyday Hormuz was described by visitors as 'a vast emporium of the world'.

/

Control of Hormuz was hotly contested over the centuries – at various times it was ruled by Arabs, Persians and even the Portuguese (who identified it as a key strategic location in their plans to establish an empire in the East). In the seventeenth century, the island was claimed by Shah Abbas I, the great Safavid ruler. He decided that this vital trading hub would be less vulnerable on the mainland, so he moved all commerce to a small fishing village that soon became known as Bandar Abbas – the port of Abbas.

/

We are keen to see if any remnants of Portuguese occupation remain, so we charter a boat bound for Hormuz Island and soon it appears through the sea-mist: a beautiful rose-pink vision, rising from the waves. But we find the tiny tear-drop island is all but deserted, apart from a few thousand souls who live in the only remaining town. Nothing remains of its former glory except for a crumbling Portuguese castle at the northernmost tip. But it is exquisitely beautiful and its craggy red mountains are layered with striations of pink, cream, yellow and pale green. The light is going down quickly, so we dash around the island, driving close to the cliff-tops to watch the sea churning the blood-red sand below and tasting the salt on our lips. Then rocks, sand and sea sink into inky shadows.

/

BY THE TIME WE ARRIVE BACK AT THE SMALL HARBOUR IT is engulfed by darkness and there are no boats in sight. Nothing daunted, Yas makes a few phone calls and, with the promise of extra cash, persuades two islanders to take us back to the mainland. The boat is tiny and there are no life-jackets. We have a brief moment of crisis and then climb in, half-prepared for the worst.

/

The boat heads out slowly into the warm, silky darkness, then it gathers speed and begins to crash through the waves. Before long we are drenched. I have to shift about constantly on the narrow plank that serves as a seat and I have never been as uncomfortable or terrified in all my life.

/

The boatman's mate stands in the prow of the boat to weigh it down. His legs are braced, he clutches a thick rope with one hand and the other is held high in the air like a rodeo rider. He remains there for the entire journey and his sense of balance is remarkable, given the way we are bouncing about on the water. Ten minutes into the journey I slowly relax my grip on the sides of the boat. I gaze upwards into the night sky, where the stars seem to blaze so close to the earth I feel I can almost touch them, and I throw my head back and laugh out loud.

/

IT FEELS AS IF ALL THE WORLD IS AT THE MINAB THURSDAY morning market. It's an immense, colourful, messy, noisy sprawl on the outskirts of the town and soon we're swallowed up by the crowd.

/

We push our way through the outer layers, where the stalls are stocked with plastic toys, cheap clothing and gaudy fabrics, pausing to watch a thin old man haggling over the price of a few stiff sheets of dried tobacco.

/

Eventually our noses lead us toward elaborate displays of spice mixes and we plunge our hands into hessian sacks of cumin, coriander, turmeric, cinnamon sticks, dried tangerine peel, peppercorns – all the bounty of the Orient. Although it is still early spring, there is an astonishing abundance of fresh fruit, vegetables and herbs here – many of which we are unable to identify. There are heavy bundles of sabzi – mixed herbs – and mounds of coconuts, tiny rose apples, lotus fruit, guavas and bananas. We are tempted by vats of syrupy dates flavoured with lemon zest and fennel seeds, and by tubs of tahini in varying shades of beige. But we make do, instead, with a big bag of blood oranges. Less appealing is mahyaveh, a thick red sludge unique to the Persian Gulf. An intensely salty anchovy sauce mixed with red soil from Hormuz Island, mahyaveh is used to flavour bread and to pep up the local version of crêpes.

/

We are inevitably drawn to the handicrafts section where women in traditional garb sit cross-legged on the ground next to their wares. Here on the Gulf there is none of the constant adjusting of chadors that you get elsewhere in Iran, that pulling of fabric across the face by way of concealment. Here many women wear masks – in woven red cloth, shiny gold or leather – that cover the face from brow to lip. The rest of the head is swathed in cloth and I feel hot just looking at them. When they turn their heads we catch a glint of a dark eye, and I think, rather uncharitably, that they look like evil birds.

/

By now it is late morning, our fingers are sticky from the oranges, the temperature and humidity are soaring and I'm feeling hot and resentful under my own hijab. In the privacy of our car on the drive back to Bandar Abbas, I rip off my scarf for a short period of respite, and thank my lucky stars ...

/

IN THE OLD TOWN OF BANDAR ABBAS, TUCKED AWAY IN a small square in the back streets, we find a crowd gathering for the first night of a traditional wedding ceremony. Carpets have been spread out next to a wall outside the groom's house, and a group of about twenty men are sitting around drinking tea, waiting for the entertainment to begin, as more and more men arrive in a convoy of cars and motorbikes. The groom is pacing nervously, but politely invites us to stay and watch the fun.

/

Yas explains that traditional Iranian wedding ceremonies take place over several days. This is the first night of celebrations – the hanabandan ceremony – when the bride is decorated with elaborate henna designs and the groom and his family take gifts to her parents' house.

/

Near by three musicians are tuning their instruments and getting dressed in their costumes. As they start up, a few small children and their mothers emerge from the groom's house to watch. The leader of the group plays a ney ammbooni – a long wind instrument that sounds like a cross between bagpipes and an oboe – and before long the drums are beating faster and faster. A lone dancer jumps up to join the band, clicking his heels and shimmying his way around the square, his eyes half-closed in a slow, secret smile.

By now night has fallen and it's time for the gathered crowd to proceed to the bride's house. And off they go, cutting a vivid, noisy swathe of colour and movement through the dark city streets. They beckon us to follow, and although we would love to join them, we have a feeling that this party will go on all night – and we have a plane to catch.

/

grills and roasts

MAKE NO MISTAKE ABOUT IT, for all their love of khoresht, which combine meat, fruit, vegetables, nuts and herbs (pages 170–189), for Iranians the kebab is king. If there is any such thing as an Iranian national dish, then chelow kabab (lamb kebabs with rice) is it. The anglicisation – kebab or kebob – even comes from the Persian word 'kabab', which means 'to grill', and as you wander past the open-air food stalls and hole-in-the wall kebab restaurants dotted around the country's bazaars – from the north to the south, the east to the west – it sometimes seems as though all of Iran is permeated by the intoxicating aroma of grilling meat.

This method of cooking reaches its apotheosis in specialist chelow kabab restaurants, where an extraordinary variety of meat and poultry skewers is offered with platters of plain or saffron rice. The kebabs arrive covered with a piece of flatbread

that keeps the meat warm and soaks up some of the juices. Sometimes the rice is served with pats of butter and half-shells of egg yolks. Each diner mixes butter and a yolk into their own hot rice to add richness, flavour and sheen to the dish. Sadly, modern-day concerns about cholesterol mean that this practice tends to be reserved now for special occasions. Other essential kebab accompaniments are tangy ground sumac for sprinkling and a jug of chilled Dugh (page 318) to drink. Fresh herbs, pickles, lemon wedges, yoghurt and more warm flatbread are always on the table, of course.

The skewers for kebabs are made from metal, which conducts the heat evenly from the inside out. These are flat, and come in varying widths. The widest are around 2 centimetres, and are used for minced meat kebabs – kabab koobideh. The mince will simply fall off anything thinner. The skinniest skewers are used for spearing small chunks of meat, offal

and chicken, while medium-width skewers are used for the superlative kabab-e barg – wafer-thin strips of succulent lamb fillet.

The love of cooking over fire extends to the home as well, and many Iranians have their own small charcoal brazier or manqal for barbecuing. This is lit most evenings over the summer months and will often be packed into the boot of the car to take on picnics. Unlike the 'bells and whistles' barbecues that many Westerners seem to feel are essential, the manqal is nothing more than a simple tin box on short stubby legs that is filled with charcoal. There is no grill plate as such – rather, the kebabs rest on the edge of the box, suspended above the coals. The meat is cooked by the radiant lick of flame, instead of direct contact with hot metal – a much gentler, more aromatic way of grilling.

As for roasts, the Persians have been masters of the art for millennia.

Spit-roasting whole beasts over an open fire is one of the earliest cooking methods known to man, and by the sixteenth century the Safavid court kitchens were refining the technique by roasting beasts and fowl with ever-more elaborate stuffings laden with fruits, nuts and herbs and sprinkled with flower waters. To this day, a whole baby lamb stuffed with a complex rice filling is essential at weddings, celebrations and religious festivals. Before the days of domestic ovens, roast meats and birds were taken to the neighbourhood bakery for cooking. But these days, Persian roast dishes can be happily cooked at home.

Most of the recipes in this chapter are intended to be eaten with rice (pages 52–66), but, of course, they would be just as delicious served Western-style, with a salad or vegetable side dish.

Joojeh Kabab
MARINATED CHICKEN WING KEBABS WITH SKEWERED TOMATOES

Marinated chicken wings are irresistible whether grilled on the barbecue or baked in the oven to sticky golden goodness. And we love the Persian way of spearing them onto skewers, instead of just scattering them randomly over the flames. The yoghurt in this marinade helps to tenderise the meat, and it adds a faint, but delectable tang. I prefer to grill the tomatoes separately, rather than spearing them with the wings, as they cook at different rates and the tomatoes are easier to handle if they can maintain some shape.

If you don't feel like firing up the barbecue, the chicken wings can also be baked at 180°C for about 20 minutes, in which case you should throw in the tomatoes halfway through the cooking time.

12 free-range chicken wings, tips removed
1 clove garlic
1 teaspoon sea salt
3 tablespoons olive oil
120 g thick natural yoghurt
2 tablespoons Saffron Liquid (page 54)
juice of 1 lime
grated zest of ½ orange
½ teaspoon freshly ground black pepper
6 small vine-ripened tomatoes
splash of pomegranate molasses
1 teaspoon chopped thyme leaves
rice, lemon wedges, fresh herbs and flatbread, to serve

Cut the chicken wings in half through the joint and put them into a shallow dish.

Crush the garlic to a paste with the salt and scrape it into a bowl. Add 1 tablespoon of the oil and the yoghurt, saffron liquid, lime juice, orange zest and pepper and mix well. Pour the marinade onto the chicken wings and turn them around in it so they are evenly coated. Cover and refrigerate overnight, or for at least 6 hours. Allow to come to room temperature before cooking.

When ready to cook, preheat your barbecue or griller to high. Thread the wing pieces onto metal skewers (any width will do here), and grill, turning so they colour evenly. As they begin to colour, move them away from the direct heat to prevent them burning. They will take around 15–20 minutes to cook through.

Halfway through the cooking time, thread the tomatoes onto a skewer. Whisk the remaining oil with the pomegranate molasses and thyme and baste the tomatoes as they cook, turning them continuously so they char evenly.

Pile all the skewers onto a warm platter and serve with your choice of rice, lemon wedges, fresh herbs and lots of warm flatbread. **MAKES 6**

Kabab Koobideh
CLASSIC PERSIAN MINCED LAMB KEBABS

One of the secrets to an outstanding kabab koobideh is to mince the lamb twice; ask your butcher to do this for you, or do it yourself at home. The mince must then be energetically and thoroughly kneaded so that the fat is evenly distributed throughout the meat and it turns into a soft, smooth, sticky paste. You can do this quickly in a food processor, if you like, but chill the bowl and blade in the fridge first.

To make kabab koobideh you really must have 2 centimetre wide metal skewers (which you'll find in Middle Eastern stores), as it is almost impossible to get the mixture to adhere properly to the skinny variety.

600 g lamb (from the leg), minced twice
1 small onion, very finely diced
1 very small garlic clove, very
    finely diced
1 teaspoon ground turmeric
1 teaspoon sea salt
½ teaspoon freshly ground black pepper
splash of olive oil
60 g unsalted butter, melted
juice of ½ lemon
rice, salad onions, radishes, lemon wedges,
    pickles and flatbread, to serve

Combine the lamb, onions, garlic, seasonings and oil in a large bowl. Wet your hands with cold water, then knead the mixture very well for up to 10 minutes. Alternatively, whiz it in a food processor.

Divide the mixture into 6 even portions. With wet hands, mould a portion of the mixture around a wide metal skewer, squeezing it out evenly to create a 15 cm long kebab. You might find it easier to shape it into a long sausage on your work surface and then push the skewer lengthways through it. For the traditional pattern, use your index finger to make indentations crosswise along the length of the kebab. Make sure the meat is squeezed tightly around the skewer at either end. Repeat with the remaining meat so you have 6 kebabs, then cover and refrigerate for 1–2 hours before cooking.

When ready to cook, preheat your barbecue or griller to high. Whisk the melted butter with the lemon juice. Grill the kebabs for 2–3 minutes on each side, basting regularly with the butter mixture, until they are golden brown and cooked to your liking.

Pile all the skewers onto a warm platter and cover with a piece of flatbread. Serve with your choice of rice, salad onions, radishes, lemon wedges, pickles and more warm flatbread. MAKES 6

Kabab-e barg

SKEWERED BEEF 'LEAVES' MARINATED IN YOGHURT, CARDAMOM AND BLACK PEPPER

These Persian favourites are definitely a cut above your average kebab. Traditionally they are made from lamb fillet, which is cleverly sliced into long, wafer-thin strips that are woven onto skewers for grilling. The word 'barg' means 'leaf', which tells you how thin the meat should be. They are just as succulent and exquisitely tender when made using beef fillet – I've suggested here that you ask your butcher for a centre-cut piece of fillet, to ensure you have a piece of uniform thickness. Whether you use beef or lamb, the fillet is an expensive cut and in Iran kabab-e barg are usually served sparingly as part of a wider kebab selection.

Although Iranian kebabs are often marinated to tenderise the meat, in this instance the yoghurt is purely to add flavour, as the cut is already so tender.

100 g thick natural yoghurt
juice of 1 lemon
1 tablespoon olive oil
1 teaspoon dried oregano
1 teaspoon ground cardamom
½ teaspoon sea salt
½ teaspoon freshly ground black pepper
1 x 1 kg beef fillet, centre cut
ground sumac, rice and flatbread, to serve

Put the yoghurt, lemon juice, oil, oregano, cardamom, salt and pepper into a bowl and whisk together well.

With a very sharp knife, carefully cut the beef fillet in half lengthwise. Cut each half into 3 portions. Working with a portion at a time, cut it through the centre horizontally, but not all the way through – it should still be attached at one short end. Open it out to form one longer strip. Repeat with the remaining portions of beef so you have 6 long, thin strips. Carefully weave a medium-width metal skewer through each strip of meat and arrange in a shallow dish. Brush the marinade over the meat, then cover and refrigerate for 2–2½ hours.

When ready to cook, preheat your barbecue or griller to high. Grill the kebabs for 1–2 minutes on each side, or to your liking. Because they are so thin, they will cook in a flash.

Pile the skewers onto a warm platter and cover with a piece of flatbread. Serve with sumac to sprinkle, your choice of rice, and plenty more warm flatbread. **MAKES 6**

Offal kebabs with sumac, allspice and oregano

Iranians are very fond of offal. A favourite breakfast soup is calehpacheh, made from slow–simmered lambs' heads and feet. It's not for the squeamish, or for those who have cholesterol issues, but it is absolutely delicious. And brain or tongue sandwiches seem to be popular at any time of the day. One of our favourite quick lunches in Iran was mixed offal kebabs (variously composed of hearts, livers and kidneys) wrapped in flatbread. There's no doubt that it's a whole different approach to take-away!

This pared-back version is quite rich, so allow half a skewer of each per person for a quick lunch or winter breakfast.

250 g lamb's kidneys
250 g lamb's liver
2 tablespoons extra-virgin olive oil
1 teaspoon dried Greek oregano
1 teaspoon ground sumac
½ teaspoon freshly ground black pepper
½ teaspoon ground allspice
lemon wedges, pickles, fresh herbs and
  flatbread, to serve

Remove the membranes from the kidneys, then cut each one in half crosswise and cut out the core. Cut each half into quarters and put into a bowl.

Remove the membrane from the liver, then cut out any visible tubes or greenish bits. Cut the liver into small pieces the same size as the kidney, and put into another bowl.

Whisk the oil with the oregano and spices, then add half to the kidney and half to the liver. Use your hands to mix well, then thread the offal onto metal skewers. You should have enough to make 3 skewers of each. Cover and refrigerate while you heat your barbecue or grill to high. Grill the kebabs for 1–2 minutes on each side, or until they are brown and crusted on the outside and still pinkish inside.

Pile the skewers onto a warm platter and cover with a piece of flatbread. Serve with lemon wedges, pickles, fresh herbs and plenty more warm flatbread. **MAKES 6**

Kabab-e mahi
SKEWERED TAMARIND FISH WITH DRIED-LIME BUTTER AND CHIVES

For fish kebabs you need a firm, meaty fish, such as rockling, hapuka or blue-eye, or an oily fish, such as swordfish, marlin or even tuna. The sauce here is a little bit fancy, for when you want a change from plain lemon wedges.

Dried limes are available from Middle Eastern food stores and are worth hunting down.

1.2 kg rockling fillet, skin removed

2 tablespoons tamarind paste

50 ml hot water

120 ml olive oil

½ teaspoon ground turmeric

1 onion, grated

12 bay leaves

rice, lemon wedges, fresh herbs and
   flatbread, to serve

DRIED-LIME BUTTER

1 dried lime, cracked

100 ml water

50 ml verjuice

juice of ½ lime

3 sprigs thyme

160 g unsalted butter, diced and chilled

2 tablespoons finely snipped chives

Remove any stray bones from the fish and cut it into 24 large chunks, then transfer to a shallow dish.

Whisk the tamarind paste with the hot water until dissolved, then whisk in the oil and turmeric. Stir in the grated onion and pour this mixture over the fish. Cover and refrigerate for 20 minutes.

While the fish is marinating, make the dried-lime butter. Put the cracked dried lime into a small saucepan with the water, verjuice, lime juice and thyme and simmer vigorously over a high heat until the liquid has reduced by half. Strain and discard the solids, then return the liquid to the pan. Add half the chilled butter, then lower the heat to very low and whisk vigorously until the mixture comes together as a creamy emulsion. Slowly drop in the remaining butter, whisking all the time, until it has all been incorporated. Remove from the heat and keep in a warm place until ready to use.

When ready to cook, preheat your barbecue or griller to high. Thread the fish chunks onto 6 metal skewers, interspersing 2 bay leaves on each. Grill for 4–5 minutes, turning a few times to prevent them burning, and brush with the marinade as they cook.

Pile the skewers onto a warm platter. Stir the chives into the dried-lime butter and spoon over the fish. Serve with your choice of rice, lemon wedges, fresh herbs and plenty more warm flatbread. SERVES 6

Morgh-e zafaran

GRILLED SAFFRON CHICKEN WITH LEMON, CHILLI AND MINT

This is a slightly spiced-up version of a Persian favourite. To the standard saffron–lemon combination I've added a rather un-Persian touch of chilli heat and a mixture of dried and fresh mint. It's a brilliant way to liven up what can sometimes be a bland white meat. Serve with a fruit-and-nut-laden polow and lots of creamy yoghurt to take the edge off the chilli-heat.

800 g boneless free-range chicken
   thighs, trimmed of excess fat
1 cup loosely packed mint leaves
2 long red chillies, finely chopped
1 dried red chilli, finely chopped
3 cloves garlic, finely chopped
50 ml olive oil
2 tablespoons Saffron Liquid (page 54)
grated zest and juice of 2 lemons
1 teaspoon ground cardamom
generous pinch of dried mint
rice, lemon wedges, fresh herbs, yoghurt
   and flatbread, to serve

Cut the chicken thighs into large chunks and put into a large bowl.

Combine the remaining ingredients in the bowl of a food processor and whiz to a paste. If you prefer, you could, of course, do this by hand using a mortar and pestle. Pour the marinade over the chicken pieces and toss to coat thoroughly. Cover and refrigerate for at least 1 hour.

When ready to cook, preheat your barbecue or griller to high. Grill the chicken pieces for 2–3 minutes on each side, or until lightly charred and good and sticky. Alternatively, you can cook these on a stove-top chargrill pan.

Serve with your choice of rice, lemon wedges, lots of yoghurt, fresh herbs and flatbread. **SERVES 6**

Grilled quail with turmeric, lemon and garlic

This is one of the simplest and tastiest Iranian-style marinades and it is just as good with chicken pieces.

6 quail	1½ teaspoons ground turmeric
2 cloves garlic	½ teaspoon freshly ground
1 teaspoon sea salt	black pepper
30 ml olive oil	rice, lemon wedges, fresh herbs
juice of 1 lemon	and flatbread, to serve
1 tablespoon chopped thyme	
leaves	

To spatchcock each quail, use kitchen scissors to cut along both sides of the backbone, from base to neck. Remove the backbone and discard it. Open out the bird and turn it flesh-side up on your work surface, then use the heel of your hands to squash the bird flat. There's no need to fiddle about removing small bones for this style of informal eating – and the bones keep the meat juicier as the birds cook.

Crush the garlic to a paste with the salt and scrape it into a bowl. Whisk in the oil, lemon juice, thyme and spices.

Put the spatchcocked quail into a shallow dish and pour on the marinade, turning the birds around so they are evenly coated. Cover and refrigerate for at least 2 hours.

When ready to cook, preheat your barbecue or griller to high. Grill the quail for 2–3 minutes on each side, or to your liking. Be careful not to overcook them – the breast meat should still be a little pink. Alternatively, cook them in a heavy-based frying pan – they will need around 4 minutes on each side.

Serve on a warm platter with your choice of rice, lemon wedges, fresh herbs and flatbread. SERVES 6

Pan-fried trout with orange zest, cayenne pepper and sumac

The inspiration for this recipe came from a meal we enjoyed in the revolving restaurant atop the El Goli Pars Hotel in the north-western city of Tabriz. Freshwater fish, such as trout, are popular in the north of Iran, and the proximity to Turkey and Azerbaijan adds a touch of chilli-heat to some dishes from the region. In keeping with the Iranian custom of balancing hot and cold dishes, serving cooling herbs alongside this spicy dish would be in order.

finely grated zest of 1 orange	1 teaspoon sea salt
1 tablespoon freshly ground	6 x 350 g rainbow trout
black pepper	80 ml vegetable oil
1 teaspoon cayenne pepper	rice, fresh herbs and lemon
2 teaspoons ground sumac	wedges, to serve

Preheat the oven to 120°C. Scatter the orange zest on a small baking tray and dry in the oven for 30 minutes. Mix the dried zest with the spices and salt.

Snip the fins from each trout and trim the tails neatly. Pat dry inside and out. Heat the oil in a heavy-based frying pan over a high heat. Sprinkle the spice mix over the trout, inside and out. Fry in batches, for about 4–5 minutes on each side, until the skin is golden and the flesh cooked through. Serve straight away with your choice of rice, wedges of lemon and fresh herbs. SERVES 6

Whiting with Persian Gulf spices

The usual all-purpose coating for fried fish in Iran is turmeric-tinted flour. It does turn a lovely yellow–gold on frying, but the flavour is a little one dimensional. This rather more exotic spice blend is easy to throw together – you'll probably have most of the ingredients in your pantry already. Or if you have a batch of the Bandari Spice Mix (page 184), feel free to use that instead.

60 g plain flour
1 teaspoon ground coriander
1 teaspoon ground cumin
1 teaspoon ground turmeric
½ teaspoon cayenne pepper
½ teaspoon ground cinnamon
½ teaspoon cardamom seeds, finely
   ground
½ teaspoon freshly ground black pepper
6 x 180 g whole whiting, scaled and gutted
80 ml vegetable oil
rice and lemon wedges, to serve

Combine the flour and spices in a large shallow dish. Snip the fins from each whiting, cut off the heads and trim the tails neatly. Pat dry inside and out.

Heat the oil in a heavy-based frying pan over a high heat. Working in batches, roll the whiting in the spicy flour so they are evenly coated. Fry for about 2 minutes on each side, until the skin is golden and the flesh cooked through. Drain briefly on paper towels and serve straight away with your choice of rice and lemon wedges.

SERVES 6

Tuna steaks with dried mint, oregano and sumac

Dried herbs can often look like rather unappealing grass-clippings, but they scrub up very well as a coating for this quick-as-a-flash tuna dish. You could serve it as part of a Persian-themed dinner party, perhaps with Shaved Cucumber and Pomegranate Salad (page 99).

6 x 180 g tuna steaks
1 tablespoon dried oregano
1 tablespoon dried mint
1 teaspoon freshly ground black pepper
1 teaspoon ground sumac
sea salt
80 ml olive oil
rice or salad and lime wedges, to serve

Trim any visible bloodline from the tuna steaks, if necessary.

Combine the dried herbs, pepper and sumac in a mortar and pound to an even, fairly fine consistency. Season the tuna steaks with salt, then sprinkle on a generous layer of the herb–spice mixture so they are evenly coated on both sides.

Heat the oil in a heavy-based frying pan over a high heat. Fry the tuna steaks in two batches for 1–2 minutes, which will cook them rare. Turn them every 30 seconds to make sure they don't burn.

Serve straight away with your choice of rice or salad and lime wedges. SERVES 6

Bandari-spiced calamari with tomato—coriander sauce

Locally caught calamari, octopus and cuttlefish are all popular in the villages and towns on the Persian Gulf. They are sometimes braised slowly in a tomato-based sauce, but frying is also popular – usually in a light dusting of turmeric flour. I am not wild about slow-cooking calamari – and let's face it, everyone loves it crisp-fried and golden. I've used a spice mix that's really popular in this part of Iran to jazz up the coating. The accompanying tomato sauce is light and fresh.

6 x 120 g calamari, cleaned (tentacles reserved)
100 g fine semolina
2 teaspoons Bandari Spice Mix (page 184)
½ teaspoon sea salt
vegetable oil, for shallow-frying
rice and flatbread, to serve
1 tablespoon pistachio slivers (optional)

TOMATO–CORIANDER SAUCE
2 tablespoons olive oil
1 large shallot, finely diced
1 small clove garlic, finely chopped
1 tablespoon Bandari Spice Mix (page 184)
1 teaspoon tomato paste
300 ml crushed tomatoes
250 ml water
juice of ½ lemon
1 teaspoon sea salt
⅓ cup shredded coriander leaves

To make the tomato–coriander sauce, heat the oil in a heavy-based saucepan over a low heat. Add the shallot and garlic and fry gently until soft and translucent. Stir in the spice mix and fry for another couple of minutes. Stir in the tomato paste, tomatoes and water and bring to a boil over a medium heat. Lower the heat and simmer gently for 30 minutes.

Split the calamari tubes lengthwise, then trim the sides neatly. Use a very sharp knife to score a fine diamond pattern on the inner surface.

Combine the semolina, spice mix and salt in a bowl.

When the sauce is ready, heat a shallow layer of oil in a heavy-based frying pan over a high heat. Working in small batches, dust the calamari pieces (including the tentacles) with the spicy semolina and fry for around 30 seconds on each side. The scored calamari pieces will curl up into tight little cylinders as they cook. When evenly golden and crisp, transfer them to a plate lined with paper towels to drain.

Just before you serve, add the lemon juice and salt to the sauce and stir in the coriander. Top with the fried calamari, garnish with pistachio slivers and serve with your choice of rice and plenty of warm flatbread for mopping up the sauce. SERVES 6

Whiting in spicy chickpea batter

There's something irresistible about battered, deep-fried fish — especially if the batter is flavoured with heady spices. This dish was inspired by a recipe for pekareh (pakoras) we discovered in a local Bandari cookbook, yet another indication of the strong links between the Persian Gulf and the Indian subcontinent. This chickpea batter is one of my favourites, although to be honest, I often make it with beer instead of soda water, because of the more pronounced tangy, yeasty flavour. Either way, it is light and crunchy, tastes wonderful and is also really attractive, all flecked with spices.

If you're serving this as part of a generous Persian spread, you'll only need one whiting fillet per person, otherwise serve two per person for a main course.

12 whiting fillets
vegetable oil, for deep-frying
plain flour, for dusting
salad and lemon wedges, to serve

SPICY CHICKPEA BATTER

500 ml soda water
150 g chickpea flour
250 g self-raising flour
50 g cornflour
1 teaspoon ground turmeric
1 teaspoon cumin seeds, roasted and
   lightly crushed
1 teaspoon coriander seeds, roasted and
   lightly crushed
½ teaspoon freshly ground black pepper
1 dried red chilli, seeded and finely
   chopped
1 shallot, grated
1 clove garlic, grated
pinch of sea salt
pinch of bicarbonate of soda

To make the batter, pour the soda water into a bowl and whisk in the flours, spices, chilli, shallot and garlic. Add the salt and bicarbonate of soda and leave to rest for 30 minutes before using.

When ready to cook, cut the fins away from the whiting fillets and remove any stray bones. Heat the oil in a deep-fryer or large saucepan to 185°C. Test by dropping in a little batter. If it sizzles slowly to the top, turning golden brown in 10–15 seconds, the oil is hot enough.

Working in batches, dust the whiting fillets lightly with flour, then dip into the batter, allow the excess to drip off, and gently lower into the oil. Fry for 1–2 minutes, or until the batter is golden brown.

Drain briefly on paper towels and serve with a salad and lemon wedges. **SERVES 6**

Brain fritters with lime, coriander and hot paprika

While we were in Mashhad, the large pilgrimage city in the north-east of Iran, we had a simple but delicious lunch of delicately spiced poached brains stuffed into a long, soft white roll. This region is prime saffron-growing country, so, unsurprisingly, that spice features in many dishes – even in the poaching liquid for the brains, tinting them pale yellow. That dish was the inspiration for these fritters, which you could serve as a small course with salad leaves, or stuff into a bread roll, Iranian-style, with lots of tangy pickles.

Many offal lovers only ever eat brains when they see them on restaurant menus because they're concerned the preparation is too involved. Lamb's brains are a cinch, don't require the peeling and attention to detail that calf's brains do, and are absolutely delicious – but, then, you know that already. Be brave – and be rewarded!

6 sets of lamb's brains
cold milk
1 tablespoon Saffron Liquid (page 54)
1 bay leaf
6 sprigs thyme
1 cinnamon stick
1 shallot, cut in half
3 tablespoons olive oil
lime wedges and pickles or dried chilli
   flakes, to serve

LIME-PAPRIKA BATTER
50 g self-raising flour
1 teaspoon hot paprika
½ teaspoon dried mint
½ teaspoon freshly ground black pepper
½ teaspoon sea salt
2 eggs
zest of 1 lime
juice of ½ lime
½ cup shredded coriander leaves
2 tablespoons snipped chives

Soak the brains in cold milk for 2 hours. Drain well.

Put the brains into a large, non-reactive saucepan with the saffron liquid, herbs, cinnamon and shallot. Cover with water, then bring to a gentle boil over a medium heat. Skim, then lower the heat and simmer gently for 2 minutes. Remove the pan from the heat and allow the brains to cool in the poaching liquid. When they are cold, remove them from the pan and split each set in half. Cut out and discard the stem at the base of each lobe, then pat the poached brains dry with paper towels and cut into 15 mm dice.

To make the batter, mix the flour, paprika, dried mint, pepper and salt in a large bowl. Crack in the eggs and whisk until very smooth. Whisk in the lime zest and juice, followed by the fresh herbs. Fold the diced brains into the batter.

Heat the oil in a large heavy-based frying pan over a high heat. Stir the batter briefly, then drop spoonfuls into the hot oil. Lower the heat to medium and fry the fritters for 4–5 minutes on each side. Remove from the pan and drain briefly on paper towels. Serve with lime wedges and pickles or a pinch of dried chilli flakes – stuffed into a long bread roll, if you like. SERVES 6

Mahi-e mast-gerdu

YOGHURT BAKED FISH WITH WALNUT–HERB CRUMBS

Although it might at first seem a little strange to bake fish in yoghurt, I guarantee that this wonderful dish from the north of Iran, with its crunchy walnut and herb topping, will surprise and delight you. You'll need to select a firm white fish that becomes succulent and tender as it cooks — I find rockling ideal. While chelow rice is good with this, I also particularly like Baghali Polow (page 54) or Sabzi Polow (page 55).

unsalted butter, for greasing

1 kg firm white fish fillet, skin removed

sea salt

freshly ground black pepper

rice and fresh herbs, to serve

WALNUT–HERB CRUMBS

150 g fresh breadcrumbs

150 g shelled walnuts, coarsely chopped
   and sieved

¼ cup shredded flat-leaf parsley leaves

¼ cup shredded tarragon leaves or
   dill sprigs

90 g unsalted butter, melted

YOGHURT SAUCE

250 g thick natural yoghurt

½ teaspoon cornflour

1 large egg

1 small shallot, finely diced

2 tablespoons finely snipped chives

juice of ½ lime

1 tablespoon extra-virgin olive oil

sea salt

freshly ground black pepper

Preheat the oven to 180°C. Lightly butter a baking dish just large enough to fit the fish comfortably.

To make the walnut–herb crumbs, combine the ingredients thoroughly in a bowl.

To make the yoghurt sauce, whisk the yoghurt with the cornflour and egg. Stir in the shallot, chives, lime juice and oil and season lightly with salt and pepper.

Remove any stray bones from the fish, then cut the fillet into 6 even pieces. Season the fish lightly all over with salt and pepper and arrange in the baking dish. Pour the yoghurt sauce over the fish. Pack a generous layer of the walnut–herb crumbs on top of each piece of fish. Season lightly again and bake for 15–20 minutes, or until the topping is golden and crunchy and the fish is cooked through.

Serve straight away with your choice of rice and fresh herbs. **SERVES 6**

Baby snapper with walnut–raisin stuffing and barberry butter

In the north of Iran, fish is sometimes served with fesenjun – a sauce of toasty walnuts and sour pomegranates. I've drawn on this surprisingly delicious combination for the stuffing given here. Instead of pomegranates, though, I've used sweet golden raisins, and the sourness comes from the lovely buttery barberry sauce that is drizzled over the fish as you serve.

This is a terrific dinner-party dish as it looks impressive and the flavours are wonderful. You can prepare the rice stuffing ahead of time, but don't add the coriander leaves and lime juice until you are ready to stuff the fish.

6 x 300–400 g baby snapper
sea salt
freshly ground black pepper
salad, lemon wedges and flatbread,
  to serve

WALNUT–RAISIN STUFFING

1 tablespoon olive oil
50 g shelled walnuts, coarsely chopped
1 shallot, finely diced
1 clove garlic, finely chopped
180 g basmati rice, rinsed and soaked
  for 30 minutes
1 tablespoon Saffron Liquid (page 54)
¼ cup golden raisins, coarsely chopped
sea salt
freshly ground black pepper
2 tablespoons shredded coriander leaves
juice of 1 lime

BARBERRY BUTTER

1½ tablespoons dried barberries, stems
  removed
water
juice of ½ lime
few drops of Saffron Liquid (page 54)
120 g unsalted butter, diced and chilled

To make the stuffing, heat the oil in a small saucepan over a medium heat. Add the walnuts and fry for a minute, tossing continuously so they colour evenly. Add the shallot and garlic to the pan and toss with the nuts for 30 seconds, until they start to caramelise. Keep an eye on them to ensure they don't burn. Tip into a small bowl and set aside.

Add the drained rice to the same pan with the saffron liquid, golden raisins and enough boiling water to cover by a finger's width. Season lightly with salt and pepper and simmer over a very low heat, covered, for 12 minutes, or until the rice is just tender and the liquid has been absorbed. Remove from the heat and leave to cool.

When the rice is cold, stir in the fried walnut mixture, coriander and lime juice. Taste and adjust the seasoning to your liking.

When ready to bake the fish, preheat the oven to 180°C and line a large baking tray with baking paper.

Snip the fins off each fish and trim the tails neatly. Rinse the cavities and pat dry. Season the fish lightly all over with salt and pepper. Divide the stuffing mixture into 6 even portions and use to fill the cavities. Transfer the fish to the baking tray and bake for 14–15 minutes, or until just cooked.

Meanwhile, to make the barberry butter, soak the barberries in cold water for 2 minutes, then drain and roughly chop. Put the barberries into a small saucepan with 3 tablespoons water, lime juice and saffron liquid. Simmer vigorously over a high heat until the liquid has reduced by half. Add half the chilled butter, then lower the heat to very low and whisk vigorously until the mixture comes together as a creamy emulsion. Slowly drop in the remaining butter, whisking all the time, until it has all been incorporated. Remove from the heat, then taste and adjust the seasonings to your liking

Towards the end of the cooking time, brush a little of the butter onto the fish and cook for another minute or so to glaze the surface. Spoon the remaining barberry butter over the fish and serve with your choice of salad, lemon wedges and lots of warm flatbread. SERVES 6

Chicken roasted with barberry butter

It's no big secret that roasting a chicken with a herb- or spice-flecked butter underneath the skin is a simple but effective way of keeping the breast meat moist and infusing the flesh with extra flavour. The magic is all in the way you combine ingredients, of course, and this sour–sweet barberry butter with a hint of aniseedy chervil provides a real lift. Because of the butter, with this method you won't achieve very crisp skin over the breast, but the succulence of the meat more than makes up for this.

2 x 1.4 kg free-range chickens

2 limes, cut into quarters

8 sprigs thyme

8 cloves garlic, peeled

2 long red chillies, split and seeded

sea salt

freshly ground black pepper

olive oil

rice and salad, to serve

BARBERRY BUTTER

½ cup dried barberries, stems removed

1 clove garlic

1 teaspoon sea salt

200 g unsalted butter, softened

finely grated zest of ½ lime

1 tablespoon icing sugar

⅓ cup roughly chopped chervil sprigs
    or tarragon leaves

½ teaspoon freshly ground black pepper

To make the barberry butter, soak the barberries in cold water for 2 minutes, then drain and pat dry. Crush the garlic with the salt. Heat a knob of the butter in a small frying pan over a low heat and fry the barberries and garlic for 4–5 minutes, stirring constantly. Stir in the lime zest and icing sugar, then remove the pan from the heat and leave to cool.

Put the remaining butter into a bowl. Tip in the cold barberry butter and add the chervil and pepper. Beat vigorously to combine.

Preheat the oven to 180°C. Wipe the cavities of the chickens thoroughly with paper towels, and pat dry all over.

Working from the neck-end of each bird, carefully insert your fingers underneath the skin that covers the breast meat. Ease it gently away from the flesh to create a pocket, being careful not to tear the skin. Work back as far as you dare – even over the drumsticks, if you can. Push knobs of the barberry butter deep into the pocket, again as far as you can, until it covers most of the meat, then smooth it evenly over the surface with your fingers. Gently pull the breast skin forward again, so that the meat is covered.

Divide the limes, thyme, garlic and chillies between the birds and stuff them inside the cavities. Sprinkle in a generous amount of salt and pepper. Tie the chicken legs to the parson's nose as firmly as you can, then sit the birds side by side on a rack set inside a large roasting pan. Rub the skin with the oil and season generously with salt and pepper.

Roast for 20 minutes, then lower the temperature to 160°C and roast for a further 30 minutes, turning the chickens around and basting them every 15 minutes or so to ensure the skin colours evenly. After 50 minutes, turn off the oven and leave the chickens to rest for 10 minutes. Remove from the oven and pierce the thighs with a skewer to check that the juices run clear. If not, return to the oven, turn the heat up to 180°C and cook for a further 10 minutes. Serve with your choice of rice and salad. **SERVES 6**

Sardast-e bareh tu por

SLOW-ROASTED SHOULDER OF LAMB WITH JEWELLED-RICE STUFFING

Special occasions demand special dishes, and in Iran this still often means a whole lamb will be stuffed with an exciting mixture of rice, fruit, nuts and herbs before being roasted and presented as a banquet centrepiece. This more modest adaptation uses a rolled shoulder to fit domestic ovens, but achieves an equally sumptuous result.

Shoulder of lamb benefits from very long, slow roasting, which transforms the marbling of fat and connective tissue into melting softness. My approach with this recipe is to poach the lamb gently and then finish it in a hot oven for a lovely crunchy, golden exterior. I find that this way the flesh is exceptionally moist and tasty.

This is another wonderful dish for dinner parties. Because of the rice stuffing, it only needs a simple salad or vegetable dish by way of accompaniment.

1 x 1.8 kg boned lamb shoulder

sea salt

freshly ground black pepper

olive oil

2 teaspoons cumin seeds, roasted and ground

salad or vegetables, thick natural yoghurt and flatbread, to serve

JEWELLED-RICE STUFFING

60 g basmati rice

50 g dried sour cherries, cut in half

50 g dried apricots, diced

20 g unsalted butter

1 shallot, finely diced

225 ml good-quality chicken stock, boiling

sea salt

freshly ground black pepper

80 g shelled walnuts

2 tablespoons unsalted shelled pistachios

8 dried rosebuds, petals separated

2 teaspoons cumin seeds, roasted and crushed

splash of rosewater

squeeze of lime or lemon juice

To make the stuffing, soak the rice, sour cherries and dried apricots in separate bowls of cold water for 20 minutes, then drain. Melt the butter in a small saucepan over a low heat and fry the shallot gently until soft and translucent. Stir in the drained rice, then cover with the boiling stock. Season lightly with salt and pepper and simmer over a very low heat, covered, for 12 minutes, or until the rice is just tender and the liquid has been absorbed. Tip the rice into a large bowl and leave to cool. When cold, stir in the remaining ingredients and toss gently to combine. Season with a little more salt and pepper and set aside.

Open out the lamb shoulder on your work surface, skin-side down. Season with salt and pepper, then cover the meat with an even layer of stuffing. Roll it up fairly tightly into a sausage shape, securing with kitchen string at intervals. Wrap the rolled shoulder tightly in several layers of plastic wrap, squeezing gently to ensure there are no bubbles. Twist and tie the ends to make the whole package air- and watertight (remember, the wrapped parcel is to be poached).

Fill a fish kettle or large, deep roasting pan with water and bring to a boil. Carefully lower in the plastic-wrapped lamb shoulder and simmer, covered, for 2 hours. If using a roasting pan, cover it loosely with a sheet of foil. You won't be able to submerge the meat completely, so turn it around in the water after 1 hour. Remove the poached lamb from the water and set it aside to rest, still in its plastic wrap, for at least 30 minutes or up to 2 hours.

Preheat the oven to 200°C. Carefully unwrap the rolled lamb and transfer it to a roasting pan, then brush it liberally with oil. Sprinkle on the cumin and season lightly with salt and pepper. Roast for 20 minutes, rolling the meat around in the pan so it browns evenly.

Rest in a warm place for 15–20 minutes, then serve with your choice or salad or vegetables as well as plenty of yoghurt and warm flatbread. SERVES 6

Run-e bareh

SPICED ROAST LAMB WITH PUMPKIN AND SULTANAS

I am always looking for interesting new ways to brighten up a roast leg of lamb, and a spice paste is a surefire way to add flavour. Persian spice mixes range from simple combinations of one or two flavours to complex creations that include esoteric spices such as angelica, dried rose petals and dried-lime powder. This is an easy Persian-inspired spice blend that's turned into a paste with the addition of garlic and oil and features a touch of chilli heat. The pumpkin and sultanas really bring out the underlying sweetness of the meat.

1 x 2.5 kg leg of lamb
80 ml olive oil
600 g peeled pumpkin, cut into chunks
2 purple onions, cut into quarters
¼ cup sultanas
splash of verjuice
rice and yoghurt, to serve

SPICE PASTE

2 cloves garlic, roughly chopped
1 shallot, roughly chopped
1 long red chilli, roughly chopped
1 teaspoon sea salt
1 teaspoon caraway seeds, ground
1 teaspoon freshly grated nutmeg
½ teaspoon ground cardamom
½ teaspoon ground cinnamon
½ teaspoon freshly ground black pepper
50 ml olive oil

Preheat the oven to 200°C.

To make the spice paste, combine the garlic, shallot, chilli and salt in a mortar and pound to a paste. Add the remaining spices and pound again to incorporate thoroughly. Stir in the oil. Use your fingers to rub the paste all over the lamb, working it in thoroughly.

Pour half the oil into a heavy-based roasting pan, then add the lamb and cook in the centre of the oven for 20 minutes. Turn the oven down to 180°C and cook for a further 20 minutes. Remove the pan from the oven and add the remaining oil. Scatter in the pumpkin, onion and sultanas, tossing them around in the spicy oil to coat. Return the pan to the oven and cook for a further 20 minutes. Check from time to time and turn the vegetables to ensure they cook evenly.

Check for doneness – at this stage, the lamb should be cooked medium-rare. Return to the oven for a little longer, if you prefer it less pink. Allow the meat to rest for at least 15 minutes before carving – the vegetables can be kept warm in the oven if they are done. Serve with the pan juices and vegetables, your choice of rice and lots of yoghurt. **SERVES 6**

SHIRAZ: CITY OF WINE, POETRY, ROSES AND NIGHTINGALES. AND ALSO, IT SEEMS, OF RAIN. We arrive late at night and our plane descends through the clouds amidst a spring shower. This is the first real rain we've seen on our travels around Iran, and after the heat and wilting humidity of the Persian Gulf it is bliss to feel a cool breeze and the reviving raindrops on our faces once we are on the tarmac.

/

The next morning we draw back the curtains on a new day, a new city and thin, watery sunshine. The streets have a just-washed feel and visitors to the Naranjestan Gardens are rugged up against the wind. For the first time, I am grateful to be wearing a headscarf and tuck it in tightly around my ears and chin.

/

Because it's a Friday, the pretty gardens are full of sightseers and the place is bustling with families, school groups and shy couples. The sour-orange trees that give the gardens their name are beginning to blossom and their perfume scents the air. Classical Persian music is playing through the loudspeakers – just a touch too loudly – and we spend a delightful hour admiring the opulently decorated rooms of the late-nineteenth-century pavilion.

/

I'm especially drawn to the gul-o-bul-bul decoration of the exterior façades around the garden. This 'rose and nightingale' motif is popular in Persian poetry and nineteenth-century art, and we are not surprised to learn that many historians believe it originated here in Shiraz. In this style, a mass of birds and flowers are depicted intertwined, representing the lover and the beloved, in earthly or divine union. On these walls there are not just roses and nightingales, but also irises, peonies and tulips and peacocks, lapwings and the mythical phoenix and simorgh. After the preponderance of blue, white and green tiles we've seen at other Persian monuments, the lavish use here of yellows, pinks, reds and lilacs is enchanting.

/

A BOLD USE OF COLOUR CAN BE SEEN AT THE NEARBY NASIR-OL-MOLK
Mosque, also known as the Pink Mosque because of its striking rosy-hued
tilework. Inside the airy prayer room the caretaker is busy at his midday
prayers and we move quietly so we don't disturb him. We weave our
way through rows of squat carved pillars that twist and turn in alternate
directions beneath a canopy of tiled cupolas, and then, as we turn to leave,
the sun bursts through the stained-glass windows and we walk back out to
the courtyard through streaks and splashes of a brilliant rainbow.
/

Happy in her hometown, Yas now leads us through a series of archways into
a tiny jewel-like prayer room, tucked away secretly at the rear of the mosque.
Inside, the walls and ceilings are painted in pale, sugared-almond tones
of lavender, pistachio, cream and pink. One vaulted corner is covered in a
kaleidoscope of tiny mirrors and I tell Yas that I've noticed the use of mirror
seems to be a popular decorative element in Persian buildings.
/

'It's because the idea of light is so important,' Yas explains. 'Inside many
mosques, mirror is used to increase the light, which symbolises God, of
course. But mirrors are also used to decorate houses and in ceremonies such
as Nowruz – Persian New Year – and at weddings, and they are also used
in poetry and literature to symbolise reflection.' She pauses for a moment,
then a smile breaks over her face. 'There is a famous line of poetry,' she says:
'*Ayaneh chon naqshe to benmood rast. Khod shekan ayeneh shekastan khastast.*
Don't break the mirror for showing you what you really are. In other words,
if you are unhappy with what you see, you must change yourself.'
/

There is more symbolism later that afternoon, but this time it comes in a simple bowl of soup. Greg has been longing to taste ash-e reshteh, so Yas has invited us to meet her sister Farideh, an expert home cook.

/

Farideh lives with their mother in the family home, and when we arrive she is already in the kitchen, picking over a mountain of fresh herbs. She tells us that the category of dishes known as ash is one of the earliest known, dating back to Zoroastrian times, and falls somewhere between a soup and stew. The word 'ash', she continues, derives from the Farsi word for a cook – ashpaz – which literally means 'soupmaker', and this gives us an idea of its significance in the Persian kitchen. We learn that there are endless varieties of ash, for all manner of different occasions, but the main ingredients are meat, pulses, grains and fresh herbs.

/

Farideh pauses to stir onion and spices in a battered old pot, then in go chickpeas, lentils, and borlotti and kidney beans and plenty of water. Once the pot is simmering away happily, she ushers us into the cosy living room to make the noodles. Kneeling on the floor in front of a large wooden board, she rolls a simple semolina dough out into large, thin sheets and then shreds these into fine strips before dropping the noodles into a shallow basket to dry.

/

It's the noodles that distinguish ash-e reshteh, and as we look at the tangle gathering in the basket, Farideh explains that they represent the problems we all have to manage in our lives. It comes as no surprise, then, when she tells us that this soup is often eaten on the first working day of the Persian New Year, to symbolise a fresh start.

/

A little later the chopped herbs and noodles are added to the pot and as Farideh stirs, we watch the noodles unravel before our eyes. 'You see,' says Farideh, 'in the end life is as simple as this soup.'

/

WE VISIT THE SHRINE OF HAFEZ, THE REVERED FOURTEENTH-CENTURY PERSIAN POET, IN THE LATE afternoon. His tomb lies in a rotunda at the centre of a pretty garden of sloping shadows, cypress trees and roses. It's a peaceful spot, despite the number of visitors milling around, and Ebi tells us it's one of the country's most popular monuments.

/

Like many Westerners, before visiting Iran I knew virtually nothing about Persian literature, and I've been startled to learn of the sheer number of Persian poets and of the influence the poetic canon has on the Persian psyche. The era of classical poetry dates back more than a thousand years and encompasses epic works such as Ferdowsi's *Shahnameh*, the mystic Sufi poetry of Rumi, and Omar Khayyam's *Rubaiyat*. I was familiar with Khayyam as will be many Westerners, but, interestingly, in his homeland he has always been more famous as a mathematician and an astronomer than as a poet. But of them all, I've learned that it is Hafez who reaches deepest into the Persian soul.

/

Hafez's poetry explores eternal ideas of life, love and spirituality, but one of his most enduring themes is of unrequited love and longing – both earthly and divine – and of finding solace in wine. And this in a land and time of Islam! But most particularly, over the centuries, his poetry has given rise to a kind of fortune-telling – you pose a question, open his poetry at random, and find guidance from the words within. And if you don't have a book of poetry with you when visiting Hafez's tomb, outside the gardens a budgerigar will pluck a card at random, and offer insight from a Hafez verse for the cost of a few tomans.

/

We circle the tomb slowly, then draw back to watch as others approach. Most visitors are clutching a book of verse and they pause to bend or kneel in front of the tomb, tapping the surface tenderly and muttering beneath their breath. There's no mistaking their sincerity. So cherished is Hafez that many Iranians can quote his poetry by heart, and Yas tells us that copies of his works outsell the Koran.

/

YAS IS TAKING US OUT TO LUNCH. SHE'S BEEN TEASING US ABOUT A LOCAL SPECIALITY CALLED chakhol parhol, a sandwich filled with fried chopped lung, but it transpires she has something more substantial in mind, and is taking us to one of her favourite local restaurants. At first, the idea of a restaurant meal leaves us a little less than excited. By now we have learned not to expect too much from Iranian restaurants. Everyone here knows that if you want really good food it's best to eat at home, and most restaurants dole out the same predictable offerings of kebab and chelow rice. But, admittedly, we have discovered the odd gem on our travels, and this is Yas's hometown, after all, so we cross fingers and head off.

/

A good sign: although we arrive early at Brentin Restaurant, the dining room is already filling up and we are lucky to find a table in the corner. 'Here you will find completely Shirazi food, but also some food with a modern twist,' Yas tells us happily. We've barely had time to sit down before two small plates are set on the table before us. One contains hot cashew nuts that have been roasted with salt and lime juice, the other a pretty sliced arrangement of watermelon and white cheese. Good service and attractively presented food! Things are looking promising.

/

There's no Shiraz wine on the menu, sadly, but chilled pomegranate beer and fresh lime and mint sherbet are just the thing to go with the hot cashews. Before long the table is crowded with dishes. There's kalam polow, a rice dish with tiny meatballs and chock-full of tarragon, savory and dill; and khoresht-e gheimeh, a wonderful thick stew of lamb and split peas flavoured with dried limes. In Shiraz, this khoresht is served with shirin polow, a sweet saffron rice tossed with almonds, pistachios and shredded orange zest – a combination I find irresistible. We feel obliged to have a Shirazi salad, a dish we've eaten all around Iran. In the local version, cucumber, shallots and tomatoes are chopped finely and tossed with mint and verjuice – unfermented, sour grape juice. 'This verjuice is typically Shiraz,' explains Yas. 'We have to find something to do with all those grapes after all!'

/

The famous shiraz grapes may no longer be used to make wine, but Yas tells us that every visitor to the city makes time to stock-up on bottles of the local verjuice. It provides a much-loved sourness to many Persian dishes, as do fresh lemon and lime juice, and we've seen an entire row of shops devoted to these products behind the eighteenth-century Citadel in the city centre. But Shiraz is also famous for its flower waters, and Ebi has plans for us to visit an araghiat – arak shop – before we depart for the ancient city of Persepolis.

/

The first thing we notice as we push open the gate to the Jaleh family araghiat is the pungent herbal aroma. Arak, which literally (and rather unappealingly) means 'perspiration', are distilled extracts from flowers and herbs. We're very familiar with rosewater and orange-flower water, but here in Iran there is a dazzling array of arak varieties. A few, such as golab – rosewater –

are used in cooking, but more often these distillations are combined with sugar syrup and ice to make thirst-quenching drinks or sherbets.

/

Today's brew, bubbling away beneath the steaming domed stills, derives from walnut blossom, but all around the small yard are vast tanks of other types of arak. Yas translates some of the labels for us: oregano, cumin, eglantine, cinnamon, chicory, sweetbriar, pussy willow – it seems there are waters made from every conceivable flower, twig and leaf in Iran.

/

While we study the vats, a steady stream of customers arrives. Most of them are equipped with their own bottles and seem to know exactly what they want. Ebi explains that there is another reason for the popularity of arak – their use as natural remedies. Above the cashier's office is a chart that outlines the medicinal properties of each water and Yas again reads some of them out to us: cinnamon for diabetes, oregano for the blood, borage for the heart, mint for stomach ache.

/

Iranians set great store by arak, and will usually try dosing themselves with the appropriate herb or flower water before making a trip to the doctor. Ebi has been talking to the owner and now he comes over to us with two enormous containers under his arms and a gleam in his eye. 'This is pure and natural medicine,' he declares. 'And here in Shiraz it is the best in the country.' Greg's interest is piqued when Ebi explains that he's choosing cumin water for weight loss and dill water to lower cholesterol. Greg hurries off to find a couple of empty bottles. 'Anything's worth a try!', he calls back to us over his shoulder.

/

By the time we reach persepolis the landscape is washed in a strange, steely-mauve light and it feels as if a storm is brewing. In the distance, on a dusty plateau, the shattered columns of the ancient city jut like broken teeth under the dark, bruised sky. But even in ruins, it is dramatic.

/

Persepolis was established around 515 BC, and for two hundred years it was a dazzling symbol of Persia's power, and its most sacred site. To this day it remains the best-preserved monument to the achievements of the Achaemenid kings; its destruction by the young Alexander the Great and his army, in a night of wanton vandalism in 331 BC, was the death-blow to the greatest empire the world had yet seen.

/

There is only one approach to Persepolis and, like every visitor before, we climb the broad but shallow stairway to the palace complex, which rises high above us on an immense stone platform. It's impossible not to think of the other feet that have trodden here before us, of the subjects who gathered from all corners of the empire to pay homage to the king. And as we pass beneath the towering Gate of Nations, topped with mythical double-headed creatures, we surely feel the same sense of awe.

/

Yas tells us that it was Cyrus the Great who laid the foundation for this unique empire, one that was built on tolerance for other cultures and religions. And as she talks, a bell rings in my mind, and I remember Ali telling us about the Cyrus Stone all that time ago.

/

Cyrus and his successors expanded their territories across Asia, Africa and Europe, bringing twenty-three nations together under one rule. That early Persian ideal of inclusiveness and mutual respect is reflected in the very fabric of these buildings, which were constructed in an eclectic mix of Greek, Assyrian and Egyptian styles by skilled craftsmen brought in from the subject nations.

/

Clues to understanding the function of Persepolis are carved into the walls – and there are carvings *everywhere*. Yas points out twelve-petalled lotus flowers, radiant suns and great leaping lions – all of which are ancient metaphors for kingly power. In fact there are endless depictions of lions tearing at the flanks of horned bulls, and Yas explains that this also symbolises the victory of spring over winter, of day over night.

/

It seems that Persepolis was not a military or political capital, but a ceremonial complex, and spring was the highlight of the year. Then, as now, the Persian New Year was celebrated on 21 March, and on this first day of spring delegations from across the empire congregated at the palace with gifts for the king of kings.

/

After making our way through gateways and courtyards, we walk slowly up the great Apadana staircase to the Central Hall, flanked by a silent procession of carved stone dignitaries bearing bowls of gold and lapis lazuli, folds of gorgeous fabric, jewels, wine and rare beasts. There are no depictions of wars or fights between humans – indeed some figures hold hands in friendship. It seems certain that these visitors to Persepolis brought with them not just precious gifts, but also their various ideas, skills, languages and religions. Despite the undoubted magnificence of the buildings around us, I can't help but feel that the greatest achievement of the empire was not material wealth, but the human kind.

/

There is only one hotel in persepolis and this evening we are its sole guests. It feels suitably splendid to have the place to ourselves, although the hotel staff tells us that in a fortnight it will be Nowruz, the Persian New Year, and the place will be heaving.

/

Hamid, the chef, is over the moon to meet a fellow professional from the other side of the world, and with the help of Yas translating, he and Greg manage a lively conversation, swapping recipes and notes.

/

After our long day travelling and sightseeing, none of us is very hungry, and hotel food is the last thing that we feel like eating. Rather than be irritated by his difficult customers, Hamid rises to the challenge and offers to prepare a homely dish called eshkeneh. It's a suggestion that sends Ebi and Yas into transports of delight.

/

Eshkeneh turns out to be a lovely, simple onion soup flavoured with fenugreek and with egg whisked in at the last minute. Hamid brings it to the table with a basket of flatbread and a small jug of vinegar for sharpening the soup to our own taste, and explains that eshkeneh is a traditional peasant dish that dates back several thousand years. It's the perfect comfort food for a chilly spring evening and we all agree that it seems very appropriate in these ancient surroundings.

The next day, after leaving our hotel at Persepolis, we stop at Naksh-e Rostam to admire the Sassanian bas-reliefs and massive cruciform cliff tombs of four of the Achaemenid kings – Darius I and II, Xerxes and Ataxerxes. And then it's on to see the tomb of Cyrus the Great, which stands alone on a vast dusty plain.

/

It seems inconceivable that this is almost all that remains of Pasargadae, the first capital city of the mighty Achaemenids. But so it is. After Persepolis, we can't help but think about the fleeting nature of power. And when we read the inscription on Cyrus's tomb, it seems as if he has had the last word – again.

/

Welcome traveller, I have been expecting you.
Here lies Cyrus, King of Asia, King of the World.
All that is left of me is dust. Do not envy me.

CYRUS THE GREAT

sweets

ALTHOUGH IRANIANS ARE WELL known for having a sweet tooth, they don't tend to eat desserts after a meal in the same way we do at the Western dinner table. If there are guests, ice-cream or cream-stuffed pastries might be bought from a fancy pastry shop, but in the main most meals finish with seasonal fresh fruit – perhaps plucked fresh from the household's own walled garden. Also popular are refreshing chilled fruit salads or 'cocktails' of crushed fruit combined with ice and perfumed with flower waters; watermelon and melon are favoured for these simple granitas.

/

Ice-creams and dairy desserts are popular all day long as between-meals treats, or as much-needed refreshment on hot summer's days. Bastani – traditional ice-cream – comes in two tones: white and saffron-tinted yellow. It is made with sahlab, the ground root of an orchid that produces a characteristic stretchy texture.

Both versions are usually mixed with pistachios and flavoured with sweet rosewater.

/

Faloodeh is a traditional sweet chilled concoction that is often sold in Iranian ice-cream shops. With a texture somewhat unusual to a Western palate, faloodeh is made from fine noodles that are drenched in a lime or sour-cherry syrup. In the stifling heat of an Iranian desert summer, this sweet treat is blissfully reviving.

/

Rice- and dairy-based sweet dishes, such as shir berenj (rice pudding), yakh dar behesht (a thick milk pudding that translates rather charmingly as 'ice in heaven') and shollehzard are eaten as daytime treats. In fact they are thought to have originated as nourishing, wholesome dishes to tempt children or revive invalids rather than as desserts to eat after a big meal. Shollehzard, a rich, thick, saffron-yellow pudding, is often distributed

to the neighbourhood as nazri – a food offering to commemorate significant events, bereavement or religious anniversaries, or to give thanks for recovery from sickness.

/

Although the range of traditional Persian 'dessert' options is fairly limited, when it comes to shirini – which translates literally to 'sweet things' – it is a different story. This category encompasses cakes, cookies and confectionery, pastries, wafers, fritters, sugared nuts and fruits – in fact, any little sweet morsel you can think of. In Iran a cup (or glass) of tea is unthinkable without some kind of sweet accompaniment, however simple, and most households will have cookies or candies on hand to offer guests.

/

The fact that there is no real dessert tradition in Persian cuisine has encouraged us to adopt a rather freewheeling approach to the recipes in this section. Although we've included a few traditional favourites,

in the main the recipes that follow were inspired by ingredients, techniques and flavour combinations we discovered on our travels. These dishes are predominantly fruit-based and many are intended to be served as a dessert at the end of a Western-style meal, while some of the pastries work well either as a dessert or as a treat with a cup of tea or coffee. Finally, the selection of sweetmeats are lovely with coffee after dinner – or to give as gifts.

/

Pomegranate and blood-orange sorbet with flower water

Pretty as a picture, this is a light, cleansing sorbet that combines sweet–sour blood orange and pomegranate juices with the delicate perfume of orange-flower water.

250 g caster sugar

250 ml water

250 ml blood-orange juice

150 ml pomegranate juice

juice of ½ lime

1 tablespoon orange-flower water

50 g liquid glucose

Combine the caster sugar and water in a heavy-based saucepan over a low heat until the sugar has dissolved. Increase the heat, then bring to a boil and simmer for 1 minute. Remove from the heat and leave to cool slightly.

Mix the fruit juices with the orange-flower water. Stir in the warm syrup and the liquid glucose, then transfer to the fridge to cool completely.

Tip the cold mixture into an ice-cream machine and churn according to the manufacturer's instructions. Transfer to a plastic container and freeze for up to 3 days. MAKES 1 LITRE

Plum sorbet with nougat

Plums are often overlooked in favour of other more exotic soft fruits, but they have many virtues – not least of which is that they are widely available, especially at the end of summer. They are copiously juicy, which makes them ideal for jams, jellies, juices – and sorbets. A sprinkle of chewy nougat cubes provides textural interest and a pleasing colour contrast to the vibrant purple–pink of the sorbet itself.

600 g ripe blood plums, stoned and roughly chopped

200 g caster sugar

300 ml water

30 g liquid glucose

1 tablespoon rosewater

100 g almond nougat, finely diced

Combine the chopped plums, sugar, water and liquid glucose in a heavy-based saucepan over a low heat until the sugar has dissolved. Increase the heat, then bring to a boil and simmer for 1 minute. Remove from the heat and leave to cool slightly.

Blitz the fruit mixture in batches in a food processor to a very smooth purée. Push through a sieve into a bowl, using a rubber spatula to extract as much juice as possible. Stir in the rosewater and set aside to cool completely.

Tip the cold purée into an ice-cream machine and churn according to the manufacturer's instructions. At the end of the churning, add the nougat and churn briefly to distribute it evenly. Transfer to a plastic container and freeze for up to 3 days. MAKES 1 LITRE

Roasted hazelnut–chocolate parfait with mulberry syrup

Parfaits are ideal if you don't have an ice-cream machine as they require no churning but instead are set in a mould and then turned out. This toasty hazelnut parfait is smoothed with chocolate and flavoured with spices, and makes an impressive, albeit rich, dinner-party dessert.

Mulberry syrup – or cordial – is available from Middle Eastern stores, but other good-quality fruit syrups would do just as well, or you could, of course, make your own from fresh seasonal berries. Choose one you think will give a pleasing complementary tang to the smooth chocolate and nut flavours of the parfait.

100 g caster sugar

3 tablespoons water

2 teaspoons finely grated orange zest

½ teaspoon fennel seeds, ground

8 egg yolks

80 g dark chocolate

300 ml thickened cream

60 g currants

100 g hazelnuts, roasted and coarsely chopped

MULBERRY SYRUP

100 ml mulberry syrup

juice of 1 lime

2 tablespoons water

few drops of vanilla extract

To make the mulberry syrup, bring all the ingredients to a boil in a small saucepan, then remove from the heat and allow to cool. Strain to remove any bits of lime flesh and reserve the syrup.

Line a 1 litre terrine mould or loaf tin with plastic wrap.

Combine 80 g of the sugar with the water, zest and fennel seeds in a heavy-based saucepan over a gentle heat, stirring occasionally, until the sugar dissolves. Increase the heat and bring to a boil, then simmer for 5–10 minutes or until the mixture reaches the soft-ball stage (the mixture will form a soft ball when a little is dropped into cold water) or 125°C on a candy thermometer.

Meanwhile, whisk the egg yolks and the remaining sugar in an electric mixer until pale, thick and fluffy. With the motor running at medium speed, slowly pour the hot sugar syrup onto the egg mixture. Increase the speed to high and continue whisking for about 5 minutes, or until the mixture cools. It will bulk up into a soft, puffy mass.

While the mixture is whisking, melt the chocolate in a microwave oven or in a bowl set over a saucepan of simmering water. Add the chocolate to the whisked egg mixture, whisking briefly to incorporate, then transfer the mixture to the refrigerator to chill.

Meanwhile, whip the cream to soft peaks and chill. Soak the currants in a little hot water for 20 minutes, then drain and allow to cool.

Fold the chilled cream, currants and hazelnuts into the chilled chocolate parfait mixture until thoroughly combined. Tip into the prepared mould and freeze for 10–12 hours until really firm. The parfait will keep in the freezer for up to 3 weeks.

To serve, dip the mould into warm water for a few seconds. Cover with a board or serving platter and invert. Carefully lift away the mould, then peel away the plastic wrap. Use a sharp knife to cut the parfait into slices and serve straight away, drizzled with a little mulberry syrup. **SERVES 8–10**

Saffron–honey ice-cream with candied ginger and ginger lace wafers

Traditional Persian ice-cream is thick, smooth and strangely stretchy; sometimes tinted yellow with saffron, but nearly always flavoured with rosewater and garnished with chopped pistachios. It's hard to recreate at home because you need sahlab, the ground root of an orchid, to create the distinctive stretchy consistency.

Instead, here is an alternative saffron ice-cream that uses a duo of molten gold – saffron liquid and honey – and chunks of sparkling candied ginger. It is rich, luscious and intensely flavoured: fit for a Shah!

100 ml honey
350 ml water
200 g caster sugar
25 g liquid glucose
3 tablespoons Saffron Liquid
   (page 54)
1 teaspoon ground ginger
juice of ½ lime
250 g thick natural yoghurt
3 tablespoons pure cream
80 ml sour cream
⅓ cup crystallised ginger

GINGER LACE WAFERS

250 g caster sugar
125 g golden syrup
125 g unsalted butter,
   softened
1 tablespoon orange juice
1 teaspoon finely grated
   orange zest
125 g plain flour
1 teaspoon ground ginger

Preheat the oven to 180°C. Line 2 baking trays with baking paper.

To make the ginger lace wafers, combine the sugar, golden syrup, butter, orange juice and zest in a saucepan over a low heat until the butter has melted. Stir thoroughly, then remove from the heat.

Sift the flour and ground ginger into a bowl and make a well in the centre. Pour in the golden syrup mixture and stir until well combined and smooth. Drop small teaspoons of the batter onto the prepared baking trays, leaving 5 cm between each one to allow for spreading. Bake for 8 minutes, until an even golden brown. Remove from the oven and transfer to a wire rack to cool.

Bring the honey to a boil in a small saucepan over a medium heat and simmer to form a dark caramel – 145°C if you have a candy thermometer. As the caramel darkens, swirl the pan constantly and move it on and off the heat to ensure you don't burn the honey.

Remove from the heat straight away and stir in the water (be careful, the caramel will spit and splutter). Stir gently to combine, then return to the heat. Stir in the sugar, liquid glucose, saffron liquid and ground ginger. Return to a boil, stirring gently to dissolve the sugar and glucose, then simmer for 3 minutes. Remove the pan from the heat and leave to cool. Refrigerate until chilled, then stir in the lime juice.

Whisk the yoghurt, cream and sour cream together, then gently fold in the chilled honey–saffron syrup. Tip into an ice-cream machine and churn according to the manufacturer's instructions. At the end of the churning, finely dice the crystallised ginger, add to the ice-cream and churn briefly to distribute it evenly. Transfer to a plastic container and freeze for up to 3 days.

For an attractive presentation, sandwich a scoop of ice-cream between ginger lace wafers. Alternatively, serve the ice-cream in bowls with the wafers on the side. **MAKES 1 LITRE**

Shir berenj

SAFFRON RICE PUDDING WITH CARAMEL BLOOD ORANGES

In Persian cooking, saffron and rice are not just combined in savoury polows but also in sweet desserts. This saffron-scented pudding is etherial, delicate and creamy – the antithesis of gluggy Anglo-style rice puddings. Ruby-hued blood oranges make a lovely colour contrast, but you can, of course, use normal oranges – or any sweet citrus – instead.

1.2 litres full-cream milk

120 g caster sugar

1 tablespoon finely grated orange zest

1 small cinnamon stick

½ vanilla pod, split and seeds scraped

1 tablespoon Saffron Liquid (page 54)

160 g short-grain rice

1 egg yolk

200 ml thickened cream

CARAMEL BLOOD ORANGES

4 small blood oranges, peeled and
    pith removed

100 g caster sugar

100 ml orange juice

1 tablespoon orange-flower water

To make the caramel blood oranges, use a very sharp knife to slice the orange segments out of their skin casings (make sure there's not a trace of pith or membrane) and set aside.

Combine the sugar and orange juice in a small saucepan over a low heat until the sugar dissolves, swirling the pan occasionally. Bring to a boil, then simmer for 8–10 minutes or until a deep golden brown. Remove from the heat straight away and stir in the orange-flower water and orange segments (be careful, the caramel will spit and splutter). Stir gently and refrigerate until ready to serve.

To make the rice pudding, combine the milk, sugar, zest, cinnamon stick, vanilla pod and seeds and saffron liquid in a large, heavy-based saucepan over a medium heat. Bring to a boil, then stir in the rice and boil briskly for a minute, stirring. Lower the heat and simmer very gently for 50 minutes, or until the rice is creamy and the milk has been absorbed. If you have a heat-diffuser, this is the time to use it. You don't need to stir constantly – especially for the first 20 minutes or so – but you do need to keep an eye on it to make sure the rice doesn't stick to the bottom of the pan.

Remove the pan from the heat and allow to cool for a few minutes. Meanwhile, whisk the egg yolk with a few tablespoons of the cream, then whisk this into the rice. Leave to cool completely – you can speed this up by scraping it into a bowl set in cold water. Fish out the bits of vanilla and cinnamon stick.

Whip the rest of the cream to stiff peaks. Fold it into the cold rice, then cover with plastic wrap and refrigerate until chilled.

Serve the saffron rice in pretty bowls, accompanied by caramelised orange segments and a drizzle of caramel. SERVES 6

Buttermilk ice-cream with dried fruit compote

Iranians are big consumers of dairy products – milk, cream, yoghurt and buttermilk are all enjoyed regularly. Buttermilk is not quite as well known in the West, but its faint sour tang makes for a light and refreshing ice-cream. We serve it here as a delicate accompaniment to an autumnal spiced fruit compote. Most of these dried and candied fruits are available from Middle Eastern stores or good providores.

250 ml thickened cream
150 g caster sugar
6 egg yolks
250 ml buttermilk

DRIED FRUIT COMPOTE
250 g caster sugar
250 ml water
½ cinnamon stick
2 cloves
4 cardamom pods
1 long strip orange peel, all pith removed
1 small strip lime peel, all pith removed
4 cm piece ginger, peeled and
    thinly sliced
6 slices dried apple
6 slices dried pear
6 small dried wild figs
1 candied clementine, finely diced
¼ cup currants
¼ cup golden raisins
6 fresh dates, pitted
60 g shelled walnuts, coarsely chopped

To make the ice-cream, combine the cream and half the sugar in a heavy-based saucepan over a low heat and bring to a simmer.

Whisk the egg yolks and the remaining sugar in an electric mixer until the sugar has dissolved. With the motor running, slowly pour the hot cream mixture onto the egg mixture and whisk until well combined. Pour the custard mixture back into the saucepan. Cook over a low heat for about 8 minutes, stirring frequently, or until the custard thickens enough to coat the back of a spoon. Strain into a bowl and allow to cool. When cool, stir in the buttermilk and refrigerate until cold.

Tip the cold custard into an ice-cream machine and churn according to the manufacturer's instructions. Transfer to a plastic container and freeze for up to 3 days.

To make the dried fruit compote, combine the sugar and water in a heavy-based saucepan over a low heat, stirring occasionally until the sugar dissolves. When the syrup is clear, add the spices and citrus peels, then increase the heat and bring to a boil. Add the ginger, apple, pear, figs, clementine, currants and golden raisins and simmer for 5 minutes. Remove from the heat and gently stir in the dates and walnuts. Leave to cool completely, then transfer to an airtight container and refrigerate until ready to use. The compote will keep for up to a week.

Serve the compote at room temperature, or gently warmed through, with the buttermilk ice-cream. **SERVES 6**

Rhubarb-and-rose cream with rhubarb twirls

In her lovely book *The Legendary Cuisine of Persia*, Margaret Shaida writes that the Persian word for rhubarb – reevas – means 'shining light'. Rhubarb is a plant with ancient and holy connections: Zoroastrians believe the human race emerged from the rhubarb plant, which in turn grew from supreme being Ahura Mazda's first earthly creation. Certainly, Persians make great use of it in their cooking – for both savoury khoresht and sweet sherbets – and it has important medicinal value as a digestive and as a 'cold' ingredient.

Rhubarb's tart flavour marries beautifully with sugar, orange, ginger and rosewater in this creamy dessert. Serve in pretty bowls, or set in dariole moulds and turn out. Garnish with Rhubarb Twirls or accompany with Ginger Lace Wafers (page 258).

370 g rhubarb stalks, chopped
50 ml orange juice
2 1/2 tablespoons caster sugar
1 cinnamon stick
1 vanilla pod, split and seeds scraped
150 g soft brown sugar
2 leaves titanium-grade gelatine
2 teaspoons rosewater
squeeze of lime juice
370 g thick natural yoghurt
300 ml thickened cream
molasses or caramel (optional), to garnish
1 teaspoon ground ginger

RHUBARB TWIRLS

100 g caster sugar
100 ml water
4 long rhubarb stalks, trimmed to an
    even length

Preheat the oven to 100°C and line a baking tray with baking paper. To make the rhubarb twirls, dissolve the sugar in the water in a small, heavy-based saucepan over a gentle heat, stirring from time to time. Increase the heat and bring to a boil, then remove from the heat and set aside to cool a little.

Using a vegetable peeler, slice each stalk lengthwise into wafer-thin, pink-edged ribbons. You can do this side-on or down the face of each stalk, depending on how wide you'd like your ribbons. Dip each one in the sugar syrup, then lay them out flat on the lined tray. Bake for 50–60 minutes, or until the ribbons are starting to colour a lovely golden brown. Remove a ribbon from the tray and allow to cool. If it doesn't crisp up as it cools, return the tray to the oven and cook for a further 5 minutes.

Transfer the rhubarb to a wire rack and gently twist each ribbon along its length to form long twirls. Leave to cool completely. Store in an airtight container for up to 3 days. If the twirls soften, they can be re-crisped in a warm oven.

Bring the rhubarb, orange juice, caster sugar, cinnamon stick and vanilla pod to a boil in a heavy-based saucepan over a medium heat, then cover the pan and simmer for 10 minutes, stirring from time to time. When the rhubarb has collapsed to a pulp, remove from the heat and cool for a few minutes, then push through a sieve into a measuring jug – you need about 250 ml purée.

Return the measured purée to a clean saucepan, then add the soft brown sugar and warm gently. Meanwhile, soften the gelatine leaves in cold water for 2 minutes, then squeeze dry. Stir the gelatine into the warm rhubarb, then add the rosewater and lime juice and remove from the heat. Set aside to cool completely.

Gently whisk the yoghurt and cream together. Fold in the cold rhubarb purée until evenly combined. Pour into little serving dishes or lightly oiled dariole moulds and leave to set in the refrigerator for 4–6 hours.

Turn out the creams, if using dariole moulds. Garnish with rhubarb twirls and a drizzle of molasses. SERVES 8–10

Sweet souffléed kuku with honeyed mulberries

Kukus are a hugely popular kind of savoury omelette in Iran – but sweet versions also feature. This dessert is a slightly more elaborate version, as I like to separate the whites and make a souffléed omelette. Served hot from the pan, with whipped or clotted cream, it makes a lovely wintry dessert or Sunday brunch.

You can substitute currants or raisins for the dried mulberries, if you like. Both dried mulberries and mulberry molasses can be found in Middle Eastern food stores.

50 g dried mulberries

3 tablespoons orange juice

1 tablespoon honey

splash of orange-flower water

splash of mulberry molasses (optional)

100 g plain flour

3 eggs, separated

125 ml milk

½ vanilla pod, split and seeds scraped

1 tablespoon vegetable oil

40 g unsalted butter

icing sugar

dried rosebuds, petals separated (optional)

whipped or clotted cream, to serve

Combine the mulberries, orange juice and honey in a small saucepan over a low heat until the honey dissolves. Bring to a boil, then lower the heat and simmer until the liquid has reduced by half. Take the pan off the heat and leave to cool. Stir in the orange-flower water and the molasses, if using.

Whisk the flour, egg yolks and milk to a smooth batter in a bowl. Tip in the honeyed mulberries, then add the vanilla seeds and pod and set aside to rest for 20 minutes.

Preheat the oven to 180°C. Whisk the egg whites to stiff peaks. Remove the vanilla pod from the batter. Carefully fold the batter into the egg whites – be gentle, so you don't lose volume – and make sure the mixture is evenly combined.

Heat the oil in a 20 cm heavy-based frying pan over a medium heat. Pour in the batter and leave the pan to sit, undisturbed, for 2–3 minutes. Transfer to the oven for 6–8 minutes until set, then return the pan to the stove top. Carefully turn the omelette over in the pan and use a sharp knife to cut it into wedges or squares. Dot knobs of the butter around the edges of the pan, lifting the omelette to let it melt underneath. Sprinkle on 1 tablespoon icing sugar and gently turn and toss the omelette pieces in the buttery sugar for a few minutes until lightly caramelised.

Tip onto a serving platter, dust with icing sugar and sprinkle with rose petals, if using. Serve with a bowl of whipped or clotted cream, and let everyone help themselves. **SERVES 6**

Coconut-cream flakes with toffeed mango

Many Iranian pastry shops offer a pastry selection that is distinctly French, and reflects the European influence on the country in the early nineteenth century. Profiteroles, roulades and mille-feuilles (or Napoleons) sit happily alongside Persian baklava, and are all hugely popular. Napoleons, known in Iran as cream flakes, are so highly regarded that we felt we just had to include a recipe. I've given them a tropical tweak, reflecting the sweet perfumed mangoes and coconuts that appear in markets around the Persian Gulf.

Just remember that the components for this special dessert need to be cool before you start assembling the flakes. The flakes, coconut cream and toffeed mango can all be prepared in advance – the filo-pastry flakes can be made up to three days ahead of time and stored in an airtight container – which makes serving a breeze.

COCONUT FLAKES	COCONUT CREAM FILLING	TOFFEED MANGO
50 g desiccated coconut	180 ml thickened cream	3 mangoes
8 sheets filo pastry	180 ml coconut cream	60 g unsalted butter
100 g clarified butter or ghee	60 g desiccated coconut	90 g soft brown sugar
50 g icing sugar	2 tablespoons caster sugar	juice of 1 lime
	1 tablespoon coconut rum (optional)	juice of 1 orange
		½ teaspoon vanilla extract

Preheat the oven to 180°C and line a baking tray with baking paper.

Blitz the coconut to a coarse powder in a food processor. Arrange a sheet of filo pastry on your work surface and brush it liberally with clarified butter and dust with icing sugar. Top with another 3 filo sheets, brushing and dusting with butter and sugar as you go. On the fourth and final sheet, sprinkle an even layer of coconut powder over the surface, being sure to cover it completely. Fold the filo in half lengthwise and use a 10 cm pastry cutter to cut out 6 rounds. Carefully lift the rounds onto the prepared baking tray. Repeat with the remaining 4 filo sheets, butter, icing sugar and coconut powder.

Place a sheet of baking paper on top of the 12 pastry rounds (these are the flakes), then cover with another baking tray to weigh the pastry down. Bake for 8–10 minutes, until golden brown. Carefully check after 8 minutes – the flakes may be ready. Remove the tray from the oven and set aside to cool for 5 minutes before lifting away the top tray. Lift the flakes onto a wire rack to cool completely.

To make the coconut cream filling, combine thickened and coconut cream with the desiccated coconut and sugar in a small saucepan. Bring to a boil, stirring frequently to dissolve the sugar. Remove from the heat and leave to infuse for 1 hour. Strain into the bowl of an electric mixer, squeezing the coconut to extract as much flavour as you can, then cover and chill. Stir the coconut rum, if using, into the chilled cream, then whisk to soft peaks.

To make the toffeed mango, cut the cheeks from the mangoes. Cut each cheek lengthwise into 3 wedges and carefully slice the flesh away from the skin. Melt the butter in a heavy-based frying pan over a medium heat and add the sugar. When the sugar has dissolved, increase the heat, then add the mango and fry until it begins to turn golden brown and caramelises. Add the citrus juices and vanilla extract, then tip the toffeed mango into a bowl and cover and refrigerate until ready to serve.

To assemble the coconut flakes, place a filo flake on each plate and top with a generous spoonful of coconut cream, followed by 3 mango wedges. Place another filo flake on top and drizzle with some of the mango caramel. Serve straight away. SERVES 6

Sparkling grape jelly with frosted fruit

This is our homage to the city of Shiraz, famous through the centuries for its wine grapes. These days the memory of wine lingers only in the much-loved poetry of Hafez, and local grapes are grown for the table or pressed to make juice or verjuice. This easy and lovely jelly is made from sparkling grape juice that makes the finished dish refreshing and lightly fizzy on the tongue. It is lavishly decorated with sugared fruit and we like to imagine that something similar might have been served as part of a banquet spread in the Shah Abbas's summer pavilion.

We set the jelly here in a ring mould. For an alternative, and equally stunning presentation, set the jelly in pretty glasses or glass bowls so the trapped bubbles are visible. Top with the frosted fruit, or serve it on the side.

Any tender fruit may be frosted, but always select unblemished, ripe fruit, and note that varieties with firm skin work best. Try a mixture of green and red grapes, cherries, blueberries and mandarins, perhaps. Prepare the fruit no more than three hours before serving, or the sugar will start to dissolve. You'll need to prepare the jelly the day before it's needed to ensure a good set and proportion of bubbles to jelly.

750 ml sparkling grape juice
4 leaves titanium-grade
    gelatine
juice of 1 lime, strained

FROSTED FRUITS
400 g firm-skinned soft fruit
1–2 egg whites, lightly whisked
    caster sugar

To make the jelly, pour 100 ml of the grape juice into a small saucepan and reseal the bottle tightly. Bring the juice to a gentle simmer, then remove from the heat. Meanwhile, soften the gelatine leaves in cold water for 2 minutes, then squeeze dry. Stir the gelatine into the grape juice, then pour the mixture into a large jug and stir in the strained lime juice. Leave to cool for 15 minutes. At the same time, chill a jelly ring mould in the freezer.

Pour the remaining sparkling grape juice into the gelatine mixture, taking care not to let it fizz too much, otherwise you'll lose the precious bubbles. Stir very gently to combine, then carefully pour into the chilled mould. Return the mould to the freezer for 20 minutes, then transfer to the fridge to set, nudging the mould every now and then to create more bubbles. Leave at least overnight, which also allows the bubbles to develop.

To make the frosted fruits, line a baking tray with baking paper. Brush each fruit lightly with egg white and sprinkle liberally with caster sugar until evenly coated. Leave to dry on the lined tray.

When ready to serve, briefly dip the base of the jelly mould in hot water. Loosen the edge with a small knife, then carefully invert onto an attractive serving plate and shake gently to release. Mound the frosted fruits in the central cavity and serve any extra fruit on the side. **SERVES 6**

Noon khameii
PROFITEROLES WITH THICK FIG CREAM

The joy of profiteroles is that you can make them as fancy – or as simple – as you please. Sweetened whipped cream perfumed with rosewater or with a spoonful of good homemade jam stirred through it would be almost as lovely as this thick fig cream. Fill the profiteroles at the last moment to stop the pastry going soggy.

3 teaspoons ground cinnamon
1½ tablespoons caster sugar

THICK FIG CREAM
150 g dried figs, roughly chopped
50 g caster sugar
200 ml water
juice of ½ lemon
300 ml thickened cream, chilled
2 tablespoons thick natural yoghurt
¼ cup icing sugar
lemon or orange juice (optional)

CHOUX PASTRY
75 ml water
75 ml milk
70 g unsalted butter
80 g plain flour, sifted
3 eggs
zest of ½ lemon
½ teaspoon ground cinnamon

To make the thick fig cream, bring the figs, caster sugar, water and lemon juice to a boil in a small, heavy-based saucepan over a medium heat. Lower the heat and simmer gently for about 15 minutes, or until the figs break down to a paste. Cool for a few minutes, then whiz to a smooth purée in a food processor. Set aside until ready to serve, but don't refrigerate.

Whip the cream, yoghurt and icing sugar to medium-stiff peaks, then chill until ready to use.

To make the choux pastry, preheat the oven to 180°C. Line baking trays with baking paper. Combine the water, milk and butter in a heavy-based saucepan over a medium heat until the butter melts, then bring to a boil. Add the flour all at once and beat vigorously with a wooden spoon until the dough comes together as a smooth paste. Lower the heat and continue beating until the paste thickens and dries and comes away from the sides of the pan in a ball.

Tip the choux pastry into the bowl of an electric mixer fitted with a K-beater and leave to cool for a minute. With the mixer on low speed, add the eggs, one at a time, ensuring that each is thoroughly incorporated before you add the next. Continue beating until you have a smooth, stiff paste. Briefly beat in the lemon zest and cinnamon.

Spoon heaped tablespoons of the choux pastry onto the prepared baking trays, leaving about 5 cm between each one to allow for expansion – you should get 24 profiteroles. Bake for 10 minutes, then decrease the heat to 140°C and bake for a further 15–20 minutes, or until the profiteroles are puffed and golden. Transfer to a wire rack and pierce the side of each profiterole to release the hot air – this stops them going soggy.

When ready to serve, take the chilled cream out of the fridge and loosely fold in the fig paste. If the paste is very stiff, loosen it first with a little lemon or orange juice. Use a sharp knife to cut the tops off the profiteroles and fill each with a generous spoonful of the cream, then replace the tops. Mix the cinnamon with the caster sugar and dust on the profiteroles. Serve straight away with a cup of tea or coffee or as a dessert, with fresh berries. MAKES 24

Zoolbia
CRUNCHY FRITTERS WITH SPICED SUGAR

These light-as-air, delicate spiral fritters are well known as jalebi in Indian sweet shops and in other parts of the Middle East as mushabek. Traditionally they are dropped straight from the hot oil into a sugar syrup, and become sticky and translucent. We prefer to dust them with a spiced sugar, as this way they retain their crispness and are less tooth-achingly sweet.

Some batter recipes call for bicarbonate of soda as a leavening agent but we prefer the texture and flavour yeast provides. This batter holds up really well, and if you leave it to stand overnight, the flavours develop beautifully. Serve the fritters as a sweet treat or with fried bananas and maple syrup for breakfast.

120 g icing sugar
50 g ground pistachios
½ teaspoon ground cardamom
vegetable oil for deep-frying

FRITTER BATTER
175 g plain flour
1 tablespoon dried yeast
250 ml warm water
75 g thick natural yoghurt
2 tablespoons Saffron Liquid (page 54)
pinch of sea salt

Combine the icing sugar, pistachios and cardamom well and store in an airtight jar until ready to use.

To make the batter, sift the flour into a bowl. Sprinkle on the yeast, then whisk in the warm water and yoghurt to form a batter. Stir in the saffron liquid and salt, then cover and leave to stand for at least 2 hours or up to 12 hours.

Pour vegetable oil into a small, deep, heavy-based saucepan to a depth of 5 cm. Heat the oil to 190°C. If you don't have a candy thermometer, the oil will have reached temperature when it is shimmering, and when a blob of batter sizzles up to the surface in a few seconds.

Pour the batter into a piping bag fitted with a narrow nozzle, or into a plastic squeezy bottle. Pipe the batter into the oil, working from the centre outwards in a spiral. Use the size of the saucepan as the template for your fritter size. Don't worry if you do not make a perfect spiral, as a free-form, lacy effect is just as pretty. Cook for 1–2 minutes, moving the fritter in the hot oil with a slotted spoon so it colours evenly. Once the batter has set, turn it over in the oil to colour. Lift the fritter out of the oil with a slotted spoon and drain on paper towels for a moment. Repeat with the remaining batter. Dust the spiced sugar over the fritters and enjoy with a cup of strong coffee or tea. **MAKES ABOUT 15**

Baghlava
PERSIAN BAKLAVA WITH ROSE–LIME SYRUP

Every country in the Middle East and Eastern Mediterranean does its own thing with baklava, small, nutty pastries drenched in a lightly perfumed sugar syrup. Some versions favour ground pistachios as a filling, others prefer ground almonds or walnuts. Sometimes a touch of cinnamon is included with the nuts, or honey is added to the syrup.

Persian baklava is particularly delicious, and the preference is for ground almonds scented with cardamom, with the whole thing soaked in a light rosewater syrup. Some versions comprise two layers: a base of almond, topped with a pretty green pistachio layer. Here, we keep it simple, but the addition of a little lime juice to the syrup helps balance the intense sweetness of the baklava. Serve in small amounts; it is extremely rich.

clarified butter
300 g ground almonds
200 g caster sugar
2 teaspoons ground cardamom
6 sheets filo pastry
3 tablespoons pistachio slivers
   (optional)
dried rose petals (optional)

ROSE–LIME SYRUP
300 g caster sugar
150 ml water
2 tablespoons rosewater
1 tablespoon lime juice

To make the rose–lime syrup, dissolve the caster sugar in the water in a small, heavy-based saucepan over a gentle heat, swirling the pan from time to time. Increase the heat and simmer for 10 minutes until the syrup thickens. Remove the pan from the heat and allow to cool for 5 minutes before stirring in the rosewater and lime juice. Set aside.

Preheat the oven to 180ºC and brush a 28 cm x 18 cm baking tin with clarified butter. To make the filling, combine the ground almonds, sugar and cardamom in a bowl.

Take a sheet of filo and position it with the long side facing you. Brush the filo with clarified butter and fold it in half from left to right. Line the prepared tin with the pastry (it should be a close fit) and brush with a little more clarified butter. Repeat with 2 more sheets of filo. Use a sharp knife to trim the layers to fit the base of the tin neatly.

Tip the almond filling into the tin and use your fingers to press it in evenly and firmly. Butter another layer of filo and fold in half, as before, then brush with clarified butter and place it, buttered-side down, on top of the filling. Brush with a little more clarified butter and repeat with the remaining 2 sheets of filo. Finally, brush the top layer of pastry with more butter. Trim the edges neatly.

Cut the baklava on the diagonal into small diamond shapes with a sharp knife – you should end up with about 30 pieces. Make sure you cut right through to the bottom, and try to avoid moving the top pastry layers. Sprinkle the surface with a few drops of water and bake for 15 minutes. Check that the pastry is not browning too quickly; if it is, cover loosely with aluminium foil. Bake for a further 15 minutes, or until golden brown.

Remove from the oven and immediately drizzle the rose–lime syrup over the baklava, allowing it to seep into all the cuts. If you like, garnish with pistachio slivers or rose petals, then set aside to cool.

When completely cold, cover tightly with aluminium foil and store in a cool place until ready to serve. The baklava will keep in the refrigerator for up to a week. Return to room temperature before serving with black tea or as an after-dinner treat with strong black coffee. MAKES 30

Hazelnut–orange shortbreads

Tiny melt-in-your mouth cookies are popular in Iran – and around the entire Middle Eastern region. Some are made with rice or chickpea flour, some with wheat flour, while others incorporate finely ground nuts, but all use a high ratio of butter or ghee to give that crisp, melting 'shortness'. Iranian versions are usually flavoured with cardamom, but for a change I think hazelnut and orange work beautifully together. Perfect with a cup of tea at any time.

80 g icing sugar
110 g clarified butter or ghee
100 g plain flour, sifted
¼ cup self-raising flour, sifted
50 g roasted hazelnuts, finely ground
grated zest of 1 orange

Mix the icing sugar with the clarified butter thoroughly. Fold the remaining ingredients into the butter mixture deftly and thoroughly but take care not to overwork the mixture. The dough will be very soft, but if it feels too wet add a little more flour.

Tip the dough onto a sheet of plastic wrap and divide in half. Roll each portion into a log about 3 cm in diameter. Wrap each log in plastic wrap and twist the ends tightly. Refrigerate for 10 minutes or so to firm the dough.

Preheat the oven to 150°C. Line a baking tray with baking paper.

Use a sharp knife to cut each log into slices about 1 cm thick. Arrange on the prepared baking tray and bake for 15–20 minutes, or until the biscuits are just starting to colour and feel a bit firm to the touch.

Cool the shortbreads on the tray for a few minutes, then carefully lift onto a wire rack and leave until completely cold. They will keep in an airtight container for a week. **MAKES 24**

Walnut and candied-clementine orange cake

Moist enough to be served as dessert with softly whipped cream, or as a treat with tea or coffee, this cake was created by Odette Martini, a wonderful pastry chef and friend. It is an adaptation of the popular Middle Eastern boiled orange and almond cake, made famous by Claudia Roden, but instead combines walnuts with citrus fruit – both of which grow abundantly in the north of Iran. The addition of candied clementines (available from good providores and Middle Eastern food stores) gives a mild, but pleasing, bitter edge to the cake.

This is a flat, moist cake, not a high-risen, airy one, so it is surprisingly quick to bake.

500 g oranges, washed
4 candied clementines
75 g shelled walnuts, finely ground
½ teaspoon ground cardamom
½ teaspoon ground fennel
½ teaspoon baking powder
2 eggs
75 g caster sugar

Remove any little stems still attached to the oranges. Put them into a saucepan with enough cold water to cover. Bring to a boil, then lower the heat, cover and simmer for 1–1½ hours, or until the oranges are very soft when you pierce them with a skewer. Leave the oranges to cool in the liquid, then cut them into quarters and remove any pips. Blitz the oranges and 2 of the candied clementines to a purée in a food processor. Scrape into a large bowl and set aside.

Preheat the oven to 150°C and grease a 24 cm x 20 cm cake tin and line it with baking paper. In a bowl, combine the ground walnuts, cardamom, fennel and baking powder.

Whisk the eggs and caster sugar in an electric mixer for 10 minutes, or until pale and fluffy. Stir the egg mixture into the orange purée, then gently fold in the dry ingredients. Pour the batter into the prepared tin – it should be a very shallow layer – and bake for 25–30 minutes. The cake should be golden brown and feel lightly springy to the touch.

Remove from the oven and leave to cool completely in the tin. Turn out carefully when cold, then cover tightly with plastic wrap and refrigerate until ready to serve. Cut into squares, decorate with slices of the remaining candied clementines and serve with thick or softly whipped cream. SERVES 12

Sohan
PISTACHIO-ROSE BRITTLE

We saw several different kinds of toffee and nut brittles on our journeys around Iran, some flavoured with cardamom, others with honey, still others with saffron. This is my version of a thin, crunchy pistachio brittle, and I've added a sprinkling of exotic rose petals, just for fun.

This recipe produces a fairly large quantity, but it's a little tricky to make in small amounts. Anyway, brittles are incredibly versatile as you can serve them as is, or crush them to make a crunchy praline topping for desserts or ice-creams (keep a bag of it in the freezer for instant gratification). You'll power through it in no time!

200 g unsalted shelled pistachios
330 g caster sugar
80 ml corn syrup
50 g unsalted butter
125 ml water
½ teaspoon bicarbonate of soda
pinch of sea salt
grated zest of 1 orange
1½ teaspoons ground cardamom
10 dried rosebuds, petals separated

Preheat the oven to 160°C. Roast the pistachios on a baking tray for 10–12 minutes, shaking the tray frequently. You don't want them to colour, just to dry out a little. Tip into a bowl and cool.

Line a baking tray with baking paper. Combine the caster sugar, corn syrup, butter and water in a heavy-based saucepan over a low heat until the sugar dissolves. Increase the heat, then bring to a boil and cook over a medium heat for 15–20 minutes until the mixture is a light golden caramel – if using a candy thermometer, at 160°C it will be approaching the hard-crack stage. Remove from the heat and immediately stir in the bicarbonate of soda, salt, zest, cardamom and pistachios.

Scrape the mixture onto the prepared baking tray and use a spatula to smooth it out as thinly as you can. Sprinkle with rose petals, if using, pressing them gently into the surface of the brittle. Leave to cool completely before breaking into pieces with a rolling pin. **MAKES 500 G**

Sohan-e Qom
CARDAMOM–PISTACHIO BUTTER FUDGE FROM QOM

This wickedly buttery, cardamom-scented sweet is from the religious city of Qom, about an hour south of Tehran, and is famous all around Iran. The texture is hard to define – it is perhaps closer to fudge than brittle or toffee – but it is absolutely addictive.

Make in one large slab, and cut or break into random pieces, or drop spoonfuls of the mixture onto the prepared tray to make individual round portions. The high butter content means it can 'sweat' a little bit, so store it in a cool place in an airtight tin, rather than a plastic container. It will keep well for up to two weeks.

500 g caster sugar
80 ml corn syrup
80 ml water
300 g unsalted butter, roughly diced
2 teaspoons ground cardamom
2 tablespoons Saffron Liquid (page 54)
50 g unsalted shelled pistachios
50 g slivered pistachios

Line a baking tray with baking paper. Combine the sugar, corn syrup and water in a heavy-based saucepan over a low heat until the sugar dissolves. Increase the heat and cook until the mixture begins to become golden in colour, then whisk in the butter, cardamom and saffron liquid and cook for a few minutes more, until an even butterscotch colour.

Pour the mixture onto the prepared baking tray and use a spatula to smooth it out as thinly as you can. Sprinkle on the pistachios, pressing them gently into the surface of the toffee. Leave to cool completely before cutting into pieces with a sharp knife. MAKES 650 G

Gaz
PISTACHIO–SOUR CHERRY NOUGAT

We were in Isfahan a week or so before Persian New Year and the local gaz – nougat –shops were doing a roaring trade as all households need to have vast supplies on hand to dispense during the endless socialising that takes place at this time of year. We enjoyed sampling several different styles: some were set firmer and were chock-full of almonds or pistachios, others were soft and a little bit squidgy and came drenched in cornflour that erupted in a white cloud on eating.

To be honest, making nougat at home is hard work, and you do need basic confectionery skills and a candy thermometer. But the result is so gorgeous – and delicious – that we felt it was well worth including a recipe. We strongly recommend you read the method through carefully to be sure of the timing. It's important to have everything ready to go – no scrambling around at the last minute for a forgotten ingredient or implement – and imperative that you warm the fruit and nuts before adding them to the nougat mixture. Be organised and you'll be rewarded!

We've used pistachios and dried sour cherries here, but have also used similar quantities of roasted and chopped hazelnuts and chopped dried apricots to great effect. Candied fruit or barberries would work well with pistachios too. By all means experiment with any other pairing that you think will complement the sweetness of the nougat.

If you can resist eating it yourself, gaz makes a lovely gift. Look for edible rice paper – widely available now, including from good supermarkets – which makes for neater presentation and easier serving.

140 g unsalted shelled pistachios, roughly chopped
250 g dried sour cherries, roughly chopped
50 g (2–3) egg whites, at room temperature
380 g caster sugar
120 g liquid glucose
100 ml water
230 g honey

Preheat the oven to 110°C. Scatter the pistachios and dried cherries onto a baking tray and put them into the oven to warm while you make the nougat. It's important that the nuts and dried fruit are warm when added to the nougat mixture, or it will seize up and be unworkable.

Prepare all the ingredients: put the egg whites into the bowl of an electric mixer fitted with a whisk; put the sugar, liquid glucose and water into a saucepan; put the honey into another small saucepan. Line a baking tray with edible rice paper or baking paper.

Begin cooking the honey over a medium heat and measure the temperature with a candy thermometer. When the temperature reaches 108°C, begin whisking the egg whites on medium–high speed. Continue cooking the honey until it reaches 120°C, by which time the egg whites should have reached the stiff-peak stage. Turn off the mixer and take the honey off the heat.

Now begin gently heating the sugar, glucose and water until the sugar has dissolved, then increase the heat and bring to a boil.

Meanwhile, turn the electric mixer back on to a low speed and mix the hot honey into the egg whites. When incorporated, increase the speed to high.

Continue whisking until the boiling sugar syrup reaches 155°C. Slow the speed of the mixer down again and pour in the boiling sugar syrup slowly and carefully until incorporated. Increase the speed of the mixer again and whisk for 3 minutes.

Turn off the mixer and, working quickly, take the warm fruit and nuts out of the oven and tip them into the nougat. Fold in by hand as quickly as you can, then scrape into the prepared baking tray. Smooth out the nougat with a large, strong spatula to a rough rectangle, about 3 cm deep – don't try to make it fit the shape of the tray. The nougat will be very stiff to work with, but try to make the surface as even as possible; use a rolling pin if you like. Cover with a second sheet of rice paper or baking paper. Rest overnight, then cut into portions and store in an airtight container. **MAKES 750 G**

Roasted dates in coffee syrup

The intrinsic toffee-sweetness of dates marries beautifully with bitter coffee. This is a simple way of turning fresh dates (or even less-luscious out-of-season dates) into a delectable after-dinner sweetmeat.

12 large fresh dates, pitted
125 ml orange juice
125 ml strong black coffee
1 tablespoon soft brown sugar
2 long strips orange peel, all pith removed
1 cinnamon stick
½ teaspoon cardamom seeds, ground
40 g unsalted butter, chilled and diced

Preheat the oven to 180°C. Arrange the dates in a small ovenproof dish, just large enough to fit them and the remaining ingredients comfortably.

Bring the orange juice, coffee, sugar, peel, cinnamon stick and cardamom to a boil in a small saucepan over a medium heat, then pour over the dates.

Roast the dates for 10–12 minutes, basting frequently. Remove from the oven and leave to cool a little in the syrup. When cool enough to handle, carefully peel the dates and put into a small, deep dish or bowl.

Strain the syrup back into a clean saucepan. Bring to a boil, then lower the heat and simmer until reduced by half. Whisk in the chilled butter to make a glossy sauce and spoon over the dates.

Serve straight away with ice-cream as a simple dessert. Alternatively, cover and refrigerate and serve as a treat with tea or coffee. MAKES 12

Apricot sweets

There are various kinds of apricot sweets in the Middle East, some stuffed with thick clotted cream, others with chopped nuts, but they all rely on using good-quality dried apricots. These are incredibly simple to make – just a whiz in the food processor and a bit of gentle rolling by hand. Don't soak the apricots first, and make sure they are completely dry before blitzing. As a variation, try mixing the paste with coarsely chopped pistachios, or use desiccated coconut instead of caster sugar when rolling the mixture into balls.

500 g dried apricots
squeeze of lemon juice (optional)
icing sugar

Put the dried apricots into a food processor and whiz to a smooth paste. If the mixture seems very dry, add a squeeze of lemon juice to help it bind.

Scrape the paste out onto a work surface and with wet or lightly oiled hands, roll into balls the size of a large marble. Roll in icing sugar and serve straight away with tea or coffee. Alternatively, store in an airtight container and roll in icing sugar just before serving. **MAKES 24**

Toot
WHITE 'MULBERRIES'

Almond sweetmeats are popular all around the Middle East. In Iran they are shaped, rather charmingly, into little mulberries, with a bright-green pistachio sliver forming the stem. They are popular at any time, but especially over Persian New Year.

125 g ground almonds
160 g icing sugar
½ teaspoon cardamom seeds, finely
    ground
2–3 tablespoons rosewater or
    orange-flower water
caster sugar
slivered pistachios

Combine the ground almonds, icing sugar and cardamom in a bowl. Add the rosewater to taste and use your hands to work the mixture to a paste. Don't worry if it seems very stiff and crumbly; as you knead, the almonds will release their oil and the mixture will bind to a soft dough.

Take small teaspoons of the dough and shape into long, elegant mulberries. Stick pistachio slivers into the ends to create little stems. Arrange on a platter and serve with tea or coffee. Alternatively, store in an airtight container. **MAKES 40**

rangin

'ISFAHAN NISF-A JAHAN', GOES THE FAMOUS HALF-RHYME: 'ISFAHAN IS HALF THE WORLD.'
There is nowhere more associated with the refined glories of persia than isfahan in central Iran, and to this day it is considered by many to be the country's most beautiful city. I've been dreaming of its legendary bridges, tea houses, mosques and palaces for many months now, ever since we began making plans for a Persian adventure, and at last we are here, standing on the impressive balcony of the Ali Qapu Palace, high above the Maidan-e Naqsh-e Jahan, gazing down at the monuments to a former Shah's glory.

Isfahan had a speedy and spectacular rise to fame. It was always a bustling provincial trading town, but in the sixteenth century it fell to the Safavids, and Shah Abbas I, Persia's most celebrated ruler, decided to make it his capital. Over thirty-two years he poured money and manpower into making Isfahan one of the most gorgeous cities in the world.

We had read about the immense Maidan (or Imam Square, as it is officially called these days), but it is only now that we are here, with it stretched out beneath us, that we can fully appreciate how vast it really is. Shah Abbas wanted the square to be the focal point of his new capital, and from the palace's huge yet elegant balcony, with its carved wooden ceiling, ornamental pool and slender columns, he would have sat with his entourage, looking down at military parades, polo matches, public festivals and all the daily business of the city.

He would also have gazed upon the three new jewels of his empire: the monumental Qeysarieh Gate at the distant northern end of the square, with the sprawling bazaar beyond; the massive blue portal of the Royal Mosque (now the Imam Mosque) that rises at the southern end, and, directly opposite, the pretty little dome of the Sheikh Lutfollah Mosque, built for the Shah's own family, and connected to the palace, say some, by a secret passage beneath the square itself. It would be lovely to linger here, enjoying the view and the sunshine, but we still have half the world to see.

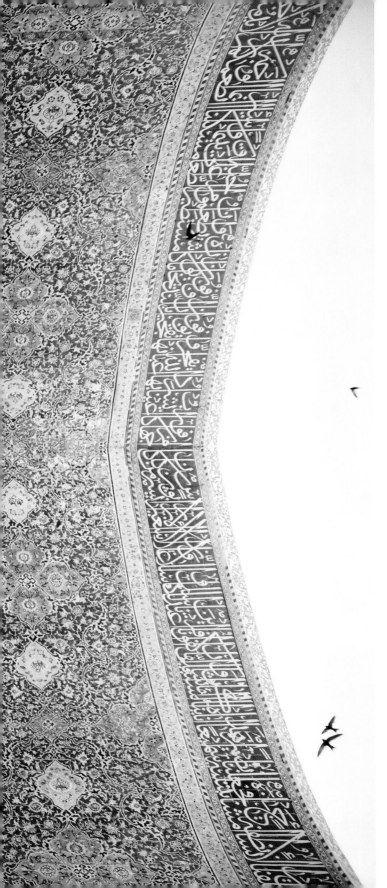

Yas has a morning of culture planned, so we stride off after her to the Imam Mosque, the grandest of all the Safavid momunents. From the balcony of the Ali Qapu Palace we were able to see that the entrance portal fronts directly onto the square but that the dome, minarets and complex of buildings behind are skewed to the right, so as to orient them, as is proper, towards Mecca.

/

Now we follow Yas through the mosque's cool entrance chamber into the light-filled central courtyard. An ablution pool in the middle is surrounded by double-storeyed arcades. Four vast portals – iwans – are spaced symmetrically around, each leading to a prayer hall or sanctuary. The first impression is of grandeur: a sense of space and sun and emptiness. There are no trees or other vegetation in the courtyard, but on the walls around us a glazed garden of leaves and flowers tumbles over every surface.

/

Yas leads us onward, and we wind our way through arcades and arches and lofty chambers, each awash with colour and movement. I think of Vita Sackville-West, who visited the city in the 1920s, and wrote, ' In sixteenth century Isfahan, Persians were building out of light itself, taking the turquoise from the sky, the green of the spring trees, the yellow of the sun, the brown of the earth, the black of their sheep and turning these into solid light.' And here it is, this 'solid light', all around us.

/

WE CUT ACROSS THE CORNER OF THE Maidan to the Sheikh Lutfollah Mosque, the first of the new monuments that Shah Abbas built here, and named after his father-in-law, a revered Shiite scholar. From a distance, the Lutfollah dome is small and elegant; it announces its presence discreetly. But we soon realise that this restraint draws the eye back, again and again. Instead of the familiar turquoise of most Persian mosques, the Lutfollah dome is a soft, milky-coffee colour inset with a tracery of black and white arabesques and the occasional splash of azure blue that sparkles when the sun catches it. It doesn't compete with the larger, more vibrantly hued dome of the nearby Imam Mosque; instead it complements it perfectly.

/

Here there is no courtyard, no iwans nor vast prayer halls. Instead, there is just one intimate chamber at the end of a twisting, dimly lit passageway. After the sun and space of the Maidan, our eyes take time to adjust

and only slowly do we make sense of our surroundings. Latticed windows set high around the base of the dome diffuse the light softly, and we realise that every surface is clothed in colour. There are blues – every conceivable shade of blue – and greens and yellows and even some gold and white and black. We move closer to appreciate more fully the intense, complex, intricate detail. Wherever we turn, our eyes are drawn to endless swirling variations of letter and leaf, flower and twisting tendril, which all seem to shimmer and change in the light.

/

Hovering overhead is a shallow dome inlaid with delicate, diminishing, lemon-shaped lozenges that draw the eye ever upward. As I move beneath it, the sun pierces the apex and a single beam of light spills down the side; all at once it becomes the fanned tail of a radiant peacock.

/

I think it is here, inside this lovely prayer room, that I am at last beginning to grasp the intention of the great Islamic designers with their emphasis on pattern and order and on elusive, constantly changing beauty. It's to remind us, of course, that God is at the centre of a divinely ordered universe that we mortals can never entirely grasp nor understand. I stop trying to analyse what I'm looking at or to work out where it all begins and ends. I feel my heart constrict as I gaze around and up and, finally, I allow my mind to surrender and float free.

/

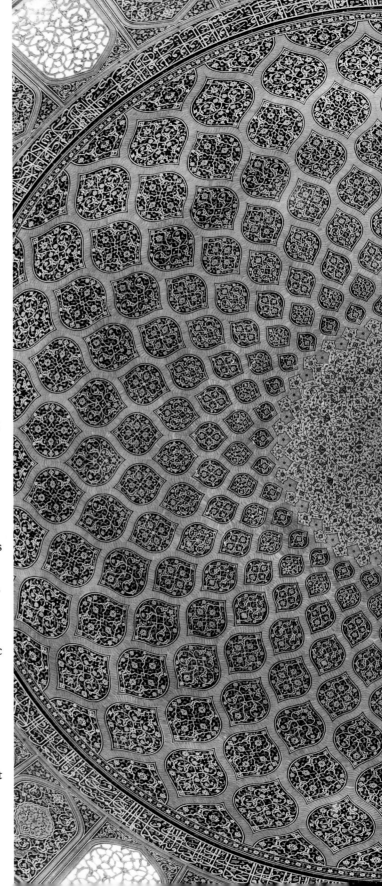

But in isfahan it's not all geometry and mathematical precision and abstract beauty. The frescoed walls of the Chehul Sotun Palace suggest that the Safavids were just as interested in the pleasures of the flesh as of the soul, and they were certainly less bound by the strictures of Islam than today's government.

/

Chehul Sotun – the Palace of Forty Pillars – was built as a glittering summer pavilion within lovely gardens that stretch back to the Maidan. In fact, there are only twenty slender columns supporting the exquisite inlaid verandah ceiling, but reflected in the still water of a long pool there appear to be forty.

/

The great interior hall was once a banqueting chamber, where visiting dignitaries, diplomats and adventurers from China, India and Europe were entertained in lavish style. The walls are adorned with vibrant scenes from Safavid life; celebrations of razm o bazm – fighting and feasting – enjoyed, it seems, with equal alacrity. Some paintings portray famous battles and historic scenes, others depict languid picnics and lavish feasts. Despite the Islamic prohibition of alcohol, wine features prominently in many of the paintings: it's poured from elegant jewelled flasks into tiny bowls that are passed between casually touching hands or raised to lovers' lips. The walls are alive with colour and movement and tell a thousand scandalous tales. Guests recline on gorgeous brocaded cloths spread with sweetmeats and exotic fruits and are entertained by musicians and sloe-eyed dancing girls. Here a falcon perches on an embroidered sleeve; there, a slender hand slips beneath silken skirts, and, elsewhere, a pale-faced eunuch collapses in a drunken stupor. What indulgence! What life!

/

Soft-boiled eggs and huge flaps of bread, straight from the baker's oven. Conserves of sour cherry, sweet orange and cinnamon-spiked apple. Thick clotted cream and honey dripping from the comb. Hot milk, fresh white cheese, soft chewy dates and tiny dried wild figs. I think I'd be happy to eat this way every morning for the rest of my life.

/

We have breakfasted early and now we are slipping through a vast sprawling network of alleyways in the old part of Isfahan – we are headed for the Grand Bazaar. The shutters are rattling up and we feel the world come alive around us. Part of the enjoyment of visiting the bazaar is the sense of uncertainty, of not quite knowing what you're going to find around the next corner. Before long the streets are thick with shoppers and we emerge from the clamour and chaos and find ourselves at the entry to the old Jameh Mosque.

/

As we watch pedestrians bustle in and out of the mosque, we are reminded that mosques are a focal point of a community and that they are always located close to the main centre of commerce. Here in Iran, religion is an integral part of daily life and the mosques are far more than just places to come and pray. Instead, people treat them as a kind of community centre; they are places to meet friends, do business, study, relax, eat – even sleep.

/

Isfahanis have been doing all these things in the Jameh Mosque – the main congregrational mosque used for Friday prayers in every district across Iran – for nearly eight hundred years. We follow an old man with a bag of shopping into the sunny central courtyard. A group of mothers sits on the edge of a stone pool as their children run through the pigeons, sending them swirling off in a flurry of beating wings.

/

We move from iwan to iwan, admiring the mosaic façades, elaborate mouldings and intricately carved stonework. And then we find ourselves inside, drifting through a forest of columns in a series of connecting, low-ceilinged halls. After the exuberant, colourful opulence of the Safavid mosques in the Maidan, these internal chambers of the Jameh Mosque feel dark, strangely gloomy and subdued. But as our eyes begin to adjust we realise that this is precisely the point. Instead of colour, here the impact comes from pattern and texture. Instead of multi-coloured tiles, here small brown bricks are arranged in a seemingly infinite variety of designs. It is strangely moving, a kind of austere, ancient beauty. A beauty of simplicity and restraint.

/

There is little restraint on display at the Kemani gaz (nougat) shop, where the crowds are ten-deep and clamouring for boxes of the delectably soft sweet treat. Unlike the other customers, we haven't ordered, so have to wait patiently in line. Yas tells us that this is the busiest time of year for Isfahan's famous nougat shops, as families buy-up in vast quantities to serve to guests over the New Year's holiday. There is a four-kilo limit per customer, yet the shop is jam-packed with entire families, hedging their bets. We are impressed to learn that the price of gaz ranges from four to fifty US dollars a kilogram, depending on the ratio of pistachios used. We restrict ourselves to several boxes of the less-expensive varieties as well as another local specialty – poolaki – that turns out to be wafers of hard toffee in flavours such as coconut, lemon, saffron and sesame.

/

Clasping our goody-boxes tightly, we squeeze out of the shop and Yaz leads us to a nearby tea house to recover. The Azadegan Tea House is tucked away in a narrow alley off the north-eastern corner of the Maidan, and is well-known for its eccentric decoration. We enter through a cramped doorway into a smoke-filled narrow room, lined on either side with banquette seating and tables. This is the men-only section, and as we pass through, a few old men glance up briefly before settling back to the business of their water pipes.

/

Suspended from the low ceiling along the length of the room is an extraordinary collection of smoking paraphernalia, tea pots, lampshades, brass bells and, what can really only be called junk. The walls are crammed with framed black and white photographs from some distant era. We can make out long-dead war-heros, mullahs, politicians, dignitaries and strong-men from a local zurkhane, a traditional Persian 'house of strength'.

/

We pass into the neighbouring room – the family section – and collapse gratefully at a vacant table. A waiter arrives promptly and Yas orders the house specialty, a delicate syrup-soaked pastry known as goosh-e feel, or elephant's ears, because of their shape. 'Really you should drink dugh with this sweet,' she tells us, but we all opt, instead, for hot, fragrant chai. Slowly the hot tea and sugary pastry work their magic, and soon we are able to gather our strength and head back out into the world to our next destination.

/

A NIPPY WIND HAS SPRUNG UP BY THE TIME WE REACH THE MARTYR'S Cemetery on the outskirts of the city. It's Thursday afternoon, and all around the country businesses are closing for the weekend. Thursday evenings and Fridays are the key times for families to visit the graves of soldiers killed in the war with Iraq, and it is a ritual that holds particular significance for Isfahanis, who lost around thirty-six thousand men during those eight terrible years.

/

We trail through a sea of Iranian flags that flutter in the breeze over the endless rows of graves. Each is crowned with a photograph of its occupant: there are young boys, scarcely more than children, and teenagers sporting wispy moustaches and 1980s hair-dos. Older men – but still only in their twenties or thirties – are thickly bearded. They all gaze out with the same implacable, clear-eyed certainty.

/

Yas clutches her shawl tightly and shivers, while Ebi wanders off on his own. It's a rare Iranian family that is untouched by a war that gained nothing and cost more than a million lives to Iran alone. Those who come here to mourn consider martyrdom an honour, and some visit every week to sit at the graves of their loved ones. But it is quiet in the cemetery this afternoon. Solitary mourners sit in silent contemplation or murmur verses from the Koran, and a few old women busy themselves with sweeping graves and watering flowers.

/

Ebi rejoins us and is looking sour. 'This mourning, this grief, it is so much part of being Iranian,' he says. 'Sometimes I think it is more important to us than anything else.'

/

On the way out we pass a family heating a pot of soup on a portable stove. They offer us a plate of sweets and Yas explains that this is nazri – offerings of food that are distributed in memory of the departed, and a vital part of the Islamic culture. By sharing nazri, the memories and the burden and the respect are shared by the community.

/

Yas points out a small child, skipping happily around her mother's knees and says to Ebi, 'I don't think the younger generation wants to think about war. They don't seem to have the energy to visit cemeteries these days. By the time this one grows up, I wonder, will anyone care anymore?'.

/

WE AMBLE ALONG THE EMBANKMENT OF THE ZAYANDEH
River in the cold, late-afternoon sunshine, admiring
the famous Safavid bridges that span its waters in single-
and doublearched tiers. It is too early in the year for the
famous river tea houses to open for business, and we
have also heard that, one by one, they are being closed
down, ostensibly because tobacco smoke from the
ever-popular water pipes is damaging the stonework.
Other people have told us that the closures are part of
the current government's continuing efforts to minimise
opportunities for young men and women to socialise.

The Khaju Bridge is, nonetheless, crowded with
pedestrians and as we duck in and out of the arches we
pass several groups of teenagers lounging in the alcoves,
listening to loud Iranian pop music and smoking water
pipes. A little further along, at the sound of our footsteps,
a young couple slips deeper into the shadows. And now
we join a small crowd that is gathering around a solo
singer. He is young, but the words and melody are
ancient. We pause for a while to listen, and the wind
catches the mournful notes and casts them out over the
rippling water.

But the afternoon is drawing to a close. This will be our
last evening in Isfahan and there is one final thing we
must do before we leave.

IT IS THE GOLDEN HOUR. THE TIME between day and night that photographers love so much, when the world is bathed in a magical light. Greg and I have returned to the Maidan for one last time, for one last glass of chai.

/

Up a narrow flight of stairs next to the Qeysarieh Gate is a tea house. Overlooking the Maidan, its balcony is empty now except for the two of us sitting quietly with our tea and sweet wafers as we wait for nightfall. It feels like a secret, peaceful place, in contrast to the bustling shoppers going about their evening business in the bazaar below. We gaze for a while at the distant elegant columns of the Ali Qapu Palace, and the domes and minarets of the city's glorious mosques, luminous in the fading light. From somewhere near by the plangent wail of evening prayer call begins and the city lights start to twinkle.

/

THERE IS BOTH PLEASURE AND PAIN IN THESE LAST PRECIOUS MOMENTS, AND now that we are going home I can hardly bear to think that we may never return here. Our journeying has given us tantalising glimpses into worlds both ancient and modern. But we have found that they are elusive dream worlds that seem to shift and change uneasily before our eyes. The beauty of this place – this country, these people – is that it steals up on you, then settles inside, as precious golden memories, that leave you yearning for more. But it's a disquieting beauty, too – capricious, intoxicating, baffling – and we are left with feelings of profound sadness as well as intense joy.

/

We know full-well that in the few months we have travelled here we cannot possibly hope to understand a country as subtle, tangled and complex as Iran, and yet we have experienced and learned more than we could ever have hoped for, thanks to the unquestioning, boundless generosity of our new Iranian friends. Of one thing we are certain, the experiences shared here will inform our lives – forever.

/

Now the moon is rising higher behind the dome of the Sheikh Lutfollah Mosque. Soon the square will empty of traffic and people and the grand buildings will be washed in silver. All colour and detail will be bleached away, and all that will remain will be darkness and light. And beyond the reaches of the great city square, where the houses, gardens, roads and mountains roll out to meet the approaching night, the country will sink slowly into shadow.

/

It is time for us to leave.

/

Seize the day, for the world is fleeting
In the eyes of the wise, the moment
is better than the whole world.

ISFAHAN, SIXTEENTH CENTURY

preserves

PERSIANS HAVE A VERY SWEET tooth – *and* a very sour tooth! To satisfy both these needs, the Iranian diet includes a bewildering array of preserved vegetables and fruits. We were in awe of the extreme conditions so many Iranians live under – the searing heat, blistering winds and endless dry of summer, and the icy cold and deep snow of winter – and grew to understand how important it is for local cooks to make the most of produce when it is available. Although pickles, relishes, jams, dried fruits and fruit leathers are widely available from the daily bazaar, many households still have a strong tradition of home-preserving – especially in rural areas. One of our great pleasures was trying the different jams on offer at breakfast (saffron jam and orange-flower jam were two extravagant favourites) and the range of home-pickled vegetables that were served alongside kebabs and rice at lunch or dinner.

Pickled vegetables and relishes – torshi – feature at every Iranian meal, as their sour crunch is the ideal accompaniment to rich soups and stews and grilled meats. Just about every vegetable imaginable is bottled in brine or vinegar and flavoured with fresh herbs and aromatics. Pickled cucumbers (kheeyar shoor) and garlic (torshi-e seer) are perennial favourites; the latter improve with age, and some versions can be anything up to ten years old, turning an alarming dark brown or even black in the jar. Many families will faithfully recreate their own mixed pickle (torshi-e makhloot) or relish (torshi-ye leeteh) recipes every year.

The other great preserving agent is sugar, which was used as a sweetener and to candy and preserve fruit several thousand years before it reached Europe. In fact the old Persian word 'shikar' is the origin of the English 'sugar', and from 'qanadi', for sweet shops, we get our word, 'candy'.

One or two fruit jams (or sometimes vegetable or flower-petal jams) will always appear on the Iranian breakfast table for eating with fresh flatbread spread with butter. Persian jams are somewhat different from thick, firm-set English jams, and closer to syrupy, dripping preserves or spoon-sweets of other Middle Eastern countries. They are fabulous drizzled onto yoghurt or ice-cream or served with thick cream or even custard for an easy dessert.

The Persian fondness for a sugar hit extends to beverages, and over the centuries syrupy fruit sherbets took on an even greater importance in this region with the Islamic prohibition of alcohol. For many centuries, Persians have made use of compressed snow and ice from the mountains, which was stored in ice houses or yakchal, then crushed and mixed with fruit syrups or distillations made from myriad fruit, blossoms, herbs and spices. This idea spread westwards in the seventeenth and eighteenth centuries, and was the origin of the refreshing fruit sorbets associated with European kitchens. In fact, the word 'sorbet' evolves from the Farsi word 'sharbat'. To this day, many Iranian families make their own thirst-quenching fruit sherbets for the baking hot summer months.

Yoghurt is another brilliant example of preserving. In this instance, fresh milk is converted into a semi-solid cultured product that stands up to the extreme heat of Middle Eastern summers. Yoghurt, or mast in Farsi, is ubiquitous. It's eaten at every meal and made in most households. It is enjoyed as much for its health-giving properties as its delicious, slightly sour flavour, and is consumed either as is, mixed with herbs and vegetables as the thick yoghurt salad borani (page 104–106), or as dugh, a refreshing minted, lightly fizzing drink. In every form, yoghurt is the ideal accompaniment to heavy meat dishes, as its 'cool' properties balance out the 'hot' aspects of meat (page 12).

Torshi-ye leeteh
MIXED VEGETABLE RELISH

This is just one version of an infinite number of mixed vegetable relishes. You can vary the vegetables, herbs or spices to your liking. I like the addition of a little apple vinegar, which adds a further sweetness to the finished result.

1 onion, finely diced

1 small leek, finely diced

2 sticks celery, finely diced

120 g white cabbage, finely diced

100 g cauliflower, broken into tiny florets

100 baby carrots, finely diced

1 Lebanese cucumber, peeled, seeded and finely diced

4 cloves garlic, finely sliced

4 long red chillies, seeded and finely diced

½ cup chopped tarragon leaves

¼ cup chopped dill sprigs

700 ml water

500 ml white-wine vinegar

300 ml apple vinegar

1 tablespoon sea salt

1 teaspoon freshly ground black pepper

1 tablespoon coriander seeds, lightly crushed

Combine the vegetables and herbs in a large bowl.

Bring the remaining ingredients to a boil in a large, non-reactive saucepan. Pour onto the vegetables and mix so that the ingredients are evenly distributed. Ladle into sterilised jars and seal while still hot. Store in a cool, dark place for at least 2 weeks before eating. Once opened, the relish will keep for 4–6 weeks in the refrigerator.

MAKES 1.5 LITRES

Torshi-ye anbeh
MANGO PICKLE

This is a version of a pickle we ate while visiting the Persian Gulf. It's a gorgeous vibrant yellow–orange colour and has a sweet, tangy, garlicky flavour that goes particularly well with grilled or fried fish.

3 mangoes, peeled and finely diced

1 teaspoon fennel seeds, lightly crushed

1 clove garlic, grated

juice of ½ lemon

pinch of sea salt

80 ml water

2 tablespoons apple vinegar

2 tablespoons Saffron Liquid (page 54)

50 g sugar

½ teaspoon ground turmeric

Combine the mango, fennel seeds, garlic, lemon juice and salt in a large bowl. Toss gently so the spices are evenly distributed.

Bring the remaining ingredients to a boil in a small, non-reactive saucepan. Simmer for a few minutes, then pour onto the mango mixture and stir to combine. Ladle into sterilised jars and seal while still hot. Store in a cool, dark place for at least 2 weeks before eating. Once opened, the relish will keep for 1–2 weeks in the refrigerator. MAKES 600 ML

Kheeyar shoor
TARRAGON-PICKLED CUCUMBERS

Wonderfully fresh and crunchy, these cucumbers are ready after only a few days' pickling.

800 g pickling cucumbers

3 long green chillies

1 head garlic, broken into cloves
   and peeled

1 cup tarragon sprigs, stalks and all

1 litre water

80 ml white-wine vinegar

50 g sea salt

2 tablespoons sugar

1 tablespoon coriander seeds

Wash the cucumbers and chillies, then prick them all over with a thin skewer or toothpick. Put the cucumbers and chillies into a bowl with the garlic cloves and tarragon and toss to combine evenly. Transfer to a sterilised 1 litre jar.

Bring the remaining ingredients to a boil in a large, non-reactive saucepan, then pour onto the cucumbers, filling the jar and making sure there are no air pockets. Seal the jar and turn it upside-down a few times to distribute the ingredients evenly. Store in a cool place for 5 days before using. Once opened, the cucumbers will keep for 4–6 weeks in the refrigerator. MAKES 1 KG

Zeytun parvardeh
PERSIAN GULF SPICY OLIVES

Much as I love plain olives in every shape and size, every now and then I feel like spicing them up a bit. Marinating them in herbs and other aromatics is a great way to do this. Serve the olives with chunks of sweet melon or spiced nuts with pre-dinner drinks. They also make a great addition to the dinner table to enjoy with fresh white cheese and warm bread.

1 kg plump green olives

3 cloves garlic, finely chopped

3 long green chillies, chopped

2 tablespoons chopped dill sprigs

2 tablespoons chopped coriander leaves

1 teaspoon fennel seeds

1 teaspoon dried chilli flakes

1 lemon, cut into quarters and thinly sliced

1 bay leaf

grated zest of 1 orange

Mix all the ingredients in a large bowl. Cover and refrigerate for 24 hours so the flavours develop, then transfer to sterilised jars. Keep, refrigerated, for up to 2 weeks. **MAKES 1 KG**

Moraba-ye khalal naranj
CANDIED SAFFRON-ORANGE PEEL

Citrus fruit breathe their warm perfume into all kinds of sweet and savoury Persian dishes. The zest is mainly used dried: sour-orange peel is the most popular, and it is available from the bazaar and in spice shops, but is easy to dry out yourself at home (see opposite).

This recipe for candied citrus peel is for use as a gorgeous sticky garnish. The saffron intensifies the golden-amber hue and adds its own subtle layer of flavour. Seville oranges are best, but you can use any oranges or citrus fruit you like. Use to garnish all sorts of creamy desserts and ice-creams or add a few strands to cake or biscuit doughs for a sweet citrus scent.

4 oranges

250 ml water

150 g sugar

2 tablespoons Saffron Liquid (page 54)

Peel the oranges, removing as much white pith as you can from the peelings – this is the zest. Cut the zest into julienne strips, then put these into a small, non-reactive saucepan and cover with boiling water. Return to a boil and blanch for 20 seconds, then drain and repeat twice more to remove any bitterness.

Combine the 250 ml water and sugar in a heavy-based saucepan over a low heat, stirring until the sugar has dissolved, then increase the heat and bring to a boil. Add the blanched orange zest and saffron liquid and cook at a gentle simmer for 30 minutes, until the zest is soft and translucent.

Spoon into a sterilised jar, then seal while still hot and store in a cool place. Keeps for up to 12 months. **MAKES 300 ML**

Khalal-e naranj

Dried orange peel is used extensively in Persian cooking and it's readily available from spice bazaars all around Iran. Traditionally the sour orange – naranj – is used for drying, but this particular variety is hard to find in other countries. Seville oranges or mandarins are a good approximation to the flavour, but you can also use the dried peel of sweet oranges with equal success, and tangelo is another favourite. Sweet oranges are available all year round, so for the freshest flavour we recommend drying in small batches. And you can really dry the peel anyway you like – in the oven, on a sunny windowsill and so on.

Seville or sweet oranges

Preheat the oven to 120°C. Use a vegetable peeler to remove the peel from the fruit as thinly as possible. Try to remove only the brightly coloured zest, without too much white pith attached. Use a sharp knife to carefully slice away any pith that lingers, then cut the strips into 10 cm lengths. Dry in the oven for 15–20 minutes and store in an airtight container.

Moraba-ye albaloo
SOUR-CHERRY PRESERVE WITH LIME

Fresh sour cherries, such as morello, have only a fleeting season, but imported dried sour cherries are available all year round. They are a bit pricey, but the beauty of this recipe is that it only uses a small quantity and you only need a small teaspoon for an intensely lime-perfumed sugar hit. Multiply the recipe by all means.

finely grated zest of 1 lime
180 g sugar
200 g dried sour cherries
500 ml water
juice of 2 limes

Rub the lime zest into the sugar to release its oils. Spoon the sugar onto the cherries and leave to macerate for 2 hours.

Tip the sugar and cherries into a heavy-based saucepan with the water and heat slowly, stirring until the sugar has dissolved, then increase the heat and bring to a boil. Lower the heat and simmer for 45 minutes or until the syrup coats the back of a spoon thickly. Stir regularly and skim from time to time to remove any scum that rises to the surface.

Ladle into a sterilised jar and pour on enough syrup to cover completely. Seal while still hot and store in a cool place. Keeps for up to 12 months. MAKES 300 ML

Moraba-ye zereshk
BARBERRY PRESERVE WITH CINNAMON AND VANILLA

Fresh from the tree, barberries or zereshk are mouth-puckeringly sour, but in countries such as Iran, where they are grown in abundance, they blend brilliantly with sugar to make intensely flavoured fruit leathers, jams and jellies. Dried barberries add lovely little jewels of flavour and colour to polows, stews and salads and they can also be turned into sweet preserves, as here.

100 g dried barberries, stems removed

260 g sugar

1 tablespoon cracked cardamom pods

1 cinnamon stick, broken in half

1 vanilla pod, split

700 ml boiling water

Soak the barberries in cold water for 2 minutes, then drain. Put the barberries into a heavy-based saucepan with the remaining ingredients and bring to a boil over a medium heat. Lower the heat and cook at a gentle simmer for 40–50 minutes, or until the syrup coats the back of a spoon thickly. Stir regularly and skim from time to time to remove any scum that rises to the surface.

Ladle into a sterilised jar and pour on enough syrup to cover completely. Seal while still hot and store in a cool place. Keeps for up to 12 months. MAKES 300 ML

Moraba-ye zardaloo
APRICOT PRESERVE WITH TANGELO

Use mandarins or clementines instead of tangelo, if you like, but in truth any citrus fruit seems to enhance the perfume of this lovely preserve. Delicious with thick cream.

It's worth looking for the very best dried apricots you can for this preserve, those that don't use sulphur in the drying process.

250 g best-quality dried
apricots
200 g sugar
1 vanilla pod, split
2 long strips tangelo peel,
all pith removed

500 ml tangelo juice
½ teaspoon cardamon seeds,
very finely ground
1 tablespoon orange-flower
water

Cover the apricots with boiling water and leave for 20 minutes to soften. Drain well, then put into a heavy-based saucepan with the sugar, vanilla pod, peel, juice and cardamom and bring to a boil over a medium heat. Lower the heat and cook at a gentle simmer for 30–40 minutes, or until the syrup coats the back of a spoon thickly. Stir regularly and skim from time to time to remove any scum that rises to the surface. Stir in the orange-flower water.

Ladle into a sterilised jar and pour on enough syrup to cover completely. Seal while still hot and store in a cool place. Keeps for up to 12 months. MAKES 300 ML

Moraba-ye anjir
WILD FIG PRESERVE WITH
GINGER AND ORANGE

So much prettier than normal fig jam, this preserve uses tiny dried wild Iranian figs that must be simmered gently so they maintain their shape. They combine beautifully with ginger and orange juice. Small dried wild figs are available from Middle Eastern foodstores or good providores.

500 g small dried wild figs
400 g sugar
1 cinnamon stick
2 tablespoons finely diced
crystallised ginger
500 ml orange juice
juice of l lemon

Cover the figs with boiling water and leave for 20 minutes to soften. Drain well, then put into a heavy-based saucepan with the remaining ingredients and bring to a boil over a medium heat. Lower the heat and cook at a gentle simmer for 40–50 minutes, or until the syrup coats the back of a spoon thickly. Stir regularly and skim from time to time to remove any scum that rises to the surface.

Ladle into sterilised jars and pour on enough syrup to cover completely. Seal while still hot and store in a cool place. Keeps for up to 12 months. MAKES 600 ML

Moraba-ye beh
QUINCE AND CARDAMOM PRESERVE

Quinces are ideal for making into jams and jellies as they have a high pectin content. This recipe is halfway between a preserve and jam, and the quince flesh turns wonderfully translucent in its jellied amber syrup.

> 3 quinces, washed and dried
>
> sugar
>
> 8 cardamom pods, lightly bruised

Cut the quinces into sixths. Remove the cores and cut the wedges into thickish chunks – there is no need to peel them.

Put the quinces into a large, heavy-based saucepan, then cover with cold water and bring to a boil over a medium heat. Lower the heat and simmer gently for 30 minutes, or until the quince is just tender.

Lift the fruit out of the pan and weigh it. Weigh out the same amount of sugar and add it to the water in the pan. Stir over a gentle heat until the sugar has dissolved, then put the fruit back into the pan. Cook at a fairly brisk boil for 1 hour, or until the quince is a deep, almost translucent amber and the syrup is very thick and sticky. Skim from time to time to remove any scum that rises to the surface. Add the cardamom pods to the pan and simmer for a few more minutes, then remove from the heat.

Leave to cool for a few minutes before ladling into sterilised jars. Seal and store in a cool place. Keeps for up to 12 months. MAKES ABOUT 1.2 LITRES

Moraba-ye toot
MULBERRY, PISTACHIO AND GOLDEN RAISIN PRESERVE

Syrupy fruit preserves are a highlight of many Iranian breakfasts. They are delicious eaten with warm bread, or dripped jewel-like onto a bowl of thick yoghurt (although this is not very Iranian). If you have a few jars of different preserves in the cupboard, a quick dessert, with ice-cream, rice pudding or thick cream will never be far away.

> 100 g dried mulberries
>
> 80 g golden raisins
>
> 150 g sugar
>
> 500 ml water
>
> ¼ cup slivered or sliced blanched
>   pistachios
>
> juice of 1 lime

Cover the mulberries and golden raisins with boiling water and leave for 20 minutes to soften. Drain well, then put into a heavy-based saucepan with the sugar and the 500 ml water and bring to a boil over a high heat. Lower the heat and cook at a gentle simmer for 30–40 minutes, or until the syrup coats the back of a spoon thickly. Stir regularly and skim from time to time to remove any scum that rises to the surface. Towards the end of the cooking time, stir in the pistachios and lime juice.

Ladle into a sterilised jar and pour on enough syrup to cover completely. Seal while still hot and store in a cool place. Keeps for up to 12 months. MAKES 300 ML

Rose-scented plum jelly

This recipe appeared in our first book, *Arabesque*, and it is still one of our favourites. Plums are high in pectin, so this is a great jam for first-time jelly-makers.

It is hard to give exact quantities of the yield with jelly recipes, as the amount varies depending on the juice produced from the fruit. As a general rule of thumb, each kilo of sugar will make around 1.5 litres of jelly.

2.5 kg plums

sugar

50 ml rosewater

Put the plums into a large, heavy-based saucepan and cook over a medium heat for 10 minutes until they are soft and pulpy and have released a lot of juice.

Strain the plums overnight through a jelly-cloth, a piece of muslin or even a clean Chux. Allow it to drip through naturally; don't be tempted to press the fruit as doing so will make the jelly cloudy. The amount of juice collected will vary, but this should yield around 2 litres.

Pour the juice into a large, heavy-based saucepan or preserving pan and for every 600 ml of juice add 500 g sugar. Stir over a low heat until the sugar has dissolved, then bring to a boil.

Boil for 20–25 minutes, or until the jelly reaches the setting point. To test, spoon a small amount onto a cold plate and refrigerate for a few minutes. The jelly is at setting point if it forms a skin that wrinkles when you push your finger through it.

Remove the pan from the heat and skim away any froth from the surface. Stir in the rosewater and allow to cool for a few minutes. Ladle into sterilised jars and seal while still hot. Keeps for up to 12 months. **MAKES 3 LITRES**

Quince and orange jelly

This jelly is best made with Seville oranges, but you could also try it with tangelos.

It is hard to give exact quantities of the yield with jelly recipes, as the amount varies, depending on the juice produced from the fruit. As a general rule of thumb, each kilo of sugar will make around 1.5 kg of jelly.

1 kg quinces, washed and dried

1 kg Seville oranges, peeled and
   pith removed

sugar

Chop the quinces roughly. There is no need to peel or core them. Chop the oranges roughly. Combine the fruit in a large, heavy-based saucepan or preserving pan, then cover with water and bring to a boil over a medium heat. Lower the heat and simmer gently for 45 minutes, or until the quince is just tender. It could take 1 hour.

Strain the fruit overnight through a jelly-cloth, a piece of muslin or even a clean Chux. Allow it to drip through naturally; don't be tempted to press the fruit as doing so will make the jelly cloudy. The amount of juice collected will vary, but this should yield around 2 litres.

Pour the juice into a heavy-based saucepan or preserving pan and for every 500 ml of juice add 400 g sugar. Stir over a low heat until the sugar has dissolved, then bring to a boil.

Boil for 20–25 minutes, or until the jelly reaches the setting point. To test, spoon a small amount onto a cold plate and refrigerate for a few minutes. The jelly is at setting point if it forms a skin that wrinkles when you push your finger through it.

Remove the pan from the heat and skim away any froth from the surface. Ladle into sterilised jars and seal while still hot. Keeps for up to 12 months. **MAKES 2 LITRES**

Guava–vanilla jelly

The perfumed tropical scent of guava wafted around the port towns of the Persian Gulf during our spring visit, and that memory has inspired this pretty pink jelly.

It is hard to give exact quantities of the yield with jelly recipes, as the amount varies, depending on the juice produced from the fruit. As a general rule of thumb, each kilo of sugar will make around 1.5 kg of jelly.

1 kg guavas, washed and cut into quarters	sugar
	lime juice
1 vanilla pod, split and scraped	

Put the guavas and vanilla pod and seeds into a large, heavy-based saucepan and cook over a medium heat for 20 minutes until the fruit is soft and pulpy and has released a lot of juice.

Strain the fruit overnight through a jelly-cloth, a piece of muslin or even a clean Chux. Allow it to drip through naturally; don't be tempted to press the fruit as doing so will make the jelly cloudy. The amount of juice collected will vary, but this should yield around 2 litres.

Pour the juice into a heavy-based saucepan or preserving pan and for every 600 ml of juice add 350 g sugar and 1 tablespoon lime juice. Stir over a low heat until the sugar has dissolved, then bring to a boil.

Boil for 15–20 minutes, or until the jelly reaches the setting point. To test, spoon a small amount onto a cold plate and refrigerate for a few minutes. The jelly is at setting point if it forms a skin that wrinkles when you push your finger through it.

Remove the pan from the heat and skim away any froth from the surface. Ladle into sterilised jars and seal while still hot. Keeps for up to 12 months. **MAKES 600 ML**

Sharbat-e beh limoo
QUINCE-LIME SHERBET

1 large quince, peeled, cored and diced
400 g sugar
250 ml water
1 vanilla pod, split
100 ml lime juice
edible flowers (optional)
lime wedges, to serve

Combine the quince and sugar in a large, heavy-based saucepan and leave to macerate for 1½ hours.

Add the water and bring to a boil over a low heat, stirring until the sugar has dissolved. Increase the heat and simmer gently for 20 minutes. Strain through a piece of muslin or clean Chux, then return the strained juice to the pan and add the vanilla pod and lime juice. Boil for 10–15 minutes until the syrup is thick. Remove from the heat and leave to cool. Transfer the cold syrup and vanilla bean to a sterilised bottle, then seal and store in a cool place. Keeps well.

To serve as a refreshing drink, mix 1 part syrup with 3 parts chilled water or soda water. Top with ice, garnish with edible flowers, if using, and serve straight away with a twist of lime. MAKES 400 ML

Sharbat-e reevas
RHUBARB-ROSEWATER SHERBET

500 g rhubarb, roughly chopped
400 g sugar
250 ml water
juice of 1 lime
2 tablespoons rosewater
a few dried rose petals (optional)

Combine the rhubarb and sugar in a large, heavy-based saucepan and leave to macerate for 1½ hours.

Add the water and bring to a boil over a low heat, stirring until the sugar has dissolved. Increase the heat and simmer gently for 20 minutes. Strain through a piece of muslin or clean Chux, then return the strained juice to the pan and add the lime juice. Boil for 10–15 minutes until the syrup is thick. Remove from the heat and leave to cool. When cold, stir in the rosewater and rose petals, if using, and transfer to a sterilised bottle, then seal and store in a cool place. Keeps well.

To serve as a refreshing drink, mix 1 part syrup with 3 parts chilled water or soda water. Top with ice and serve straight away. MAKES 400 ML

Sharbat-e sekanjebeen
MINT AND VINEGAR SHERBET

This ancient combination of sugar and vinegar is one of
the earliest Persian sherbets, and it may well have been the
inspiration for old-fashioned English fruit-vinegar cordials.
Although it's original use was as a wonderfully reviving
cordial with crushed ice over the summer, it is also popular
as a sort of dipping dressing, with baby cos lettuce leaves
(page 96).

350 g sugar

400 ml water

160 ml apple vinegar

juice of 1 lemon

12 sprigs mint

Combine the sugar and water in a heavy-based saucepan
over a low heat, stirring until the sugar has dissolved.
Increase the heat and simmer for 10 minutes. Add the
vinegar, lemon juice and mint leaves and simmer for a further
5 minutes. Remove from the heat and leave to cool. When
cold, fish out the mint leaves, and transfer to a sterilised
bottle, then seal and store in a cool place. Keeps well.

To serve as a refreshing summer drink, mix 1 part syrup
with 3 parts chilled water or soda water. Top with ice and
serve straight away. **MAKES 400 ML**

Dugh
MINTED YOGHURT DRINK

Known variously as dugh, ayran, lassi or tan across the region, this is one of
the most popular drinks in Iran and throughout the Indian subcontinent.
Iranian dugh is always lightly salted, unlike some sweetened Indian lassi
drinks, and there's no doubt it's a bit of an acquired taste, but one that is worth
acquiring. Most Iranians consider dugh is the *only* drink to go with kebabs
(it's the hot/cold balance thing), and in the summer it is strangely better at
slaking one's thirst than water alone. An added virtue is that its salt content is
just the thing for replacing that lost through perspiration – and, of course, the
'friendly' bacteria it contains are well known to have beneficial effects on the
digestive system.

Homemade dugh is easy to make. Unsurprisingly, the thicker and creamier
the yoghurt you use, the richer and more delicious the result. If you make dugh
with still water, it will keep, refrigerated, for up to two weeks.

500 g thick natural yoghurt,
  chilled

juice of ½ lemon or 1 lime

1–2 teaspoons sea salt

1–2 teaspoons dried mint

1 litre chilled carbonated
  mineral or soda water

crushed ice and sprigs of mint,
  to serve

Whisk the yoghurt with the lemon or lime juice, and add salt
and dried mint to taste. Whisk until well combined, then
gently whisk in the mineral water and pour over crushed ice.
Serve straight away, garnished with a sprinkle of extra dried
mint or fresh mint sprigs. **SERVES 6**

Mast
HOMEMADE YOGHURT

It would be hard to over-estimate the importance of 'cooling' yoghurt to the Iranian diet, and even though there are umpteen varieties of good-quality yoghurt available in Western supermarkets these days, I still think it is worth knowing how to knock up a batch yourself. Somehow the homemade kind always tastes sweeter and fresher than shop-bought – however pricey, organic or biodynamic it might be.

The main thing to remember is that to start things off you need to use plain live yoghurt that contains the natural bacteria that cause the milk to thicken and sour slightly. Any good-quality commercial brand will do. And if you can resist eating it all, a few tablespoons of your first batch can go towards the next batch. And the next … and the next …

1 litre full-cream milk
1 tablespoon natural yoghurt

Put the milk into a large saucepan and bring to a boil. When the froth rises, turn off the heat and leave the milk to cool.

As you are dealing with a living 'culture', the bacteria will only grow within a certain temperature range – between 32ºC and 49ºC. If you don't have a thermometer, dip your finger into the milk. You should be able to leave it for a count of 15 seconds without pain.

When the milk is at the right temperature, remove any skin that has formed on the surface. Mix a few tablespoons of hot milk with the yoghurt in a bowl, then pour in the rest of the hot milk and beat again.

Cover the bowl with a tea towel or plastic wrap and leave it in a warm place, undisturbed, for at least 8 hours – overnight is ideal. You can also pour it into a Thermos flask or wrap it in a thick blanket to ensure the ideal temperature is maintained. The yoghurt should thicken to a custard-like consistency. Refrigerate for up to a week. Use a little of your yoghurt to make another batch within 4 days.

MAKES 1 LITRE

Food Notes

Most ingredients for Persian recipes are pantry staples, and are readily available – you'll find mention of a few of these here, with tips for their selection and preparation. We also include here a list of some of the less familiar foodstuffs, together with explanations for their preparation and use, where necessary. Of these, a handful of ingredients will need to be bought from a Middle Eastern or Iranian food store – we encourage you to seek these out for the best result. Importantly, we also direct you to a discussion about the hot/cold balance required in a Persian meal.

/

APRICOTS, DRIED Dried apricots are hardly an unusual ingredient, but we include them here so we can encourage you to seek out the very best, preferably organic, specimens possible (that is, those that have not been treated with sulphur during the drying process), to approximate Persian flavours best.

/

BARBERRIES The small, red barberry (zereshk) is too sour to be eaten raw, but instead is dried and used extensively in rice dishes, stuffings and omelettes. They are also cooked down to a thick paste that is then dried to make lavashak – or fruit leather. Barberries should be picked over for rogue twigs or stones, stemmed and washed before use. Barberries can be found in Middle Eastern food stores.

/

CANDIED FRUIT Candying fruit in sugar syrup is very popular in Middle Eastern countries. Subtly different from jams and jellies, whole fruit (apricots, plums, baby clementines, wild figs) are preserved in syrup to be enjoyed as a sweet treat with a cup of chai (tea – see page 325) or glass of water. Slices of citrus fruit and peel are also preserved in a similar way, and in addition

to being consumed as is are often added as a garnish to sweet and even some savoury dishes. Some candied fruit can be found widely, but you may need to visit a Middle Eastern food store for more unusual varieties, such as candied clementines.

/

CHICKPEA FLOUR Chickpeas are grown extensively in Iran, and chickpea flour is used as a binding agent and to make cookies and other treats, particularly for Persian New Year. Chickpea flour is becoming increasingly available and can be found in good supermarkets and in Middle Eastern or Indian food stores (where it will be sold as besan gram) and good providores.

/

CLARIFIED BUTTER Clarified butter or ghee (roghan-karreh) is butter that has been melted and strained to remove the solids. It has a lovely nutty flavour, and is often used instead for making sweets, desserts and pastries, or in dishes where the milk solids in hard butter might burn. Clarified butter may also be used when making rice dishes. A small amount is sometimes mixed with vegetable oil for making the tah-deeg – the crusty layer at the bottom of the pot – or it may be poured over the rice just before serving, for added richness and sheen.

Ghee is readily available from Indian and Middle Eastern stores and most supermarkets, but it is easy to make clarified butter at home: melt butter (preferably unsalted) in a small saucepan until it froths. Strain through a fine, clean cloth (such as muslin or even a Chux) and discard the solids. Keep the clarified butter, covered, in the refrigerator for up to three months.

/

CHERRIES, SOUR Sour cherries or albalu are loved all around the Middle East. They are eaten fresh in the summer months, and are also turned into sherbets and preserves (page 309). They are dried, made into fruit pastes, and also mixed with salt to make an extraordinary intense condiment. Dried sour cherries are available from Middle Eastern stores and have a wonderful, almost vanilla-like quality. If you can resist eating them straight from the packet, they can be added to rice dishes or stews, or poached until soft in a lime-spiked sugar syrup and served with rice desserts or as a topping for ice-cream. Dried or fresh morello cherries may be subsituted, at a pinch.

/

FENUGREEK With its mildly bitter flavour, fenugreek (shambaleeleh) is one of the most distinctive herbs used in Iranian cooking. Both the seeds and leaves (fresh and dried) of the plant are used. The fresh herb is used, most notably, in Khoresht-e Ghormeh Sabzi (page 170), although the dried herb can be used when the fresh is unavailable. Fenugreek seeds are notoriously hard to grind, so are often sold ready-ground. Some Middle Eastern recipes also call for whole cracked seeds, which you can achieve in a mortar and pestle, while others require them to be soaked in a little water, when they release an unusual jelly-like substance. Fresh and dried fenugreek leaves can be found in Middle Eastern food stores, while whole and ready-ground seeds (sold as a powder) are readily available.

/

FIGS, DRIED Hard to find locally, we love the tiny dried wild figs that are imported from Iran. There, they come in varying qualities – some are very expensive – and they are eaten whole as a sort of candy or else combined with nuts for snacking on during the day or to offer to guests. They can also be used in fruit compotes and preserves. You will find imported Iranian dried wild figs in Middle Eastern food stores and good providores.

/

FLOWERS Scented edible flower petals have always been used abundantly in Persian cooking. Fresh or dried, they make a pretty garnish, but if using fresh, make sure they are free from insecticides. Dried petals – especially rose petals – are widely available from Middle Eastern stores. In Iran, they are scattered onto all kinds of polows and stews, and are ground to a powder and added to

spice mixes or sweets and desserts.

Roses and orange blossom are also used to make jams and sherbets, and are distilled to make essences (atr) and flower waters (arak) – see below. In pre-Islamic days rose petals were turned into wine.

/

FLOWER WATERS Many flowers are distilled into essences (atr) or waters (arak) in Iran. While the essences are more concentrated in essential oils and are used in perfume and toiletries, flower waters are an indispensable addition to the Persian kitchen. The best known in the West are rosewater (golab) and sour orange-flower water or neroli. Both are used to perfume sugar syrups in which sweet pastries are steeped, and they add fragrance and flavour to cordials, desserts and ice-creams. Add flower waters judiciously as some are stronger than others – as with all cooking, taste as you go to achieve the balance that suits you. Flower waters are widely found, but it's worth visiting a Middle Eastern food store to understand the range available.

/

GELATINE Gelatine is not Iranian at all, but included here as a pointer because of the endless confusion that surrounds its usage. We prefer to use gelatine leaves, rather than gelatine powder, because the latter can have an intrusive, slightly unpleasant flavour. There is, unfortunately, no standardisation among the various gelatine leaves (and the powders, too, can be inconsistent) and different brands and types have different setting strengths. For the recipes in this book we use the Gelita Titanium gelatine leaves, and as a rule of thumb, two leaves are required to set 500 millilitres of liquid. You

will find this gelatine in good food providores and many supermarkets.

/

GRAPES, SOUR Ghooreh – tiny immature grapes – are picked from the vines early in the season, before the natural sugars have had time to develop, and are used to add a desirable tartness to summer soups and stews. Unless you have your own vines, you will have to visit a Middle Eastern food store for the imported, bottled variety, which are preserved in verjuice (page 325).

/

HERBS, DRIED Dried herbs – particularly mint, dill and tarragon – are popular in Persian cooking and many households dry a selection of herbs to use during the winter months. Dried herbs have a more concentrated (and sometimes slightly different) flavour from fresh herbs and so should be used more sparingly. If you are buying dried herbs, do so from a store with a high turnover as they lose their potency over time.

/

HERBS, FRESH Fresh herbs are used abundantly in Persian recipes. They are eaten

in the sabzi basket that begins every Persian meal (page 95) and added to salads, omelettes, soups, stews and rice dishes. Most herbs of choice are familiar to the Western garden and table: parsley, mint, chives, garlic chives, dill, tarragon, watercress, fenugreek and coriander are all popular. Basil is also used frequently, including an indigenous Persian variety (rayhan), as well as some we are more familiar seeing in Asian cookery. Less well-known herbs – such as costmary, salad burnet and summer savory – are also popular. Although these used to feature in English kitchen gardens, they are rarely available commercially these days, but there is nothing to stop you growing your own, of course.

/

HOT/COLD Iranian foodstuffs are classified according to their 'hot' or 'cold' properties, and meals are carefully constructed to achieve a balance to suit diners and circumstance. See page 12 for a more detailed discussion, and a list of classified ingredients.

/

KASHK Kashk is made from whey – the liquid that remains after making butter, yoghurt or soft cheese – that is then sun-dried and rolled into hard little white chalky balls that can last for years. Kashk is pounded to a powder and dissolved in water before use. Outside Iran, it is possible to find liquid kashk in specialist Iranian stores.

/

LEMONS, SWEET Native to Iran, sweet lemons (limonshirin) are very low in acid and have a delicate, sweet, almost honeyed-orange flavour. They are occasionally available from Middle Eastern stores, but otherwise the flavour of the meyer lemon is a reasonable approximation, although they are still much more sour than the limonshirin.

/

LIMES, DRIED A Persian variety of lime has been grown in Iran for many centuries. These limes are left in the sun to dry and are used plentifully in Persian recipes for the distinctive sour flavour they add. There are two types of dried lime (limu omani), one dark, the other pale. In Iran, the pale ones tend to be preferred, as they are considered to have a finer flavour, and they are certainly always used for lighter-hued stews, such as Khoresht-e Gheimeh (page 171), where the dark variety can affect the colour of the sauce. Both types are available in Iranian and Middle Eastern stores, but, really, either can be used for any of the recipes in this book.

Dried limes should be cracked with a rolling pin before adding, whole, to stews or soups. The limes soften during the cooking, and can then be squashed against the side of the saucepan to release their juice.

Dried-lime powder (gard-e limu omani) is also available commercially from Middle Eastern food stores, although some Iranians find this product bitter because it contains the ground seeds. You can make it yourself from dried Persian limes: break them open with a rolling pin and prize out the seeds, then grind the lime to a powder in a food processor and store in an airtight jar.

/

MOLASSES Molasses is a thick syrup made from boiled and concentrated fruit juice. It is used as sweetener and to enrich many savoury soups and stews. In Iran the commonly used varieties are made from pomegranate, grape

or mulberry juice. Persian molasses can be found in Middle Eastern food stores, although some good food providores may also carry some varieties.

/

MULBERRIES Mulberry (tut) trees grow prolifically in Iran, and were once a key component of local silk production (every schoolchild knows that the leaves are the staple diet of the silk worm). While silk is no longer widely manufactured in Iran, mulberries are eaten in various forms – fresh in the summer, dried throughout the year, and as molasses. Dried mulberries are available from Middle Eastern stores, as is mulberry molasses, and have an intense raisin-like flavour.

/

NIGELLA SEEDS Known in India as 'kolonji' (and mistakenly often referred to as black cumin seeds), nigella seeds will also be familiar with anyone who knows Turkish bread, for it is these that are sprinkled over the dough before baking, as they are in Iran too. Nigella seeds are becoming increasingly available through providores, and can be found in Middle Eastern food stores.

/

NUTS Many nut varieties, such as almonds (badam), pistachios (pesteh) and walnuts (gerdoo), are indigenous to Iran, and Iranians are inveterate nut eaters! Nuts are eaten fresh, roasted, salted or spiced, added to mixtures (sometimes with dried fruit) and, of course, used in cooking.

Nuts sometimes need to be roasted for use in a dish. To do this, scatter the nuts in an even layer on a baking tray and roast in a 160°C oven for 30–40 minutes. The

tray should be shaken from time to time so the nuts brown evenly. To toast nuts, heat a large heavy-based frying pan over a medium heat and scatter in the nuts. Cook for 5–10 minutes, until evenly coloured, shaking the pan regularly to prevent them burning. Both roasted and toasted nuts should be dried briefly on paper towels and allowed to cool before using or storing in an airtight container.

Some nuts, such as walnuts or hazelnuts, benefit from having their slightly bitter skins removed before eating. After roasting the nuts, tip them into a tea towel and rub vigorously to remove the skins. If the nuts are then chopped, they should be tossed in a sieve to remove any dust or remaining bits of skin.

To grind nuts, tip small amounts into a food processor and pulse until evenly ground to the required consistency. Always be careful not to over-process, or they will turn into a paste.

As with all highly perishable goods, buy your nuts from an outlet with a steady turnover to ensure maximum freshness – a Middle Eastern food store is a good bet, given their love of nuts! If you are keeping nuts for any length of time, refrigerate or even freeze them to avoid rancidity.

/

ORANGES A variety of oranges is grown in Iran: sweet oranges, including blood oranges, for eating (porteqal) and sour oranges (naranj). The latter are sour and slightly bitter, but both the juice and peel are used extensively in cooking, and wedges are sometimes served as an accompaniment to some dizi (soups) or fish dishes, instead of

lemon. The blossoms are also used to make jams and flower water (page 322).

The peel of sour oranges is used extensively in all parts of Iran, and it is usually purchased grated and dried from the spice bazaar. It is easy enough to prepare at home: pare away long strips of the peel as finely as you can (remove any white pith), then leave it to dry on a warm windowsill. Alternatively, spread it on a baking tray and dry in a 120°C oven for 15–20 minutes.

Outside Iran, the closest variety to the Iranian naranj is the Seville orange, but sweet oranges also work well. In fact we use many citrus fruit – tangelo, mandarin or tangerine, for instance – in the same way.

/

PASHMAK A spun-sugar confectionary – similar to fairy floss – eaten as a sweet treat in Iran, but also useful as a garnish for desserts. Pashmak is increasingly available in high-end supermarkets, as well as in Middle Eastern stores, often in a range of different flavours.

/

POMEGRANATES There are some who believe this ancient fruit was the original 'apple' in the Garden of Eden, and it has been cultivated in Iran for millennia. The sweet–sour seeds of the pomegranate are eaten fresh from the fruit, or crushed to make a refreshing ruby-red juice. Fresh pomegranates (anar) are becoming increasingly widely available – even in supermarkets – in the late autumn and early winter. Always choose fruit that feels heavy to ensure it produces lots of juice. In Iran we learnt this method of preparing a pomegranate: use a sharp knife to slice off the crown, then make incisions down to the base of the fruit in segments. Pull each segment out and eat as is, or tap the skin sharply over a bowl to release the seeds from their membrane.

Fresh pomegranate juice is sold on every street corner in Iran, but in the West it is becoming increasingly available in cartons and bottles. Its tart–sweet flavour is very refreshing and the juice is full of anti-oxidants. Add a squeeze of fresh lime juice or a splash of sugar syrup to make a great alcohol-free cocktail.

Pomegranate paste or molasses (rob anar) has become increasingly well known in the West and is used widely in all Middle Eastern cooking for its wonderfully intense and sweet–sharp flavour. Persian pomegranate pastes are slightly different from other widely available molasses – and in Iran there are several regional differences. In the northern province of Gilan, for instance, a much tarter variety is preferred. Rob anar is one of the key ingredients of the classic Persian stew, fesenjun. It blends brilliantly with ground walnuts to make a thick, rich, sweet–sour

sauce that is wonderful with poultry (page 176) and even thick white fish. Pomegranate molasses can be found in Middle Eastern food stores and some good providores.

/

RAISINS, GOLDEN In Iran there are myriad varieties of dried grapes, in addition to the currants, sultanas and raisins that we know so well. They come in a range of size, colour and flavour, are eaten in fruit and nut mixtures, and are added to polow dishes. Any raisin can be used for the recipes in this book, really, although we choose golden raisins for their colour and excellent clean, tangy flavour. They are available from good providores and some Middle Eastern grocers.

/

RICE Many varieties of rice (berenj) are used in the Persian kitchen, and rice is the focal point of nearly every Iranian meal, as plain chelow or more elaborate polow dishes. Originally introduced to Iran from India, rice is now grown abundantly in the cool, wet, northern provinces of Iran, although, sadly, these varieties are not often exported to the West. Check Middle Eastern food stores for availability, otherwise the closest variety is the readily available fragrant Indian or Pakistani basmati rice, a hulled long-grain white rice. See pages 51–54 for a detailed description of preparing and cooking Persian rice.

/

SAFFRON One of the distinguishing spices of the Persian kitchen, saffron (zafaran) adds a golden hue and indefinable – almost addictive flavour – to all manner of dishes. Around ninety per cent of the world's saffron is grown in Iran, particularly in the Khorasan provinces in the north-east and in lesser

amounts in Fars and Kerman. Saffron is one of the most expensive spices in the world as it is extremely labour-intensive to produce. Each saffron crocus bulb (*Crocus sativus*) produces up to three but maybe only one flower, and each flower contains three fine stigma that must be removed painstakingly by hand. Saffron has been used in Persia for several thousand years as a dye, in medicine, as an aphrodisiac and in cooking.

When buying saffron it is always preferable to buy threads rather than powder, which is sometimes adulterated with safflower that provides a startling colour but not the wonderful aroma of the real thing. Saffron threads should be lightly warmed before use to release their pungent aroma and flavour. They may be added whole to dishes, or ground to a fine powder after lightly toasting. Iranians always prefer to use saffron liquid in cooking, which can be made easily by dissolving ground saffron threads in a little warm water (page 54).

/

SEEDS Iranians enjoy eating many different seeds as a snack, or in nut mixtures (sometimes combined with dried fruit).

Known generically as ajeel, these mixtures are consumed throughout the day and on special occasions, particularly Nowruz or Persian New Year and Yalda, the ancient winter solstice festival. Pumpkin, sunflower and watermelon seeds are all popular, although the latter have symbolic importance on Yalda, the longest night of the year, when they represent the warmth of summer in the midst of chilly winter.

Seeds of all kinds are eaten hulled or whole (when the fun is cracking them between your teeth and prising out the seed), raw or roasted and sometimes salted or lightly spiced. Watermelon seeds don't seem to be quite as widely available outside Iran as sunflower and pumpkin seeds, but you should be able to find them from specialist nut stores or in Middle Eastern food stores.

/

SPICES As a general principle, for maximum freshness and flavour, we tend to buy whole spices and grind them individually as called for in a recipe. If you prefer to buy them ready-ground, then it's best to purchase in small amounts, and buy them from shops that have a large turnover, and not where they will have been sitting on a shelf for months on end (this applies to whole spices too). Having said that, we do not want to be overly prescriptive. This is reflected in the way spices appear in the list of ingredients: where the best result really depends on *whole* spices being used, the spices are given as such, followed by their preparation (roasted, toasted, ground and so on) – for example, 1 teaspoon cumin seeds, toasted and ground. You will also find listings for 1 teaspoon ground cumin, which means the dish will be fine with either the shop-bought or home-ground version. It's up to you which way you go – prefer whole spices when you can, but if using ground spices from a packet means you will make the dish rather than not, go for it.

/

SPICE MIXTURES Persian food is subtly rather than highly spiced, and spice mixtures known as advieh are commonly used. Although many Iranian cooks make up their own preferred blends, advieh are also often purchased, ready-mixed, from the bazaar. Different advieh are used for different types of dishes: kebabs, khoresht, seafood and polow recipes will use varying combinations of spices. Advieh blends also vary around the country. In the Persian Gulf some are similar to Indian garam masa, and others use black pepper and ginger to increase the heat. Inland cooks might use dried rose petals or finely ground pistachios to add a more delicate fragrance and perfume.

/

SUMAC A dried, dark-red berry with a sour citrus flavour, sumac (somaq) is often ground and added to meats or salads. In Iran it is widely used as a condiment, especially

with rice and kebabs. The whole berries are sometimes crushed and steeped in water and the resulting liquid used in cooking or to make sherbets. Ground sumac is readily available, but you may need to go to a Middle Eastern food store if you want the dried berries.

/

TAMARIND Shaped like a long brown bean, tamarind pods are popularly used as a souring agent – especially in the south of Iran.

Tamarind paste is sometimes sold in jars and may be added directly to a dish. Alternatively, you may also find tamarind (tambrehind) in the form of a compressed block of solid pulp that needs to be soaked and strained to make a sour liquid paste. All forms can be found in Middle Eastern and Asian food stores, while the paste is readily available.

/

TEA The Iranian national drink is known there as chai (but it bears no resemblance to the hot, sweet Indian beverage made with milk and spices). In fact chai is far more than just a drink as it also plays a vital social role: it is drunk throughout the day by everybody, everywhere, and is always the first thing you are offered when visiting shops in the bazaar, a business establishment or somebody's home.

Interestingly, chai's popularity in Iran is a relatively recent phenomenon. Although many historians believe that varieties of tea leaves were introduced during the early days of trade with China, it didn't really take off as a drink of choice until the nineteenth century. Up until then, coffee was far more widely consumed, as it is still in other Middle Eastern countries.

In Iran, chai is usually prepared in samovars (introduced from nearby Russia) or

special stove-top kettles that have a tap for the boiling water. In both instances, the tea is made in a teapot that is then placed on top of the samovar or kettle where the rising steam keeps it hot. The strong brew is diluted with extra boiling water to taste, and the resulting amber-hued chai is surprisingly light and refreshing.

Many different varieties of chai are served in Iran. By choice Iranians drink the delicate and fragrant variety grown in Gilan in the north of the country, but local production is not nearly enough to satisfy the massive daily consumption, and so the more commonplace daily brew is made from imported varieties. To approximate Gilan tea, people will often blend Ceylonese or Darjeeling with earl grey tea leaves. Sometimes the tea is infused with a stick of cinnamon, dried lime (see above), cardamom pods, a few saffron threads, mint leaves or flower petals for added fragrance and flavour. Chai is always drunk black, but sweetened to taste with hard rocks of sugar (qand) that are held in the mouth, rather than stirred in the glass.

/

TURMERIC Indigenous to India, turmeric (zardchubeh) is now one of the most widely used spices in Iran, adding a vivid yellow hue to many savoury dishes. Although often considered a sort of poor man's saffron, it is in fact never used as a substitute in Persian dishes, but only in its own right. Turmeric comes from a dried, ground rhizome (part of the ginger family), and has a slightly acrid flavour. Ready-ground turmeric is widely available.

/

VERJUICE Made from unripe grapes, verjuice (abghooreh) has been used widely in Persian cooking for many centuries. It came into its own once the Islamic prohibition on alcohol started to take hold, when it was used to replace wine and wine vinegar in cooking. Verjuice has a mildly 'grapey' flavour, as well as a much-prized sourness, although it is less harsh than vinegar and less sharp than lemon juice. Verjuice is becoming increasingly available and can be found in some supermarkets and many good providores.

/

VINEGAR A popular souring agent, as well as a medium for pickling and making relishes, vinegar and verjuice (see above) came to the fore in the Persian kitchen after wine was banished following the arrival of Islam. Persian cooks still use both, although today Iranian vinegars are no longer made from wine. For those who don't drink alcohol, any fruit or malt vinegar may be used. As it happens, we often like to use apple vinegar, instead of cider vinegar, as it is less harsh and has a lovely fruity, mellow flavour.

/

Timeline

PREHISTORY 8000–2000 BC Early agricultural communities form in western Iran./Site of Susa founded around 4200 BC. /

ELAMITES 400–539 BC Elamites settle in lowlands near Tigris and Euphrates Rivers./ First great cities are established centred on Susa and Anshan./Zoroaster is born and preaches a new religion sometime between 1000–700 BC. /

MEDES 612–550 BC Waves of Indo-European Aryan tribes begin arriving from the steppelands around the Caspian Sea./ The Medes settle in the Zagros Mountains creating a capital at Ectabana and becoming a regional power as Elamites' power declines. Shortly afterwards, Farsi people – Persians – settle around Fars on the Iranian plateau. /

ACHAEMENID PERSIAN EMPIRE 550–330 BC Cyrus the Great overthrows the Median empire by defeating King Astyages (his grandfather) at Pasargadae. Subsequently establishes his first capital here. /Cyrus the Great captures Babylon in 539 BC and orders a clay cylinder (the Cyrus Stone) to be engraved announcing that as 'king of

the world' he would be a benevolent ruler and tolerant of local religions. This philosophy is informed by the Zoroastrian religion, which remains the dominant faith in Iran until the arrival of Islam./Capitals also established at Ectabana and Susa and rulers move between here and Pasargadae./Under Darius I, the empire is extended from Greece and Egypt to Central Asia and India./It is governed by twenty-three local authorities known as satrapies and is linked by a network of paved roads. The world's first postal service is introduced. /Persepolis is constructed in 515 BC as a great ceremonial centre for the empire./Invasion of Alexander the Great of Macedon 331 BC. Persepolis is looted and destroyed. /

SELEUCIDS 323–162 BC On Alexander's death, the empire is split by warring dynasties. Seleucids eventually seize power and attempt to establish Greek culture and language in Persia. /

PARTHIANS 247– 224 AD A tribe of nomads from the Caspian region overthrows the Seleucids and establishes what is often called the second Persian empire. Expert

horsemen and archers, the Parthians challenge Rome for control of Syria, Mesopotamia and Armenia. They trade with China via the Silk Road, foster a love of miniature paintings and introduce a distinctive style of architecture, including the iwan, a vaulted three-sided space opening onto a courtyard. /

SASSANIDS 224–642 The third, highly resilient Persian empire is founded by Ardashir I, the leader of a small dynasty in the Fars province. The Sassanids continue to fight Rome and Byzantium for control of east–west trade routes, and become the world's largest empire – called Iran – as Rome declines. They have their own language – the root of modern Farsi – and a golden era of culture prevails, rivalling Byzantium. Advances are made in science, medicine and astronomy, while philosophy, art, sculpture and textiles all flourish. Persian carpets (such as the famous 'Khosro's Spring') are woven, and architectural innovations such as the squinch (enabling the erection of domes) are devised. / Sassanids establish Zoroastrianism as the state religion, but over time the priesthood becomes tainted by its strong links with royalty./

ARABS 641–945 The Sassanid empire is eventually weakened by continued conflict with Byzantium, which leaves it vulnerable to Arab armies spreading Islam after the death of the Prophet Mohammad in 632./Persians abandon Zoroastrianism and adopt Islam, however they maintain their own language in the main (incorporating some Arabic words) as well as their own culture and style of government./Ummayad Caliphs govern from the capital at Damascas, but in 750 a Shiite rebellion sees the Abbasid Caliphs move control to Baghdad./Shiite and Sunni factions vie for power, but Sunni dominates.

Islam becomes increasingly 'Persianised' and sees its Golden Age under the Abbasids, with a flowering of intellectual, philosophical and scientific life. /

SELJUKS 1051–1220 Turkic dynasty from Central Asia become new rulers of eastern Islamic lands. They take over Baghdad in 1050 and a new era of creativity in arts and architecture emerges, distinguished by scholars such as Avicenna and Omar Khayyam. /

MONGOL ILKHANIDS 1256–1335 Under the leadership of Genghis Khan, the

Mongols take control of China and then sweep westwards. Subsequent Mongol rulers seize all of Persia and Turkey and establish a capital at Tabriz./After devastating many Persian cities, the Pax Mongolica is established, creating an era of tremendous trade and cultural exchange./Marco Polo (and other European merchants) follows the re-established Silk Road across Persia to China 1271–95./All manner of goods are traded between East and West as well as ideas, religions, information and newly emerging technologies./Khanate disintegrates after death of Abu Sai'id Bahadur in 1335, and several rival states vie for succession.
/

TIMURIDS 1380–1502 The Turco-Mongolian ruler Timur the Lame – Tamerlane – comes to power after entering Iran in 1380. He moves the capital from Tabriz to Qazvin and in 1402 defeats the Ottoman Turks./Timurid rulers become enthusiastic patrons of the arts, and great poets, such as Rumi, Saadi and Hafez, come to the fore during Iran's poetic Golden Age.
/

SAFAVIDS 1502–1736 Taking its name from a Sufi order from Ardabil in north-western Iran, the Safavid dynasty reunifies Iran and embraces Shia Islam. The Safavids reach their peak under Shah Abbas I (1587–1629), who moves the capital to Isfahan. The centrepiece of his capital is the Maidan-e Naqsh-e Jahan (now the Imam Square), with the Royal (Imam) Mosque as its focal point. Abbas I forges a new sense of national identity within the country./ The Safavid period is recognised as an era of political and military reform. Twelver Shiism comes to the fore and there is a flowering of

Persian art and architecture, calligraphy, carpet weaving, textiles and tilework. This Golden Age comes to an end with the death of Shah Abbas II in 1666./Afghan groups on Iran's borders launch invasions against a weakening Safavid empire, culminating in 1722 in the occupation of Isfahan.
/

NADER SHAH 1736–1747 Afghans are driven from the country by Nader Shah, a warlord from Khorasan. He establishes himself as monarch, but his oppressive regime provokes many revolts and he is eventually assassinated and Iran descends into civil war.
/

ZANDS 1750–1795 Karim Khan of the Zand dynasty grabs power. He establishes his capital at Shiraz, where he builds extensively, and rules peacefully until his death in 1779./ Another period of civil war follows in which the Qajars, an Azari dynasty, eventually triumphs.
/

QAJARS 1795–1925 The Qajar dynasty brings an end to a long period of political instability within Iran with transition from tribal to centralised government. However, corruption is rife and the country becomes embroiled in superpower rivalry between Britain and Russia. It eventually loses significant territory in the Caucasus./The Qajar dynasty nevertheless sees a period of artistic innovation and the revival of classical poetry. The British become interested in Persian culture and history and mount an exhibition of Persian art in London. Persian carpet design influences the Arts and Crafts movement./The Bahai religion emerges in the mid-nineteenth century, pushing for more

liberal and less corrupt government./Nasir al-Din Shah moves capital to Tehran./Iran remains neutral during the First World War, but is occupied by British and Russian troops and sees heavy fighting./Towards the end of Nasir al-Din's reign various concessions are granted to European companies, fuelling opposition to the regime and resulting in the Constitutional Revolution (1905–1911).
/

PAHLAVIS 1925–1979 Reza Pahlavi establishes a new dynasty as the result of a military coup and begins the 'westernisation' of Iran via industrialisation and education./ The country's name is formally changed from Persia to Iran in 1935./Reza Shah's pro-German allegiance in the Second World War leads to the Anglo-Russian occupation of Iran and his eventual removal from leadership./ Reza Shah's son, Mohammed Reza Pahlavi, replaces him. His strong pro-Western leanings make him increasingly unpopular within Iran and eventually he is forced to flee./ In 1953, a coup engineered by Britain and the CIA overthrows his successor, Prime Minister Mossadeq, and Mohammed Reza Shah returns./Ayatollah Ruhollah Khomeini emerges as the figurehead for the opposition movement, and is banished from Iran by the Shah's increasingly oppressive regime./ In 1971 the Shah organises extravagant celebrations at Persepolis for the 2500th anniversary of the Persian empire. This, and other examples of economic mismanagement, lead to a groundswell of opposition. In January 1979 Mohammed Reza Shah is forced to flee once again and Ayatollah Khomeini returns from exile.
/

ISLAMIC REVOLUTION 1979–PRESENT DAY Ayatollah Khomeini declares Iran the world's first Islamic Republic after a referendum and is appointed Supreme Leader for life./Iraq invades Iran in September 1980 over a territorial dispute. Iran–Iraq War lasts eight years, ending after a UN resolution. Nearly one million Iranians are killed./Ayatollah Khomeini dies in 1989. Former president Ali Khamenei appointed new Supreme Leader. /1989 constitutional referendum further strengthens position of Supreme Leader, and abolishes position of Prime Minister./After a period of moderate reform, governments become increasingly conservative, widening the rift between conservatives and reformists within the country and between Iran and the West.
/

Bibliography

The following is a list of resources for anyone interested in finding out more about Iran, its history, culture and cooking. Robert Byron's *The Road to Oxiana* is a classic piece of travel writing and would be a great place to start any reading on Iran, while Ryszard Kapuscinski's *Shah of Shahs* is a journalist's eyewitness account of the Islamic Revolution, and a wonderful portrayal of a country on the verge of change. *Persepolis*, a graphic novel by Marjane Satrapi, is a clever, wry depiction of growing up in post-revolution Iran. For an erudite and fascinating glimpse into the country today, we urge you to read *Mirrors of the Unseen*, by Jason Elliot.

For those with an interest in culture and history, Penelope Hobhouse takes you on a gorgeous meander in her *Gardens of Persia*, and the British Museum catalogue *Shah 'Abbas: The Remaking of Iran* by Sheila Canby provides an insight into the Golden Age of the Safavids. For food and recipes, Margaret Shaida's lovely book *The Legendary Cuisine of Persia* is a comprehensive collection of traditional Persian recipes, while Sally Butcher's more irreverent – and funny – book, *Persia in Peckham*, also describes what it's like being married into an Iranian family.

Finally, we would encourage you to delve into some Persian poetry: you will almost certainly know Omar Khayyam's *Rubaiyat*, and you might already be vaguely familiar with Rumi, but any of the translated works of Hafez are a revelation to those who think poetry begins and ends with the English poets. And they will really help you get a feel for the Persian soul.

/

Afrashi, Neda. *The Persian Kitchen: Home Cooking from the Middle East*. Mitchell Beazley, London, 2006.

Aryanpad, Farah. *Farah's Persian Cuisine*. Peacock Publications, Adelaide, 2004.

Batmanglij, Najmieh. *A Taste of Persia*. I.B. Tauris & Co Ltd, New York, 2003.

Beazley, Elisabeth and Harverson, Michael (contrib. by Susan Roaf). *Living with the Desert: Working Buildings of the Iranian Plateau*. Aris and Phillips, Warminster, 1982.

Bird, Christiane. *Neither East nor West*. WSP Pocket Books, New York, 2001.

Bird, Isabella. *Journeys in Persia and Kurdistan*. Long Riders' Guild Press, Geneva, 2004.

Burke, Andrew and Elliott, Mark. *Iran*. Lonely Planet, Melbourne, 2008.

Butcher, Sally. *Persia in Peckham*. Prospect Books, Totnes, 2007.

Byron, Robert. *The Road to Oxiana*. Picador, London, 1981.

Canby, Sheila. *Shah 'Abbas: The Remaking of Iran*. The British Museum Press, London, 2009.

Curatola, Giovanni and Scarcia, Gianroberto. *The Art and Architecture of Persia*. Abbeville Press Publishers, New York, 2007.

de Bellaigue, Christopher. *In the Rose Garden of the Martyrs: A Memoir of Iran*. Harper Perennial, London, 2005.

Ebadi, Shirin. *Iran Awakening*. Rider, London, 2006.

Elliot, Jason. *Mirrors of the Unseen*. Picador, London, 2007.

Ferdowsi, Abolqasem. *Shahnameh: The Persian Book of Kings*. Penguin Books, London, 2007.

Hafez. *Drunk on the Wine of the Beloved* (trans. Thomas Rain Crowe). Shambhala Publications, Boston, 2001.

—*The Gift: Poems by Hafiz the Great Sufi Master* (trans. Daniel Ladinsky). Penguin Compass, London, 1999.

Hattstein, Markus and Delius, Peter. *Islam Art and Architecture*. Tandem Verlag GmbH, Potsdam, 2004.

Hekmat, Forough. *The Art of Persian Cooking*. Mehr-e Amin, Tehran, 2001.

Hobhouse, Penelope. *Gardens of Persia*. Cassell Illustrated, London, 2006.

Holland, Tom. *Persian Fire*. Anchor Books, New York, 2007.

Humphries, John. *The Essential Saffron Companion*. Grub Street, London, 1996.

Kapuscinski, Ryszard. *Shah of Shahs*. Penguin Books, London, 2009.

Khayyam, Omar. *The Rubaiyat of Omar Khayyam* (trans. Edward Fitzgerald). Oxford University Press, Oxford, 2009.

Lewis, Bernard. *The Middle East*. Phoenix, London, 1997.

—*From Babel to Dragomans: Interpreting the Middle East*. Phoenix, London, 2005.

Majd, Hooman. *The Ayatollah Begs to Differ*. Penguin Books, London, 2009.

Montazemi, Roza. *Honar-e Ashpazi* (The Art of Cooking). Ketabe Iran, Tehran, 2007.

Mouaveni, Azadeh. *Lipstick Jihad*. Public Affairs, New York, 2006.

Nafisi, Azar. *Reading Lolita in Tehran*. Hodder Headline, Sydney, 2004.

Polo, Marco. *Travels* (trans. R.E. Latham). Penguin Books, London, 1958.

Pourdaryaeinejad, Mona. *Hormozgan Kitchen*. Ilaf Publishing, Iran, 1987.

Rodinson, Maxine, Arberry, A.J. and Perry, Charles. *Medieval Arab Cookery*. Prospect Books, Totnes, 2001.

Rumi. *Selected Poems* (trans. Coleman Banks).
  Penguin Books, London, 2004.

Sackville-West, Vita. *Passenger to Tehran*.
  I.B. Tauris Publishers, London, 2007.

Satrapi, Marjane. *Persepolis: The Story of a
  Childhood*. Pantheon Books, New York, 2003.

Shaida, Margaret. *The Legendary Cuisine of
  Persia*. Grub Street, London, 2000.

Simmons, Shirin. *Entertaining the Persian
  Way*. Lennard Publishing, Harpenden, 1988.

Simpson, John and Shubart, Tira. *Lifting the
  Veil, Life in Revolutionary Iran*. Coronet
  Books, London, 1995.

Stark, Freya. *The Valleys of the Assassins
  and Other Persian Travels*. Modern Library
  Paperbacks, New York, 2001.

Thubron, Colin. *Shadow of the Silk Road*.
  Vintage, London, 2006.

Upham Pope, Arthur. *Introducing Persian
  Architecture*. Oxford University Press,
  Oxford, 1971.

Zanganeh, Lila Azam. *My Sister, Guard Your
  Veil; My Brother, Guard Your Eyes*. Beacon
  Press, Boston, 2006.

Zaouali, Lilia. *Medieval Cuisine of the Islamic
  World*. University of California Press,
  Berkeley and Los Angeles, 2007.

Acknowledgements

A book of this magnitude owes its existence to many, many people. All of the following have contributed, in one way or other, and there are countless others who played a part too. We thank you all.

We are very grateful to Etihad Airways for their ongoing support and generosity, which enabled us to make not one but two trips to Iran. In particular, we'd like to thank C.E.O. John Hogan and Anne Tullis in Abu Dhabi, and Jonathan Spring and Elizabeth Graham in Australia. We also thank the Etihad staff who helped us in a time of family crisis, and smoothed the way for an unexpectedly early return to Melbourne.

More practical assistance came from Helen Fuge of Passport Travel, and her colleague in Tehran, Mr Farhad Towfighi Namin, and we thank them for guiding us through the visa application process. We also express our sincere thanks to Mr Ali Rastgou, at the Embassy of the Islamic Republic of Iran in Canberra, for his interest in our project.

Before the travelling began, there were a number of people who encouraged and inspired us, and offered us practical help for the journey ahead. We thank Andrew Burke, Kerryn Burgess and Manuela Darling, all of whom gave us the benefit of wisdom acquired from their own Iranian travels. We also thank Professor Aliakbar and Nasrin Akbarzadeh, Zakieh and Reza Jafari, Paloma Hatami and Sina Samiee, not just for their enthusiasm but also for feeding us delicious Iranian food, teaching us Farsi, introducing us to their families, colleagues and friends and, most of all, for offering us their friendship so unreservedly.

In Iran we were blessed to have two wonderful sarabans, both of whom acted as guide, translator and 'fixer', rolled into one. We thank with all our hearts Ali Taheri from Tehran and Farkhondeh Zareie from Shiraz for all they did to make our two journeys so extraordinary, rewarding and inspirational. Their assistance went way beyond their brief, and we thank them for sharing their country, friends and family with us. Ali ...Yas ...we could not have done it without you!

During the months we spent in Iran we experienced countless acts of kindness and hospitality. We thank in particular: Dr Mohammed Reza and Mozhgan Akbarzadeh; Ali Ahmady and family; Mahnaz Ave; Mr Azmoodeh; Saeed Dastmalchi; Maziar Ale Davoud; Esmaeel Fasihi and family; Noushin Gheyasi; Alelah and Soufi Golestani; Mahmoud Hassani and family; Adnan Kamaly; Alireza Karimi; Javar, Ali and Sakineh Moradi; Dr Ali Mortazavi; Hamid Rezaie; Farah, Ramin and Armin Taheri; Dr Ali Tootoonchi; Mr Touraji; Bita Yazdani; Farideh Zareie and Hosein Zareie and family.

Also in Iran we would like to thank the following: His Excellency, Mr Marc Innes-Brown, Mark Davidson and Nasrin Haddad from the Australian Embassy, Tehran; Samaneh Golestan of the excellent Gardeshgaran Travel and Tour Agency in Shiraz, and Ebrahim Khadem Bayat. Indeed, if there is any one person who has given his very soul to our project it is Ebi, who began the journey with us as a photographer but who became, along the way, a dear and treasured friend. His talent, love and understanding of his country shine through in the travel photography within this book.

In Melbourne, Greg thanks all the MoMo kitchen staff – particularly Brooke and Troy Payne – for ensuring things ran so smoothly during his many absences. We both thank Odette Martini and Aleesha Pratt for their brilliant cooking skills and for their tireless work assisting Greg during the photo shoot. We also thank the wonderful suppliers who provided us with outstanding ingredients for the recipe testing and food photography: in particular we thank Syd and Maria from The Essential Ingredient; Peter at Flavours Fruit and Veg; Roger, Simon and Sylvio at Largo's Butchers; John and George at Ocean Made Seafood, and the team from Senselle Foods.

Sincere and grateful thanks also to Aeria Country Floors, Altamira, Cote Provence, Husk, Izzi and Popo, Mauviel Cookware, Safari and The Works for so generously lending us equipment and exquisite props to enhance the food photography.

And what a team we had for the food shoot! Thanks to photographer Mark Roper – and his assistant Peter Tarasiuk – for understanding and depicting Greg's food so brilliantly, and to Glen Proebstel, stylist extraordinaire.

A very special thank you to designer Sandy Cull, whose creative energy and vision sings out from every single page of this book – thank you for your dedication to making *saraban* a work of such evocative and glowing beauty.

Recipe index

To Sandy Grant and Julie Pinkham at Hardie Grant, we owe you a huge debt of thanks for encouraging us to undertake this Persian adventure. And thank you to the team who brought the book into being: Mary Small and Ellie Smith, who were there to light the spark at the beginning and Paul McNally and Gordana Trifunovic who did such a brilliant job in seeing things through to the end. And to our lovely, unflappable, patient and extraordinarily thorough editor, Caroline Pizzey, thank you, thank you, thank you!

And so we finish where it always begins, with our families. George, Chalice, Bronte and Tarkyn – and all the other Maloufs, Komoneskis and Rushbrookes: we thank you all for your unwavering love and support. We dedicate this book to the memory of May Malouf, Greg's much-loved mother, who sadly passed away while it was being written. We know she would have loved it.

/

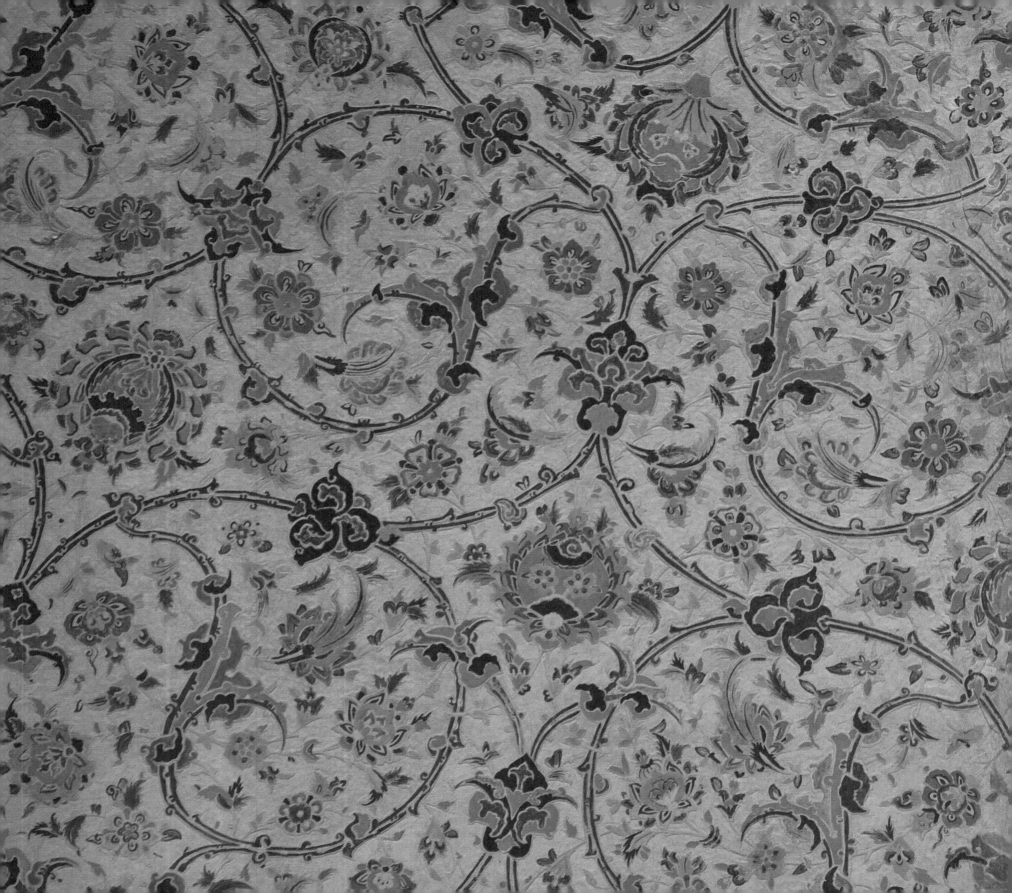